CITY FORM AND NATURAL PROCESS

CITY FORM AND NATURAL PROCESS

TOWARDS A NEW URBAN VERNACULAR

MICHAEL HOUGH

VNR VAN NOSTRAND REINHOLD COMPANY

Printed in Great Britain

Typeset by Columns of Reading

Published by Van Nostrand Reinhold Company Inc.
135 West 50th Street
New York, New York 10020

Van Nostrand Rienhold Company Limited
Molly Millars Lane
Wokingham, Berkshire RG11 2PY, England

Van Nostrand Reinhold
480 LaTrobe Street
Melbourne, Victoria 3000, Australia

Macmillan of Canada
Division of Gage Publishing Limited
164 Commander Boulevard
Agincourt, Ontario M1S 3C7, Canada

16 15 14 13 12 11 10 9 8 7 6 5 4 3 2 1

Library of Congress Cataloging in Publication Data

Hough, Michael.
    City form and natural processes.

    Includes bibliographies and index.
    1. City planning — Handbooks, manuals, etc.
2. Architecture and climate — Handbooks, manuals, etc.
3. Architecture and energy conservation — Handbooks,
manuals, etc. 4. Urban ecology (Biology) — Handbooks,
manuals, etc. I. Title.
NA9031.H66   1984   711'.4   84-15210
ISBN 0-442-26400-3

CONTENTS

Contents

PREFACE

When the history of the decades between 1960 and 1980 comes to be written, the attitudes expressed by Michael Hough and the solutions he proposes here will have a firm place in the development of a new worldview. For unbridled exploitation of land, water, air and other natural elements of this life on Earth had reached a destructive apogee.

By the early 1960s — often going against the dominant received opinion — the most perceptive minds in North America were at work to uncover a new rationale for survival of the human race. I say rationale inasmuch as the dominant view then, and the one which persists today, was that the function of humankind was and is to subdue the natural environment for present purposes, and exclusively in the service of its contemporary occupants. To think about posterity ('What the hell has it done for us?') or to act constructively on behalf of generations yet unborn, is still a minority enterprise in North American culture.

In this pervasive devil-take-the-hindmost selfishness common to both the USA and Canada, a small but growing band of environmental designers who include Michael Hough has been hacking away at old exploiters and their habits — not by personal attacks but by organising and presenting their thoughts on behalf of a new form of evolutionary change.

At the root of this new attitude, laid out in the following pages, is a revealing mixture of old and new. Michael Hough does not insist that the human use of energy is inevitably destructive (although he would be the last to argue against the workings of the Second Law of thermodynamics). Rather, he presents here a brief, in full detail, for the more efficient and effective use of both human and natural resources within our cities.

Anyone who has watched the still-mysterious unfolding of a stalk of corn from a tiny and seemingly lifeless yellow seed, anyone who has calculated the awesome yield of food from a collection of pitiful potato sproutlings, will have some suspicion of the vast energies potent in every square metre of land, even in the midst of teeming asphalteries called cities. Michael Hough explores some of this mysterious presence and peels away some of the arcane mumbo-jumbo that has infected the engineering approach to city planning and design. He opens up new vistas for designing and inhabiting the livable city that we would all do well to put into practice.

Grady Clay
Louisville, Kentucky

ACKNOWLEDGEMENTS

Many friends and colleagues have helped me in the writing of this book and I am very much indebted to them all. A few, however, must be acknowledged with particular gratitude. Professor Suzanne Barrett for her thoughtful and constructive criticism of my numerous draft manuscripts; Professor Alexander E. Rattray and Simon Miles for their continued support of this venture and for many stimulating discussions; David Croom who never gave up on my early efforts to get the book written; Richard Dober who provided much needed encouragement and advice. My thanks too, to my colleagues among the staff and students at the Faculty of Environmental Studies at York University in Toronto, for providing the stimulating academic environment that helped shape the concepts I have tried to express here; and also to my associates at Hough, Stansbury & Michalski Ltd with whom I have collaborated for many years in exploring and realising creative ideas.

Credits

The illustrations were mostly drawn by Ian Dance; the remainder were drawn by Tim Hough. Except where noted photographs were taken by the Author.

To Bridget, Timothy, Adrian and Fiona.

INTRODUCTION

This book is about natural process, cities and design. Its overall thesis is that the traditional design values that have shaped the physical landscape of our cities have contributed little to their environmental health, or to their success as civilising, enriching places to live in. My purpose is to find new and constructive ways of looking at the physical environment of cities. There is an urgent need for an alternative basis for urban landscape form that is in tune with the growing awareness of, and concern for, the issues of energy, environment and natural resource conservation. This is at the core of the themes that are explored throughout this book, which has been written with two purposes in mind. The first is to offer a conceptual, philosophical base on which urban design can rest, one that has received only scant attention in the literature. The second is to illustrate with examples drawn from real life how the practical application of theory is relevant and useful to the urban designer. The book deals with five general areas of concern.

First, there is the alienation of urban society from environmental values and cultural connections with the land. The technology that sustains the modern city has now touched every corner of human life, every landscape and wilderness, no matter how remote, and reinforces this isolation. This fact was forcefully demonstrated to me on a journey I made to the Hudson's Bay lowlands in 1967. I searched for an image of the great unspoiled Canadian wilderness, free from the sights, sounds and pressures of the urbanised south. Armed with hip waders and binoculars, I spent many days tramping through a landscape of water, muskeg and granite boulders, the dome of the sky creating a feeling of extraordinary wildness and beauty. Forget the dense clouds of hungry mosquitoes and blackfly, the discomforts of permanently wet boots; here was wild nature in the best Thoreau tradition. Yet, one day, a pink object, lying in the tangle of sedges at the edge of the pond, caught my eye. It was the rubber nipple from a baby's bottle, abandoned there by a passing group of Eskimo. The rude shock of this relic of urban man, so alien to the environment around me, brought me abruptly back to reality. The

1

incident was a forceful reminder that the products of the city are everywhere, even in the remoteness of the Hudson Bay Arctic. The nipple, my hip waders and binoculars and the fact that I was there, transported by plane hundreds of miles from Toronto, verified that urbanism is a fact of life. This is so, not only for Western man, but for the modern Eskimo who uses the white man's canned foods and machinery, hunts with a rifle, travels by skidoo, and now lives in permanent Arctic communities. The perceptual distinction between city and countryside has been a root cause of many social and environmental conflicts and the lack of attention to the environment of cities where most problems begin.

Second, little attention has been paid to understanding the natural processes that have contributed to the physical form of the city and which in turn have been altered by it. In the presence of cheap energy, the urban environment has been shaped by a technology whose goals are economic rather than environmental or social. The explosive growth of urban areas, particularly since the Second World War, has brought about fundamental changes, not only to the physical landscape, but to people's perceptions of land and environment. An affluent and mobile urban society now takes refuge in the countryside in search of fresh air and natural surroundings that are denied at home. Consequently, unsustainable pressures are placed on environmentally sensitive landscapes. The advancing city has often replaced complex natural environments of woods, streams and fields, with biologically sterile man-made landscapes that are neither socially useful nor visually enriching. At the same time a new concern for reclaiming mined or derelict land has replaced naturally regenerated sites for new horticultural deserts, perpetuating the very conditions that it intends to cure.

Third, there are issues that concern the use of urban resources. Vast areas of land lie idle and unproductive within the city, while parks departments struggle to provide parks with inadequate acquisition and development budgets. There are enormous water, energy and nutrient resources that are the by-product of urban drainage, sewage disposal and other urban processes. Having no perceived value, these contribute instead to the pollution loads of an already overstressed environment.

Fourth, there are questions of aesthetic values and formal doctrine from which the landscape of urban parks and open spaces has evolved. These values have little connection with the dynamics of natural process and lead to misplaced priorities. Recreation and amenity are seen as the exclusive function of urban parks. Horticultural science, not ecology, determines their development and maintenance. At the same time, another landscape, the fortuitous product of natural and cultural forces in the city, flourishes without care or attention. These two landscapes symbolise a fundamental conflict in the perception of nature: the desire to nurture the one and suppress the other in a perpetual and costly struggle

2

to maintain order and control. At a time when biological determinants are being professionally recognised as central to rural and resource planning, they are virtually ignored in cities. It is clear that the conventional framework for the design of urban open space must be re-examined. In-built assumptions about traditional open space priorities and standards must give way to more unconventional approaches. Questions must be asked about the role of parks and open spaces. Are there alternative functions for parks? What role should the vast non-park areas of the city serve? What is a relevant basis for aesthetics in urban design?

Fifth, there are questions of environmental values and perceptions and how we respond to the environment around us. If it can be shown that there are cheaper, more socially valuable ways of shaping the urban landscape than present practice, then we have a realistic and practical basis for action. The biologist and planner Patrick Geddes once remarked that 'civics as an art has to do not with imagining an impossible no-place where all is well, but making the most and the best of each and every place, especially of the city in which we live'.[1] So Utopian ideals of the perfect city set in bucolic landscapes that were once the fashion in planning and architectural philosophy are not relevant to our concerns. The era of new town building in both Britain and North America has come to an end. Over the next thirty to forty years at least, the bulk of development will be in urban renewal. So this book is concerned primarily with approaches to urban design that focus on existing cities. It is here that the opportunities lie and where the effort must be made.

The forthcoming chapters explore these issues in further detail. Chapter One suggests the design framework within which urban natural processes should be examined. It describes the general character and evolution of the urban landscape in both the pre-industrial and modern city and examines the constraints of energy, environment and social necessity that helped shape their form, character and use. The attitudes and values that pervade urban life today are reviewed in terms of the environmental problems they have generated and the opportunities that exist for creating a rational basis for design. Some basic principles that derive from the application of ecology to the design process are suggested. These become the frame of reference for subsequent discussions of the city's open space resources.

The chapters on climate, water, plants, wildlife and city farming examine the various components of the natural and human environment in several ways: first, as they operate as natural systems, or in balance with nature; second, how they are affected or changed by urban processes and the attitudes and cultural values that these changes have engendered. Some alternative values based on ecological insights are suggested that would tip the balance in favour of a constructive relationship to the urban environment. Such a change of perspective also reveals opportunities in lieu of problems and substitutes economy for high cost. Practical examples of opportunities that are often unrecognised, but occur everywhere in the city, serve to illustrate the potential that exists for beneficial change. The implications of the ecological view on urban form are then examined through various case studies as the foundation for a philosophy of design. The final chapter connects the parts and develops an integrated concept for urban design based on ecological principles and conserver values.

Note

1. Philip Boardman, *The Worlds of Patrick Geddes* (Routledge and Kegan Paul, London, 1978).

Chapter ONE

URBAN ECOLOGY, A BASIS FOR DESIGN

Since the 1960s there has been a growing awareness of the need to bring environmental values to the development of land and the management of natural resources. McHarg, Lewis and other eloquent exponents of the environmental planning movement have brought into focus the evolving philosophy that ecological processes provide the indispensable basis for planning and design. The dependence of one life process on another; the interconnected development of living and physical processes of earth, climate, water, plants and animals; the continuous transformation and recycling of living and non-living materials; these are the elements of the self-perpetuating biosphere that sustain life on earth and which give rise to the physical landscape. They become the central determinants of form for all human activities on the land. The design doctrines that have provided the inspiration for the built environment since the Bauhaus movement of the 1920s[1] can no longer be seen as a valid basis for form. 'Form follows function' was the manifesto, but it was proclaimed as if Darwin, Wallace, D'Arcy Thompson, biology and morphology had never existed.[2] The application of the 'Design with Nature' philosophy has become, to a growing body of practice, an accepted basis for land planning and management of natural resources. It concerns every landscape where human goals are in actual or potential confrontation with natural process.

If we consider the urban landscape in this context, we find some fundamental contradictions and paradoxes in the way the city and the larger environment are perceived. In a world increasingly concerned with the problems of a deteriorating environment, be they energy, pollution, vanishing plants, animals, natural or productive landscapes, there is a marked propensity to bypass the environment most people live in — the city itself. It has become conventional wisdom to see the modern city as the product of cheap energy, economic forces, high technology and a denial of nature; as the epitome of environmental deterioration. Yet urban landscape design continues to operate on the premise that ecological processes are either non-existent in cities, or have little relevance to design process and form. Its underlying disciplines are to be found in horticulture and engineering, in aesthetic priorities that are now regarded as secondary to the new-found insights of ecological determinism. If urban design can be described as that art and science dedicated to enhancing the quality of life in cities; to providing civilising and enriching places for the people who live in them, then the current basis for urban form must be re-examined. It is necessary to rediscover, through the insights that ecology provides, the nature of the familiar places we live in. Thus the basic premise on which this book rests is twofold. First: that an environmental view of the city is an essential component of urban design that has long been ignored. The often unrecognised natural processes occurring within cities provide us with an alternative basis for form in the urban landscape. Second: that problems in the larger landscape have their roots in cities and solutions must, therefore, also be sought here. And so, the task is one of integrating the concept of urbanism with nature. My purpose in this chapter is to identify current problems and examine the structure and principles for design that are central to this point of view.

The Contradiction of Values

Towns and cities are perceived largely through their exterior environment. The average urban dweller going about his daily life will experience the city through its patterns of streets and pedestrian ways, shopping areas, civic squares, parks and gardens and residential areas. There is another generally ignored landscape, however, lying beneath the surface of the city's public places and thoroughfares. It is the landscape of industry, railways, public utilities, vacant lots, urban expressway interchanges, abandoned mining lands and waterfronts. Thus two landscapes exist side by side in cities. The first is the nurtured 'pedigree' landscape of lawns, flowerbeds, trees, fountains and planned places everywhere that have traditionally been the focus of civic design. Its basis for form rests in the formal design doctrine and aesthetic priorities of established convention. Its survival is dependent on high energy inputs, engineering and horticultural technology. Its image is that of the design solution independent of place. The second is the fortuitous landscape of naturalised urban plants and flooded places left after rain, that may be found everywhere in the forgotten places of the city. Urban weeds emerge through cracks and gratings in the pavement, on rooftops, walls, poorly drained industrial sites, or wherever a foothold can be gained. They provide shade and flowering groundcovers and wildlife habitat at no cost or care and against all the odds of gasoline fumes, sterile soils, trampling and maintenance men. There is also a humanised landscape hidden away in back alleys, rooftops and backyards of many an ethnic

6

neighbourhood that can be described as the product of spontaneous cultural forces. It is here that one may find a rich variety of flourishing gardens and brightly painted houses. The turfed front yard of the well-to-do neighbourhood gives way to sunflowers, daisies, vegetable gardens, intricate fences, ornaments and religious icons of every conceivable variety, expressing rich cultural traditions.

These two contrasting landscapes, the pedigree and the natural and cultural vernacular, symbolise the inherent conflicts of environmental values. The first has little connection with the dynamics of natural process. Yet it has a high value in the public mind as an expression of care, aesthetic value and civic spirit. The second represents the vitality of altered but none the less functioning natural and social processes at work in the city. Yet it is regarded as a derelict wasteland in need of rehabilitation, the unredeemed blight on the urban landscape, the disorderly shambles of the poorer parts of town. If we make the not unreasonable assumption that diversity is ecologically and socially necessary to the health and quality of urban life, then we must question the current values that have determined the image of nature in cities. A comparison between the plants and animals present in a regenerating vacant lot, and those present in a landscaped residential front yard, or city park, reveals that the vacant lot generally has far greater floral and faunal diversity than the lawn or city park. Yet all efforts are directed towards nurturing the latter and suppressing the former. The rehabilitation of 'depressed' or 'derelict' areas involves reducing diversity, rather than enhancing it. A case in point which will be discussed further in later chapters will illustrate this problem.

The Outer Harbour Headland on the Toronto waterfront is a spit of land two and a half miles long, built by the Toronto Harbour Commission to create a new harbour. Begun in 1959, its purpose was to accommodate greatly increased shipping tonnage that was expected to enter the city as a consequence of the construction of the St Lawrence Seaway. This additional shipping never materialised, however, and since that time the future of the Headland has remained in limbo. Environmentally, though, the Headland represents a fascinating example of the power of natural process. From the loose rubble, subsoil and sand from which it was built, a new landscape has begun to evolve. Wind and wave are grinding bricks and concrete to sand; marshland and mudflats have appeared that now provide habitat for thousands of breeding and migratory gulls, terns and ducks. Some 150 species of plants have migrated here and established themselves. Within the open space resources of the waterfront, the Headland now represents a unique resource for education, scientific study and passive recreation. Yet there are overwhelming political pressures to reclaim this 'derelict' site, to transform it to a formal landscape of boat slips, parking lots, picnic sites, turf and cultivated plants. The only thing

a

b

Two urban landscapes A cultivated landscape; and abandoned waterfront site.
(a) supports over 150 species of plants and is visited by 185 species of birds. (b) has
five species of plant and supports no wildlife. Which is the derelict site?

saving it from the sterilising influence of established landscape development is a poor economic climate that makes such a project currently not
feasible. The question that arises, therefore, is this: which are the derelict
sites in the city requiring rehabilitation? Those fortuitous and ecologically
diverse landscapes representing urban natural forces at work, or the
formalised landscapes created by man?

It is my contention that the formal city landscape imposed over an
original natural diversity is the one in urgent need of rehabilitation. While
it will be obvious that such a landscape has a place in the city, its
universal application as the basis for making urban space is the most
persuasive argument for considering it as a derelict landscape. Other
paradoxes become apparent when we apply ecological insights to our
observation of the city environment.

(1)   Attitudes and perceptions of the environment expressed in town
planning since the Renaissance have, with some exceptions, been more
concerned with Utopian ideals than with natural process as determinants
of urban form. Many examples of North American towns and institutions
laid out over the last hundred years attest to the aesthetic and cultural
baggage of a past era, transported to hostile climatic environments and
wholly inappropriate to them. The arrival of cheap fossil fuel has enabled
the inorganic structure of planning theory to persist and maintain the
illusion that the creation of a benign climate outdoors has little relevance
to urban development.

(2)   Traditional storm drainage systems, the conventional method of
solving the problem of keeping the city's paved surfaces free of water,
have until recently been unquestioned. As the established vocabulary of
engineering, water drains to the catchbasin. But the benefits of 'good
design' — well drained streets and civic spaces — is paid for by
environmental costs of eroded streams, flooding and impairment of water
quality in downstream water courses.

(3)   Sewage disposal systems are seen as an engineering rather than a
biological solution to the ultimate larger problem of eutrophication of
major water bodies and wasted resources. We have the paradox of the
city as the centre for enormous concentrations of nutrient energy, while
urban soils remain almost totally sterile and non-productive.

The resolution of these contradictions and the alternatives for design
must be found in an ecological view that encompasses the total urban
landscape. This includes the unstructured spatial environments that are
not currently seen to contribute to the city's civic image as well as those
places that do. To explore this point of view further we must examine the
legacy that pre-indusrial as well as modern cities have left.

Vernacular Landscapes and the Investment in Nature

As I have already indicated, towns and cities are perceived through their exterior environment. The way urban spaces are used is a measure of the attitudes and values of people in relation to the places they live in. While the pressures of modern times have greatly influenced the old pre-industrial cities, many still maintain something of their original character. They have a quality that creates a variety of unmistakable impressions. One is that they are places for walking. There is a human scale to the streets as they wind their way informally but purposefully through the town, sometimes narrow and enclosing, sometimes opening to vistas of squares, market places, common green, churchyards. Another is the countryside that suddenly opens up over rooftops, or at the end of a street; fields and woods forming a hard and defined edge between urban and non-urban places. Another is their work. There is business in the market place and in the street. Livestock graze on the common and in the churchyard; crops ripen in the fields. Towns like this aptly but superficially fit the postcard image of picturesque quaintness that has long attracted tourists. But at heart their shape, the arrangement of their open spaces, their relationship to the countryside and harmonious siting, are the historical product of economic and social forces and the physical constraints of the land. These old places were built as working urban and rural landscapes. A symbiotic relationship existed between land and settlement. The land produced the food and raw materials for the settlement, which in turn returned the by-products, organic wastes, to the land to enrich the soil. While city and country remained distinct and separate places, each depended on the other. Early settlement, as Mumford has pointed out, could not grow beyond the limits of its water supply and food sources until better transportation and a more sophisticated administration could evolve.[3] This early association with food production maintained a connection between the country and the city in some form until the Industrial Revolution. For instance, fruit and vegetables consumed in New York and Paris came from market gardens whose soil had been enriched with night refuse. A good part of the population had private gardens and practised rural occupations within the city, as American towns did up to 1890. Mumford also notes that the amount of usable open space within medieval cities throughout their existence was greater per head of population than any later form of city.[4]

From a design viewpoint, the most significant impression one receives of the pre-industrial town is that it made the most of what it had within the means and technology available. Since it was built and operated on solar power, it was limited by what stored energy was available from organic materials; running water and direct sunlight. It induced a respect for variations of climate, topography, agricultural soils and water supply.

Expressions of the vernacular urban landscape (a) places for walking; (b) connections with the working countryside; (c) sheep mowing the churchyard

Open spaces were functional, producing a variety of fruit and vegetables; the common and churchyard provided grass and were kept trim by livestock — a practice still kept up by many towns and cities in Europe. Groupings of houses around greens and courtyards were arranged on the basis of functional necessity to conserve heat, minimise winds and provide access to sunlight and space. Adaptations to the constraints of nature and the inherent rightness of the siting, the relationship between rural resources and the city, and the limited energy available from sun, vegetation and water gave the cities a stake in the countryside and determined their physical and aesthetic form.

Books on architecture have marvelled at the subtle sequence of spaces, the proportions of squares, the powerful architectural statement of important buildings, and other aesthetic urban qualities. Rudofsky has shown how history has been preoccupied with 'pedigree', that style of building that was based on formal rules of design and commemorating power and wealth.[5] It excludes 'vernacular' building whose basis for form was to be found in its response to environment, to social and functional necessity. We can draw relevant parallels in the landscape. The literature on historical landscapes deals almost exclusively with the development of the artistic philosophies in the great parks and gardens of the times, from which much of our urban park tradition can be traced. It ignores the working vernacular landscape of town and country created out of necessity that symbolised the investment in nature and land. But it is these that hold crucial lessons for us today in our search for a relevant basis for form.

Energy Landscapes and the Industrial City

The patterns of space in the modern city are the product of market forces, transportation systems and design ideologies that are radically different from the older city building tradition. Visually, the advent of the tower block and the freeway of post-war development has created a landscape of extraordinary scale, relating more to the automobile than the pedestrian. The dimension of speed creates new and powerful experiences of the city. It is appreciated from the highway as broad outline — a series of changing images and fleeting impressions from a distance that are visually stimulating but sensually remote. Buildings tend to float in a sea of space rather than containing it. Tower blocks rise from open plazas which are often windswept and shadowed in winter, or sunbaked in summer. Economic forces have created a landscape of uncontained plazas, parking lots, vehicular thoroughfares, highway interchanges and vacant sites. It is a landscape sterilised by ineffective use and a lack of co-ordination of various public and private agencies that

12

a

b

Expressions of the energy urban landscape (a) the universal turf landscape; (b) the loss of visual connections

control it. Aesthetic conventions and values have created a development landscape of parks, playgrounds, recreation spaces and front yards, whose character rests on a universal application of cultivated turf, asphalt and chainlink fences occasionally punctuated by an ornamental tree or exotic shrub. Of all the varied impressions that come to mind as one looks at the modern city, there are, maybe, four that reveal the most about the subject at hand: lack of visual connections to the countryside, use of urban parks solely for leisure, the mutually exclusive nature of the relationship between town and countryside, and the abundant use of energy in the cities.

Visual Connections to the Countryside

The view to the countryside from the town, the symbol of the pre-industrial investment in the land, has disappeared. The old symbiotic relationship between city and farmland has been replaced by an industrialised agriculture that has no direct .connections with the city. Land that once produced crops and livestock is now more valuable as real estate. The massive exploitation of resources that permitted the growth of cities, and the lack of management and husbandry to ensure the continued health and perpetuation of the resource, has not traditionally been seen as a relevant problem in North American cities.[6] So the countryside immediately surrounding the city, known as the urban shadow, is the object of land speculation and sporadic development, defying planning solutions and perpetuating an unproductive landscape.

Parks are for Recreation

Recreation has become the exclusive land use for the city's public open spaces. The migration of people from the countryside to the cities that began in the Industrial Revolution did more than create poverty and slums. The skills and knowledge of the countryside and traditional patterns of rural life were replaced by the living and working patterns of the city. The psychological and physical separation between urban and rural environments widened as cities grew larger, more industrialised and more remote from the rural areas with which they had originally been connected. The urban park had an entirely different purpose from the countryside it replaced. The crops, orchards and livestock that had originally been the function of many open spaces in the pre-industrial settlements were now replaced by open spaces that catered exclusively to amenity and recreation. Parks originated in the late seventeenth century as private residential squares at a time when some cities in Britain were becoming attractive places to live for the upper classes. Among them were the famous Bloomsbury garden squares of London (1775-1850) and the crescents of Bath, developed by the brothers Wood (1730-67).[7] The development of the public parks in the expanding cities of Europe and

14

the United States in the nineteenth century evolved out of the Romantic movement. They were created in the conviction that nature should be brought to the city to improve the health of the people, by providing space for exercise and relaxation. It was felt that the opportunity to contemplate nature would improve moral standards. A new preoccupation with the aesthetics of natural landscape led to the notion that parks would improve the appearance of cities.[8] The introduction of the Royal Parks in London, Olmsted's Central Park in New York, the Boston Commons and Mount Royal Park in Montreal are testament to a period of extraordinary social convictions and purpose.

But the continuing expansion of the city since the nineteenth century and the decline of park priorities have created new conditions. There is greater wealth and leisure among more people, greater mobility, and a desire to escape the city and renew contact with rural settings that the urban park is now unable to satisfy. Work and play have come to be perceived as separate and distinct activities. These have turned leisure into an all-consuming occupation for urban people. The notion that the countryside exists solely as an urban playground is borne out every weekend when its lakes, forests and farmlands are invaded by people who have little or no direct contact with the landscape as a place of work. Thus recreation contributes little to the land on which it occurs. In reality it is parasitic. Its social effects create conflict between those who earn their living by the land and those who use it for leisure. Its environmental effects are often destructive of streams, soils and vegetation. There is no long-term investment or dependence on the land for livelihood, as a place of work. Few, therefore, with the exception of conservationist groups, have the motivation to protect it. This attitude is reflected in the urban environment. Apart from the established parks, vast land resources, evident in industrial areas, forgotten river valleys, waterfronts and similar places, lie idle and unproductive and outside the parks system. Leisure has become the prime function of urban parks, while other environmental and productive functions that the city's land resources must serve have largely been forgotten.

The City and Countryside are Mutually Exclusive Places

'. . . today it is nature beleaguered in the country, too scarce in the city which has become precious'.[9] It is not hard to understand how this mental dissociation takes place. Perceptually we miss the obvious evidence of natural surroundings, the woods, streams, marshes and fields. We fail, however, to see nature as an integrated connecting system that operates in one way or another regardless of locality. Water supply and disposal systems leave no indication that the water supplied to the kitchen tap had its origins in the forests and landscapes of distant watersheds; or that rain falling on rooftops and paved surfaces and disappearing without trace into

15

catchbasins and underground sewers is part of a continuous hydrological cycle. The turf and specimen trees of the urban park and garden, its plants brought from Korea and the Himalayas, its turf maintained like a billiard table, are difficult to associate with the diverse community of plants that convert sunlight into energy, and produce food and materials necessary for survival. The frozen and heremetically sealed plastic package one finds in the meat section of the local supermarket bears not the slightest resemblance to the animal from which it came. Maintenance has usurped natural succession. The regulated air-conditioned climate and tropical plantings of the shopping centre have substituted for the cycle of the seasons. Sanitary sewers and the garbage truck break the life cycle of nutrients and materials of natural systems.

Yet, the essential creativity of nature, the processes that continue modified and often degraded, continue to function. Rich and diverse natural habitats, remnants from a pre-urban era, occur on quasi-public or private land where public access is restricted and where the gang mower has not penetrated. A new community of plants, mostly alien species, has established itself, flourishing in the warmer climate that the city affords. These plants, like the mosses, common dandelion, plantain, sumac, Tree of Heaven and Manitoba maple, are what we know as weeds. Weeds, botanically speaking, are plants that colonise disturbed land. But from a cultural viewpoint, they are plants growing where they are not wanted. They represent the fortuitous communities of the urban environment. Hydrological systems are in evidence in the rainfall impounded on the poorly drained parking lot and playing field, where the processes of evaporation and groundwater recharge continue the cycle, by accident rather than intent. The sewage lagoon perpetuates the process of decay of organic material and release of nutrients and provides new urban marshland for large populations of shore birds. Flat-topped roofs provide nesting places for night hawks; garbage dumps and waste places attract small rodents which in turn attract the hawks and owls which feed on them. It is these natural systems operating within the city that are the basis of an ecological framework for urban design.

An Abundance of Energy

The availability of cheap energy has been the overriding determinant of urban form. The energy flow through a city, with its factories, automobiles, heating and cooling systems and high power consumption, is about a hundred times greater than the energy flow through a natural ecosystem.[10] Thus cities place enormous stresses on natural systems, depending on them for resource inputs and for the disposal of unwanted products. There is input of food from agricultural regions and output into the environment of heat and concentrated nutrient energy from sewage treatment plants. Industrial processes draw water from rivers and streams for cooling and return waste heat energy. Solid waste and organic refuse are disposed of in landfill sites (at an approximate rate of 2 to 3 cubic yards per person per year for the city of Toronto),[11] generating large quantities of methane and other gases in the process of decomposition.

With respect to building design, cheap and abundant energy has permitted building to evolve, whose climate, form and style are no longer determined by natural constraints. Steadman has pointed out that the external containing envelope of buildings becomes the consequence of their internal organisation and material structure, in contrast to traditional architecture, where the design of the exterior shell was a response to the problem of keeping out the weather and protecting the interior from heat and cold.[12] What came to be known as the 'International Style' of architecture is also true of the designed urban landscape. The problem of establishing natural elements in the hostile urban environment has produced a landscape whose creation and survival depends not on natural determinants, but on technology and high energy inputs. The creation of rooftop landscapes, for example, involves a building structure capable of withstanding the weight of soil for trees between 500 to 600 lb per square foot. Planting requires artificial irrigation to survive exposure and drying winds. Soil, imported from elsewhere, must be lifted great heights at many times its normal installation cost at ground level. Drainage, paving and other support elements involve considerable energy and capital cost. When we consider maintenance in terms of machinery, fuel, fertilisers and herbicides, whose objective is to perpetuate an unchanging plant community, we are faced with long-term consumption of energy to sustain a landscape whose sole function is its aesthetic amenity. We have, in effect, an international style of landscape design that has little to do with the inherent characteristics of the place. It is established and maintained in isolation; predetermined design imposed on its site.

Finally, perhaps the most striking aspect of the city is the amount of wasted energy and effort that is expended to create and maintain such an unrewarding environment. The wealth of opportunity that exists to create a better one remains largely unexplored. The integration of urbanism and ecology achieved through the design process is our concern here. Design is by definition a problem-solving activity — a process of integration. It makes connections between disparate elements to reveal potentials that may not otherwise be apparent. The insights that urban ecology provides, when put together with social and economic objectives, creates a rational basis for design. We should now review the principles that seem the most applicable to this view, since they form a frame of reference for the discussions of urban open space in the chapters to come.

Some Design Principles

Process

Processes are dynamic. The form of the landscape is the consequence of the forces that give rise to it; geological uplift and erosion of mountains; the hydrological cycle and forces of water, plants, animals and man working on the land. The form of the place reveals its natural and human history and the continuing cycles of natural process. An incident that occurred some years ago demonstrates the difficulty that is often experienced in understanding the dependence of form on process.

In 1964 the American Falls International Board convened a conference on the most magnificent urban geological feature known — the falls at Niagara. The issue facing the delegates was the talus that had broken off on the American Falls, forming enormous piles of rock at its base. This had created much adverse publicity in the press and consequently greatly concerned the branch of the International Joint Commission responsible for its care. The aesthetic of the falls, badly marred in the public mind, threatened to create an international incident. What was to be done? Should the rock be removed? Should it be removed entirely or only partially? And if so, how much? What form should the rocks that remained take to create the most pleasing effect? This and other problems prompted detailed landscape studies to be done with the help of a large-scale model by none other than the great Garrett Eckbo himself. The aesthetic impacts of various alternatives were tested, over a considerable length of time. The real issue that eventually surfaced, however, was how one perceives natural phenomena in terms of process. It was apparent that the Niagara Falls are a natural feature of astounding drama and grandeur that are a source of wonder for all who come to see them. Consciously or unconsciously, this sense of wonder is rooted in the idea that we are face to face with overpowering natural forces, a part of a continuum of geological time and process that has evolved over tens of thousands of years. The erosional processes that originally created the falls continue to do so. What we see today is different from what Father Hennepin (the first white man to visit them in 1679) saw, or what our distant descendants will see a hundred or a thousand years hence.

Thus, our current appreciation must be seen in this context; a mere instant of time within the evolving continuum of nature. The aesthetic of the falls is a consequence of this evolution. The tendency to view natural phenomena as static events, frozen in time, is the root cause of the aesthetic dilemmas that we face. When nature is seen as a continuum, the argument of what is beautiful and what is less so becomes meaningless. The rock falls at Niagara are simply visible evidence of nature at work. They cannot be regarded as some gigantic engineering toy that has somehow gone wrong and must, within the limits of technological

18

wizardry and irrelevant aesthetic standards, be put right. The same applies to cities that work well. They have their own inherent beauty. The commercial towns of Holland and many agricultural towns of Britain and Europe are examples of working and changing environments that have this quality. The concept of process also has radical implications for landscape design. The creation and upkeep of urban landscapes are largely seen as a static endeavour; once created the object is to maintain the *status quo*. The dynamics of natural plant communities follow quite different laws, that change and evolve in response to natural forces. Thus design and maintenance, based on the concept of process, become more than separate and distinct activities but an integrated and continuing management function, guiding the development of the man-made landscape over time.

There is a prevailing opinion among conservation-minded people that man's influence on the land is inherently destructive. There is no question that to a large measure this view is well founded. The blunt statement of the manager for State parks in New York that open space is like virginity — once lost it can never be regained — rings true when we are faced with the destruction of priceless landscapes in the face of urban development. The preservation and protection of plants, animals and landscapes can be argued, in the context of today's values, on the basis of moral and aesthetic values, of maintaining genetic diversity and the validity of keeping options open for the future. Design, however, is less concerned directly with these values than it is with the notion of change, and the constructive opportunities that change provides. Loenthal makes the point that the manager for New York State parks may not be altogether correct in his assertion, since only non-virgins can produce more virgins.[13] This remark contains an important truth when man is seen as part of natural process. Landscapes may be created that are different from the original, but may result, none the less, in diverse and healthy environments. Man as an agent of change has historically been concerned with modifying the land for survival; draining land to create productive fields, exploiting natural resources for fuel and raw materials, but often unconscious of the effects of his activity on the original landscape. While the world today exhibits countless examples of destructive change, it is important to remember that there are also many that have been beneficial. W. G. Hoskins has shown that the origin of the Norfolk Broads, a landscape of water and marshland in south-east England of great diversity and beauty, was for many years a subject of speculation, one theory being that they had resulted from a marine transgression in fairly recent times. In the 1950s it was conclusively shown that they were the result of deep peat cutting in medieval times, some four hundred years ago. Since the region was naturally treeless, peat was a valuable fuel. Water seepage into excavated areas eventually caused the abandonment of peat cutting. Marshes developed and finally enough water filtered in to create the 'artificial' lakes that form the present landscape.[14] In an urban context one may find flourishing natural landscapes that have evolved from old quarries abandoned long ago. The newly rehabilitated landscapes of the industrial Midlands brought back into productive use in Britain are examples of the purposeful modification of natural process to bring formally ravaged landscapes back to health. Human or natural processes are constantly at work modifying the land. The nature of landscape design is one of initiating purposeful and beneficial change, with ecology and man as its indispensable base.

Economy of Means

This could also be called the principle of least effort. As Steadman has so aptly stated, Mies Van de Rohe's dictum 'less is more' describing the formal aesthetic style of his buildings is little more than a bad joke in the context of their energy performance.[15] Jane Jacobs has predicted that in the future the city will assume the role as supplier as well as consumer of resources.[16] The city's used or unwanted materials, its heat energy, garbage and stormwater, vacant lands, become useful resources at less environmental and economic cost when the right linkages are established.

Victor Papanek describes an elegant example of this principle of economy of means in industrial design.[17] The problem requiring solution involved communications in pre-literate and low-power areas of the world. As most of the local people were unable to read and as there was neither power for radios nor money for batteries, the problem had to be solved in ways other than shipping out technologically sophisticated radios from the West. The unit that was developed consisted of a used tin can (of which there is a world-wide abundance) containing paraffin wax, or any local fuel, and a wick that produces enough heat via a thermo-couple to operate an ear plug speaker. The non-directionality of the radio was not important since there was only one radio station. The gadget, costing (in the 1960s) only 9 US cents, was manufactured locally as a cottage industry product. Decoration of the tin-can radio could now become a prerogative of the user, thus bypassing the problem of imposing institutionalised 'good taste'. The simplicity of the technology, its relevance to the social and physical environment where it would be put to use and the relationship of its aesthetic to the place illustrate the economy of means principle. From minimum resources and energy, maximum environmental and social benefits are available. In a landscape context there is the aspect of maintenance. Designers who have included plants such as staghorn sumac in their planting plans, whose natural tendency is to spread by root suckering, will understand the consequences of mowing underneath them, a common maintenance practice to keep the grass at the regulation two inches. Suckering is inhibited and the plants develop as individual trees rather than as a group with a dense canopy which naturally suppresses turf growth — a classical and all too common case of getting the least for the most.

The cutting of grass verges along highway rights of way is another case in point. It is reported that the budget spent in the city of Winnipeg in 1978 to cut the grass on public streets and boulevards approached $2 million;[18] this, with a population of 500,000 and a growing season of only five months.

A policy in Britain aimed at reducing maintenance costs permits less grass maintenance of verges on the motorways. Properly managed to succeed naturally and develop variety, they assume the character of wildlife corridors. This has been found to have benefits in a more varied open space network, an increase in natural plant and animal diversity and an altogether more pleasing visual character at less cost in money and energy.

Diversity

If health can be described as the ability to withstand stress, then diversity may also imply health. Odum has this comment: 'the most pleasant and certainly the safest landscape to live in, is one containing a variety of crops, forests, lakes, streams, roadsides, marshes, seashores and waste places — in other words, a mixture of communities of different ecological ages'.[19] Diversity makes social as well as biological sense in the urban setting. The quality of life implies, among other things, being able to choose between one place and another, between one life-style and another. In design terms, it implies interest, pleasure, stimulated senses and varied landscapes. The city that has places for foxes and owls, natural woodlands, trout lilies, marshes and fields, cultivated landscapes and formal gardens, old as well as new buildings, busy and quiet urban spaces, is a more pleasant and interesting place to live in.

Environmental Education Begins at Home

Environmental literacy strikes at the heart of urban life and consequently design. It has been said that children know more about nature in distant lands than they do about the natural things in their own backyards, neighbourhoods and cities. Marcus writes that 'for as long as cities have had a major place in American life most American writers on nature and the city have taken the two terms as opposites. . . . We must leave the city to be in nature.'[20] The media reinforce this perception in the treatment of natural phenomena. Children are given almost daily doses on television of programmes that focus on threatened wildlife in the East African Serengeti Plain, the Florida Everglades, or the tropical forests of Brazil. But there is little recognition of the natural systems that operate in the city itself, and little opportunity to study them in most government

a

Diversity in the urban environment
(a) places for wildlife, wild landscape, solitude and education;
(b) places for work, recreation and strolling along the waterfront

b

education programmes. The 'Watch' Trust for Environmental Education identifies one problem that comes from this dissociation of 'City' and 'Country'. 'To understand nature in towns, we have to start by forgetting many long held ideas. What we are looking for is not imitation countryside. Town nature lives by the same rules as country nature, but the "classic" habitats of the countryside . . . are not found in built-up areas.'[21] It is also wrong to assume, as many people concerned with children's play and education do, that 'In large cities, their environment is . . . devoid of greenery, birds and stars.'[22] It is evident in many places that have escaped the attention of civic authorities or tidy-minded people.

The value of diverse environments for the healthy development of children is now generally recognised. Lady Allen of Hurtwood has shown in her pioneering work with play and learning how children need to be challenged, to take risks, to make their own discoveries and their own environments.[23] These opportunities can be provided in the city. Moore reflects a general view that the natural environment provides one of the most appropriate, flexible, manipulable and diverse settings for play and learning.[24] This conviction is reflected in some of the recent Dutch housing landscapes and environmental education programmes, about which more will be said in a later chapter. It may be said that environmental education is more than the biology lesson taught in the classroom, or the yearly trip to the rural nature centre. These provide no substitute for constant and direct experience assimilated through daily exposure to, and interaction with, the places one lives in. The temporary pond in the playground left after a rainstorm is a focus for play and learning while it lasts. It can provide the best basis for discussion of water cycles in cities and in the natural environment. Similarly, the common dandelion presents everyday opportunity for observing urban vegetation as a prelude to understanding plant communities as a whole. Plants form a link that teaches us something about ourselves as well as about natural systems.

At a community level, gardening has been found to enhance community interaction, reduce vandalism, and improve the physical surroundings of low-income areas.

'Plants are non-threatening and non-discriminatory in a world that is constantly judgemental.'[25] They help fulfil a vital element of emotional well-being by enhancing self-esteem. Gardening provides for adults what water, mud and plants provide for children: a manipulable environment that provides a feeling of control — of proof that one is able to change one's physical surroundings. The task of urban design is to enrich the home environment by recognising the existence and latent potential of urban natural systems to enrich the city. This provides the best chance of spiritual growth and creative learning, which is at the heart of environmental education.

Human Development: Enhancement of the Environment

There is a common tendency to regard environmentally sensitive planning and design as that process which minimises destruction to plants, soil, water and related natural resources. The questions normally posed in environmental planning, for instance, suggest an acceptance of negative values. 'To what extent can an area be urbanised while *minimising* unacceptable water pollution or soil erosion?' This implies that some loss, wastage or disruption to the environment is inevitable. The approach is a useful tool for constraint mapping where the least number of environmental constraints against a proposed use provide a guide to understanding the limitations of a site. It maintains, however, the aspect of *negative constraint*, and inhibits the creative solutions that come from a fully integrated marriage of ecology and design. Design must go further and ask: 'How can human development processes *contribute* to the environments they change?' Habitat building, creating those conditions that permit a species to survive and flourish, is a basic animal and human motivation. In nature the byproducts of these activities create situations where the altered environment provides opportunities for other species to profit by the change. The action of beavers damming streams, making ponds and cutting forest clearings has extensive impacts on the forest ecosystem. The temperature of the pond may rise above the tolerable level for brook trout, or the dam may impede the migration of salmon up the stream. On the other hand, drowned trees, while they may cause the end of a food supply of some species, create favourable conditions for others. The eventual meadow encourages the growth of aquatic plants necessary to support moose. Over time a new succession of vegetation will invade and cover the area. The byproducts of one form of life become useful material for others.

In human terms, the negative consequences of man-made change on the environment occur when the necessary linkages are not made. A house is an imposition on the land when the resources necessary to sustain it are funnelled through a one-way system; water supply — bathroom tap — drain — public sewer. Or, food — kitchen — dump. The byproducts of use serve no useful function. The concept behind integrated life-support systems is to make these linkages. They actively seek ways in which human development can make a positive contribution to the environment it changes. The principles of energy and nutrient flows, common to all natural ecosystems, are applied to the design of the human environment. The wastes of one part of the life cycle become the resource for another. The recycling of organic products restores soil fertility and its capacity for production. Recycling of waste water maintains groundwater levels, water purity, forest production and agriculture. The sewage lagoon, constructed to collect and process the sewage from the urban area and operating as a man-made wetland, provides a new and rich habitat for a wide variety of wading birds that may not have inhabited the area previously. Stormwater conservation improves the quality of water entering streams and rivers and maintains soil stability. It improves urban climate and can enhance diversity of fish and wildlife habitats. Where change can be seen as a positive force to enhance an environment, rather than simply minimising its impact, the changes for a constructive basis for urban design will be enhanced. Thus development takes care of and re-uses the resources it draws on, rather than imposing them on the larger environment.

A Basis for an Alternative Design Strategy

In the preceding pages we have seen how, in the presence of cheap energy, the urban environment has been shaped by a technology whose goals are economic rather than environmental or social. This has contributed to an alienation of city and country and a misuse of urban and rural resources. We find a preoccupation with leisure as the prime function of urban parks, while other functions that the open space resources of the city as a whole must serve to maintain environmental quality are largely ignored. We find a preoccupation with aesthetic design conventions that are more concerned with 'pedigree' landscapes than with the forms that have evolved from the necessity of conservation. The amounts of energy and effort spent creating them does not justify the results when alternatives exist that are cheaper, more effective and more rewarding. Our primary concern is how the city can be made environmentally and socially healthier; how it can become a civilising place to live in. As ecology has now become the indispensable basis for environmental planning of larger landscape, so an understanding and application of the altered but none the less functioning natural processes within cities become central to urban design. The conventions and rules of aesthetics have validity only when placed in context with underlying bio-physical determinants. Design principles, responsive to urban ecology and applied to the opportunities the city provides through its inherent resources, form the basis for an alternative design language. They include the concepts of process and change; economy of means that derives the most benefit from the least effort and energy; diversity as the basis for environmental and social health; an environmental literacy that begins at home and forms the basis for a wider understanding of ecological issues; a goal that stresses an enhancement of the environment as a consequence of change — an integration of human with natural processes at its most fundamental level. We seek a design language whose inspiration derives from a vernacular that makes the most of available resources; one that re-establishes the concept of multi-functional, productive and working

25

landscapes. As environment and energy issues assume a higher profile in the future, it will become increasingly necessary to widen the horizons of urban design to meet new goals. Urban land as a whole will be required to assume environmental, productive and social roles, as fundamental components of the urban design process, far outweighing traditional park functions and civic values. Many of the problems generated by the city and imposed on the larger natural environment will have to be resolved within it. All the city's environmental and spatial resources may then be drawn into an integrated management framework, to serve according to their capabilities, as producers of food and energy, moderators of climate, conservers of water resources, plants and animals, amenity and recreation. The following chapters will examine the opportunities for achieving this strategy within the framework of the design principles that have been outlined here.

Notes

1. The Bauhaus school of design was founded in Germany by Walter Gropius in 1919. It revolutionised the teaching of painting, sculpture, industrial design and architecture throughout the Western world and marked the maturation of the modern design movement. The school continued under Mies Van de Rohe and, after closing in 1933, moved to the United States where its ideas were spread throughout North America.

2. Ian L. McHarg, 'Architecture, Ecology and Form', published paper, Department of Landscape Architecture, Graduate School of Fine Arts, University of Pennsylvania, 1965.

3. Lewis Mumford, *The City in History* (Harcourt, Brace and World, New York, 1961).

4. Ibid.

5. Bernard Rudofski, *Architecture without Architects* (Museum of Modern Art, New York, 1964).

6. Spenser W. Havlick, *The Urban Organism* (Macmillan, New York, 1974).

7. Sigfried Giedion, *Space, Time and Architecture* (Oxford University Press, Oxford, 1952).

8. Michael Laurie, 'Nature and City Planning in the Nineteenth Century' in Ian C. Laurie (ed.), *Nature in Cities* (John Wiley, New York, 1979).

9. Ian L. McHarg, *Design with Nature* (Natural History Press, Garden City, New York, 1969).

10. Reg Lang and Audrey Armour, *Environmental Planning Resourcebook* (Lands Directorate, Environment Canada, Montreal, 1980).

11. R. N. Farvolden, 'Solid Wastes in our Environment' in *A Conference on Solid Wastes* (Conservation Council of Ontario, Toronto, Nov. 1968).

12. Philip Steadman, *Energy, Environment and Building* (Cambridge University Press, Cambridge, 1977).

13. David Loenthal, 'Daniel Boone is Dead', *Natural History*, American Geographical Society (Aug.-Sept. 1968).

14. W. G. Hoskins, *English Landscapes* (British Broadcasting Corporation, London, 1973).

15. Steadman, *Energy*.

16. Jane Jacobs, *The Economy of Cities* (Vintage Books, Random House, New York, 1970).

17. Victor Papanek, *Design for the Real World* (Pantheon Books, Random House, New York, 1971).

18.   Douglas Patterson, A Parks and Recreation Open Space and Facility Review, ch.4 'Inventory and Analysis' (City of Winnipeg Development Plan Review, 1979).

19.   Eugene P. Odum, 'The Strategy of Ecosystem Development', *Science*, vol. 164 (Apr. 1969).

20.   Leonard S. Marcus, 'Within City Limits: Nature and Children's Books about Nature in the City' in *Children, Nature and the Urban Environment*, (USDA Forest Service General Technical Report NE 30, US Dept. of Agriculture, Washington DC, 1977).

21.   Watch Trust for Environmental Education, *Watch 1980*, ed. Geoffrey Young (Warners (Midlands), Bourne, Lincs., 1980).

22.   Ethel Banzer Medieros, 'Play in Human Settlements: an Integrated Approach' in Paul Wilkinson (ed.), *In Celebration of Play* (Croom Helm, London, 1980).

23.   Lady Allen of Hurtwood, *Planning for Play* (Thames and Hudson, London, 1968).

24.   Robin C. Moore, 'The Environmental Design of Children — Nature Relations. Some Strands of Applicative Theory' in *Children, Nature and the Urban Environment*.

25.   Charles A. Lewis, 'Human Perspectives in Horticulture' in *Children, Nature and the Urban Environment*.

Chapter TWO

CLIMATE

In Burma once, while Bishop Prout
Was preaching on Predestination,
There came a sudden water spout
And drowned the congregation.
'O Heav'n', cried he, 'why can't you wait
Until they've handed round the plate!'[1]

Introduction

The notion that we are at the mercy of the weather is aptly illustrated in this childhood poem by Harry Graham. The interacting variable forces of wind, precipitation, temperature, humidity and solar radiation are the great climatic forces that have shaped the landscape, and to which, historically, people have adapted. At the same time settlements have modified micro-climates to suit particular needs and local conditions. Human comfort, and in some cases survival, have depended on the skill with which building and space making have been able to adapt to the climatic environment. The modern city has had a greater impact on this environment, on living conditions and attitudes than at any other time. The old arts of creating felicitous outdoor places that take advantage of climatic elements and the material resources of the landscape seem to have been lost. As pressures for energy conservation and as the need for civilising places to live in become more urgent, we must look for environmentally sounder ways of manipulating the climate of cities than the present total reliance on technological systems. My purpose in this chapter is to review the nature of the urban climate and to explore how the exterior environment can usefully contribute to its enhancement and conserve the city's energy.

Natural Elements and Climate

The basic elements of climate — solar radiation, wind, precipitation, temperature, humidity — are affected and moderated by the elements of the landscape, including landform, water and plants. At a macro-scale, landforms form barriers to the movement of air masses. They affect moisture conditions on the windward and leeward sides of hills and mountains. They affect temperatures at different heights of land — temperatures decreasing with altitude. Landforms control the flow and temperature range of air by forming impediments and channels to movement. They create katabatic valley winds that move up during the day and flow down at night, settling in valley bottoms as pools of cold air. South-facing slopes concentrate solar energy and produce different micro-environments from shaded slopes, which affects the growth and patterns of vegetation.

Vegetation controls direct solar radiation to the ground and hence the heat radiated back from ground surfaces. A forest may absorb up to 90 per cent of light falling on it and in general. reduces maximum temperature variations throughout the year. It may reduce wind speeds to less than 10 per cent of unobstructed wind and maintain more equitable day and night temperatures than non-forested land. It regulates the amount and intensity of rain reaching forest floors and affects the deposition of snow and humidity. It reduces glare from reflective surfaces since leaves have a low reflective index.

Water has a profound impact on climate control. Large bodies of water absorb and store a high percentage of solar energy. They heat up and cool much more slowly than land masses and so act as moderators of temperature on land through the ventilation of onshore breezes. The process of evaporation of water converts radiant energy into latent heat, reducing air temperatures and acting as a natural air conditioner.

Urban Influences on Climate

While it is predicted that the energy requirements of cities will, in the foreseeable future, affect not only local but regional and macroclimate,[2] a great deal can be done to influence urban climatic conditions. To do so, we need to examine and understand the influences affecting urban climate.

It is quite apparent that the climate of cities is markedly different from rural areas. Various climatological studies have accounted for five major influences that affect the urban climate, based on the fact that energy is the basis for the climatic differences between city and countryside.

(1) The difference in materials in urban and rural environments. The

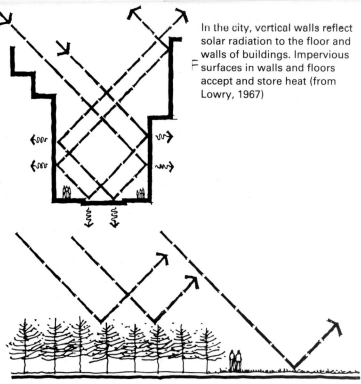

In the city, vertical walls reflect solar radiation to the floor and walls of buildings. Impervious surfaces in walls and floors accept and store heat (from Lowry, 1967)

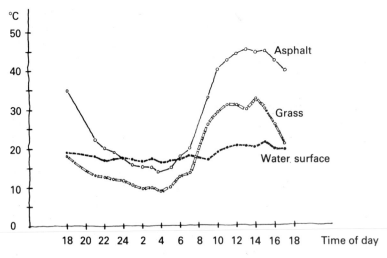

In the countryside, solar radiation is reflected back to the sky due to lack of vertical impervious surfaces. Tree canopy retains heat, while lower levels remain cool (from Lowry, 1967)

Surface temperature of materials The different physical characteristics of the various surfaces exposed to radiation give rise to a very contrasting temperature regime (from Miess, 1979)

impervious surfaces of city streets and paved spaces and the stone and concrete of building surfaces store and conduct heat much faster than soil or vegetated surfaces. In addition, the urban structures are multi-faceted. Roofs, walls and streets act as multiple reflectors, absorbing heat energy and reflecting it back to other surfaces, so the entire city accepts and stores heat. It becomes, therefore, a highly efficient system for heating large quantities of air throughout its volume. In the countryside, on the other hand, heat is stored mostly in upper layers. In wooded country the canopy receives and retains most of the heat, while lower levels remain relatively cool. Thus city temperatures are generally warmer than the areas outside. Chandler has found over thirty years that the average temperature over London was several degrees higher than in outlying areas.[3] An illustration of the considerable contrasts in temperature regime of various materials is given by Miess. In relation to a given quantity of energy received, open water is the most constant. Between early morning and midday its increase in temperature may be no more than 3° to 4° C. Asphalt, in contrast, during the period may have a temperature increase of 30° C. Grass may increase 20° C, but at the same time its temperature drops to much lower levels at night.[4]

(2)   The much greater aerodynamic roughness of built-up areas than in the countryside. The arrangement of tower blocks placed individually on their own sites presents a much rougher surface than the open country. This has the effect of slowing down prevailing winds and increasing localised gusts at street corners and round tall buildings, and diminishes the cooling power of wind in summer.

(3)   The prodigious amount of heat energy pumped into the city atmosphere from heating and cooling systems, factories and vehicles. It has been estimated that commercial energy use has grown at the rate of 5.4 per cent per year since 1960. Central air conditioning for residential building grew from 9 per cent of US households in 1969 to 15 per cent in 1973.[5] In winter, large amounts of heat are lost to the exterior and in summer, air conditioners cooling interior space pump hot air to the exterior, making the problem of high temperatures worse.

(4)   Problems resulting from precipitation. Rain is quickly carried away by storm sewers and snow is usually cleared from city streets and pedestrian areas. Evaporation converts radiated energy into latent heat, which acts as a cooling process. In the countryside, moisture either remains on the surface or immediately below it. It is thus available for evaporation and cooling. But in the city, the absence of moisture inhibits evaporation. And so the energy that would have gone into the process of cooling the environment is available for heating, a decisive factor in energy exchange.[6] The heat capacity of building materials is greater than that of air by about 1,000, and the process of transfer by means of air particles into the atmosphere is much less efficient than evaporation.

Only over open water and areas of vegetation does the process of evaporation become fully effective.[7]

(5) The heavy load of solid particles, gases and liquid contaminants that is carried in the urban atmosphere. There are ten times more particulates in city air than in the country, which reflect back incoming sunlight and heat, but also retard the outflow of heat.[8] In addition, there are gases emitted from engines and factory chimneys. One of the principal gases in many cities is from dilute sulphuric acid. Solar radiation is therefore affected and there is less sunshine. A high volume of particles in the atmosphere reduces penetration of short-wave radiation in the ultra-violet range, which is biologically important to the production of certain vitamins and the maintenance of health.

The Urban Heat Island

This phenomenon has been studied in some detail by climatologists and is the result of complex effects of the city's processes on its own climate. Lowry describes it as follows.[9]

Assuming a large city set in flat countryside with no large bodies of water nearby, the rising morning sun strikes the walls of its buildings, causing them to absorb heat. In the countryside, however, the sun's radiation is largely reflected off the surface with little heat absorbed. As the morning advances, the countryside begins to warm up, but the city already has a large lead towards maximum temperatures. The warm air in the city centre begins to rise and gradually a slow air circulation is established with air moving in, rising in the centre, flowing outwards at high altitudes and settling again in the open countryside as it cools. Near midday, temperatures inside and outside tend to equalise so that the cycle is weakened. As the afternoon passes, and the sun sinks, much of its radiation is reflected off the countryside but continues to strike building walls directly. Thus the circulation of air is repeated.

During the night the roofs and streets and other hard surfaces of the city begin to radiate heat stored during the day. A cool air layer is likely to be formed at the rooftop level. A stratification of air develops, inhibiting warmer air between buildings from moving upwards. The rural areas, however, cool rapidly at night, from light winds and unobstructed radiation to the night sky. Although both city and country continue to cool throughout the night, by dawn the city is likely to be 4° to 5° warmer.

The following day the heat, smoke and gases from the city are contributed to the heat being generated by radiation. The rising air also carries with it suspended particles of dust and smoke. Over time a dome-shaped layer of haze is formed over the city. At night the particles in the dome become nuclei on which moisture condenses as fog; this fog gets

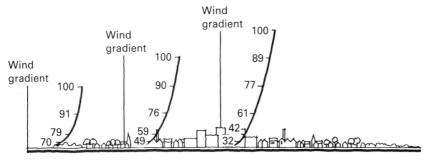

Typical wind profiles over built-up area, urban fringe and open sea Increased aerodynamic roughness of built-up areas causes rapid deceleration of wind compared with open countryside. It has been calculated that wind velocity within a town is half of what it is over open water. At the town edge it is reduced by a third (from Miess, 1979)

The urban heat island Smog dome over large cities occurs periodically due to urban activities. Air rises over warmer city centre and settles over cooler environs so that a circulatory system develops. The dome and its effect on city climate may persist until wind or rain disperses it (from Lowry, 1961)

thicker by downward growth and eventually reaches the ground as smog. Smog inhibits cooling of the air and helps to perpetuate the dome by preventing particles from moving out of the system. In the absence of wind or heavy rain, the situation continues to build up. Since less sunshine can penetrate to warm the city in winter, increased fuel consumption adds to the smog build-up. The process, in effect, is self-perpetuating and is responsible for the severe climatic problems that many cities face.

Problems and Perceptions

Mechanical Climate Control

The search for optimum human climates has been a continual process, particularly in those mid-latitude climates that are less extreme or predictable. Over the last two centuries remarkable changes have been made in man's living environment through improvements to mechanical equipment. James Burke describes the chain of events that led to the invention of the air conditioner in Charleston, South Carolina, by Gorrie in 1850.[10] As a physician, Gorrie was interested in cold air as a cure for malaria. Since obtaining ice in summer was prohibitively expensive, he developed a steam engine to compress air, which, when decompressed, cooled and was circulated in a hospital ward. Subsequently, ice-making and refrigeration machines evolved from this invention and were used to transport food in ships from Australia and also for making German beer. This was followed by the domestic Thermos flask and refrigerator for keeping food and drink cold. These inventions became the precursors of the modern air conditioning unit. One of the first large installations for comfort control of office space was the 300-ton unit installed in the New York Stock Exchange in 1904.[11] The mechanical climate control of buildings has had a number of fundamental effects on the modern city.

(1)   It has freed building from the constraints of weather that were originally imposed upon it. Stylistically, modern architectural form has become an event in its own right, responding to the constraints of mechanical engineering and design doctrine, rather than to the constraints of site and climate. Modern air conditioning has permitted the development of the megastructure; great interconnected interior complexes, whose heating, cooling, humidity and daylight are entirely dependent on mechanical systems.

(2)   It has contributed to the radical changes in urban form that have taken place since fossil fuels became abundant. The city turns its back on an outdoor environment that has become increasingly unlivable; an environment polluted by dust, smog and exhaust fumes, and alternatively swept by winter winds and cooked by summer heat.

(3)   The preoccupation with internal climate has the effect of denying a climatic role for exterior space. Air conditioning screens out the products of industrial processes — the soot, chemical pollutants and dust that threaten public health. Unhealthy outdoor climates generate greater reliance on safe, controlled interior ones, and so more and more development provides interior space for urban activities. The subterranean shopping mall is the modern alternative to the open air market.

(4)   Its effects on life-styles and perceptions of the environment have been profound. Urban life has become a series of air-conditioned experiences. The home, the office, the school, the bus that takes the children there, the movie theatre, have all been sealed off from the outdoors. It creates a world of its own; separated from the increasing problems of health and comfort of the world outside. It is remarkable how much energy and effort is expended to provide climatic comfort

a

The preoccupation
with artificially con-
trolled climate within
buildings. The cre-
ation of pleasant out-
door environments
has consequently
been ignored

b

indoors while at the same time maintaining such unrewarding environments outdoors. It has even been proposed that whole cities should be covered with geodesic domes; a suggestion that has been seriously discussed for some cities, and which takes the problem a step further to the ultimate technological solution. Yet, as Rudofsky has so aptly pointed out, the urban dweller's mania for mechanical comfort, his chances of finding relaxation, hinge on its very absence.[12] One of the reasons for the lemming-like flight from the city on summer weekends is to escape from an oppressive urban climate and the air conditioning unit for the clear air, breezes and sunshine at the summer cottage.

As I pointed out in Chapter One, planning and design doctrine has traditionally been more concerned with conceptual ideologies of built form than with the determinants of natural process. Many early North American towns and institutions, following classical planning modes, paid little heed to the extremes of climate in the regions in which they were located. Attitudes today have not radically changed.

The effort to become independent of the variables of the environment has, by today's standards, been successful. Totally inhospitable places, from the Arctic to the Equator, can now be inhabited, with mechanical heating and cooling systems providing uniform interior temperatures. But it is becoming abundantly clear that the present costs in energy to achieve such a goal are wasteful and unnecessary. The air conditioner provides evidence of this fact. The process of keeping cool in summer inside increases high temperatures outside — a non-productive transfer of heat from one place to another. There are cheaper and more effective ways of achieving similar results. Since open space comprises a large part of the city environment, it can contribute to the modification of climate. At the same time it will be apparent that some problems cannot be solved in the context of natural process alone. Air pollution, for instance, is a macro-problem requiring solutions at the source — the industries that create it. This involves many technical and institutional issues that are beyond the scope of this inquiry. But there are positive aspects to what may be seen as an environmental problem, when urbanism and natural process are seen as a whole. Design, inspired by ecology, provides solutions at less cost and effort. The vernacular forms of older towns and urban landscapes are examples of adaptation that provide some inspiration and guidance for application today.

Alternative Values

Macro-climate, moderated by landform, vegetation and water, has, in various ways, influenced the location and nature of human settlement and uses of the land. Carter has observed that the role of the environment is determined primarily by the culture of man, rather than the other way around.[13] There is no doubt, however, that man has responded in characteristic ways to climatic influences within his control. To be physically comfortable is a fundamental human need. People are affected by climate and react to it even though the response may not be conscious. There is a marked difference in the use of urban places at different seasons. On a winter's day people crowd the sunny side of the street; they seek out spaces protected from the wind; they gather where park seats and patches of lawn provide shade or a cool breeze on a hot summer's day. The manipulation of natural and man-made elements of the environment and solar energy to create felicitous and healthy places to live and work in has preoccupied urban man since the beginning of recorded history.

The business of keeping warm or cool in energy deficient societies is achieved by accepting the limitations of the climatic environment and making the most of its opportunities. This has in the past, and still does in many Third World traditional technologies, been done with great sophistication and economy of means. The Maziara cooling jar is a traditional water cooling and purification sysem used in rural areas of Upper Egypt and other parts of the world for keeping liquids and perishable food cool.[14] The action of evaporation absorbs considerable amounts of heat energy (580 calories of energy for every c.c. of water evaporated).[15] Experiments have shown that with air temperatures ranging from 19° C to 36° C water temperature in the Maziara jar remains

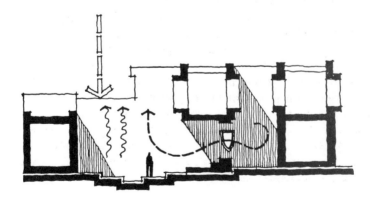

The two courtyard house In this traditional Middle Eastern design, the deep, shaded courtyard is cool; the large courtyard is warm. The difference in air pressure induces a convection draught from the cool to the warm area. Water cooling jars placed in the passageway add to the cooling effect of the breeze (from Cain, 1976)

at a constant 20° C.[16] Cities built in hot dry climates took advantage of wind for ventilation and cooling. Rudofsky illustrated a dramatic example of natural air conditioning in the Lower Sind district of West Pakistan, where specially constructed wind scoops installed on roofs channelled the prevailing wind into every room.[17] Some ingenious passive cooling system in Iran, described by Bahadori,[18] use wind towers which operate by changing air temperature and thus its density. The difference in density creates a draught, pulling air either up or down through the tower and through the building. Courtyard houses and the agglomeration of buildings along narrow streets, typical of Middle Eastern and Mediterranean towns, maintain coolness by trapping cool night-time air and retaining it by day. Many cities in Africa and Spain use awnings or arcades to shield streets from the midday sun. Cities along the

The closely packed buildings and spaces of the medieval city, built to conserve energy, trap sunlight and exclude winds

Mediterranean coast of North Africa are sited so that their streets, laid out at right angles to the shore, funnel incoming sea breezes.[19]

Plants and water have long been associated with city courtyards and gardens to provide air conditioning and places of delight. The Moorish gardens of the Alhambra are a particularly felicitous adaptation to hot dry conditions in southern Spain, where the evaporation of water off tiled surfaces and the dappled shade of plants cool its arcaded courtyards. Buildings in cold climates have employed techniques to conserve heat. The traditional Eskimo igloo, a perfect expression of adaptation, employs the highly insulating properties of snow and orientation of entrances away from wind to create a habitable micro-climate under the harshest conditions. The hemispherical shape provides maximum volume for minimum surface area, thus minimising heat loss. It is said to maintain temperatures of 60° F when temperatures outside are −50° F.[20] The narrow winding streets, enclosed squares, closely packed buildings and courtyards of the pre-industrial city provide as good a demonstration as any of response to climate and energy conservation. The streets minimised the effects of winds and the open squares trapped sunlight.

In all successful climate control, the siting and organisation of built elements and spaces, the use of landform, plants and water has achieved optimum environments for living. Faced with climatic extremes, traditional design methods greatly enhanced urban environments because there was no alternative. Adaptation of these technologies to the modern city is equally necessary if its climatic environment is to be improved. Given the limitations of industrial pollutants, open space has an important function to perform in the restoration of the energy balance. It is to the resources and the techniques available to achieve this that we must now turn.

Some Opportunities

Solar Radiation and Heat Gain

The amount of incoming radiation into a city is dependent on its layout and the pattern of buildings, streets and open spaces. Where sunlight penetrates direct to the floor, for instance in places that have large open plazas and wide streets, radiation is most effectively controlled by vegetation — in particular, trees. The capacity of the forest canopy to absorb large amounts of heat energy is considerable. Short-wave radiation in a closed canopy of maple can be reduced by 80 per cent on a clear midsummer day. The forest can also reduce maximum air temperatures by about 10° F below the temperature in the open.[21] In the city the greater the closure of a tree canopy the greater will be its air conditioning effect on surface temperatures. Surveys carried out in

39

Germany compared a well treed square with a comparable area without trees. The daily radiation balance in June of the treed area versus the treeless one showed a difference of 256 per cent.[22] Deciduous trees have the great advantage, in climatic regions that suffer from extremes of summer and winter temperatures, of providing shade in hot seasons and permitting the sun to penetrate to the floor in winter.

Wall-climbing vines perform a similar function with respect to south-facing building wall surfaces. While attention may be focused on the considerable areas of ground surface in cities requiring shading, it is easy to forget that vertical surfaces vastly increase the area subject to heat gain (see urban influences). A German calculation indicates that there is an aggregate of some 50,000 hectares of vertical surfaces in German cities.[23] In energy terms the calculation suggests that vegetation on vertical surfaces can lower summer temperatures of the street by as much as 5° C. Heat loss from buildings in winter can be reduced by as much as 30 per cent.[24] Biologically, the leaf is an efficient solar collector. During the summer the leaves are raised to take advantage of solar radiation, permitting air to circulate between the plant and the building. It cools, therefore, by means of a 'chimney effect', and through transpiration of the leaves. In winter, the overlapping leaves form an insulating layer of stationary air around the building. Even in climatic regions that are too cold for evergreens to grow successfully, summer cooling still is an important factor, lending an energy-saving and biological validity to what is generally regarded as a decorative addition to architectural facades.

Rooftops in dense urban situations also receive a high level of solar radiation paralleling the heat of ground surfaces. Rooftops constitute a large proportion of the city's upper-level open space in downtown areas and are, from taller structures, often highly visible parts of the urban landscape. Rooftop vegetation functions in the same way as it does at ground level. Rooftop gardens, therefore, can perform a functional role in climate control. The limitations to creating this kind of landscape relate to problems of structural support for soil and plants, which while they can be overcome in new projects, constitute major problems for the large areas of existing roof areas in the city. There are also severe drainage, irrigation, nutrient and (in cold climates) frost problems to be overcome. Alternative strategies must therefore be found to combat one of the major climatic and visual problems of many downtown areas. An examination of many old rooftops will reveal that fortuitous plant communities often gain a foothold. Mosses, grasses and, in places where a small amount of humus and water can collect over time, even adventitious shrubs and small trees colonise these unattended and forgotten places. The issue of fortuitous plant communities will be discussed in further detail in Chapter Four; but it is relevant here to pursue their role in climate amelioration. A research programme undertaken by the Parks Department in Berne on a concrete garage roof showed that certain plants can be grown on 7 cm of soil consisting of pea gravel and silty sand. Various sedum species were used and became well established after a year. Other experiments using grasses and climbers such as Virginia Creeper (*Parthenocissus quinquefolia*) have indicated that many vigorous plants can adapt to such environments with minimum soil depth or humus content.[25]

An experimental alternative to roof landscape has been explored in the city of Toronto in an effort to devise practical and economical ways of planting existing roofs.[26] The site was a flat roof of an old industrial building, exposed to full sunlight for about half the day during summer. On a portion of this surface, a wooden frame was installed, measuring approximately 12 feet by 10 feet. A layer of peatmoss to a depth of 10 inches was placed in the frame and planted with various urban weed species gathered from nearby waste places. A temperature gauge was placed at the bottom level of the peatmoss and the temperature checked periodically over a two-year period.

The experiment revealed several interesting results. The first was the surprising fact that over two years the plant cover readily adapted itself to this hostile climatic environment. Some species died out and were replaced naturally by others, but a viable living cover remained surviving on naturally occurring rainfall for moisture and nitrogen. The second was that temperatures at roof level under the peatmoss remained well above freezing throughout the winter, when temperatures at the surface dropped to 0° F due to the thermal insulating properties of the material. The experiment, though crude and requiring further extended research, points to potential new directions for urban landscape that have important implications for climate and energy conservation. It suggests that hardy plants adapted to city conditions can survive in hostile environments at very little cost or weight requirements on existing building structures; that the insulation value of the growth medium (in this case peatmoss) can contribute to the reduction of winter heat loss from existing urban structures; and that the creation of a new and economical landscape at roof level can contribute to the climatic conditions of the city by reducing heat absorption. It suggests, finally, that modified climates and more agreeable visual landscapes can be achieved at little cost in the existing environments of downtown areas.

Temperature Controls

City temperatures are related to solar radiation and heat gain from urban materials. Temperatures are generally higher than in the countryside. This is accounted for by reduced evaporation, greater conductivity and heat storage capacity of building materials, variation in wind around buildings and the high proportion of airborne pollutants. Temperature can be controlled in several ways.

Water. One of the most effective ways of controlling local climate is through the evaporation of water into the air. This is achieved in several ways; by direct evaporation from open water and by the evapotranspiration of plants. High run-off coefficients of paved surfaces and efficient removal of surface water by storm sewers have effectively removed its availability for evaporation and cooling. This function is greatly assisted by re-introducing water into the city. It occurs by design where pools or lakes are incorporated into the cities landscape. But it also occurs fortuitously after rainstorms where water forms ponds in parking lots, low-lying turfed areas and other open spaces, when it becomes freely available for evaporation. Introducing surface water into the city's paved and unpaved places by impounding run-off rainwater serves an important climatic function. There are also pollution and erosion control advantages in doing so that are discussed in more detail in the next chapter. The existence of natural drainage ponds and lakes in cities such as London's Hyde Park, the new town of Redditch, England, and High Park, Toronto, are examples of landscape features functioning to improve urban climate as well as providing recreation and aesthetic enhancement.

Plants. Plants evaporate water through the metabolic process of evapotranspiration. The cycle of water is carried from the soil through the plant and is evaporated from the leaves as a part of the process of photosynthesis. It has been estimated that on a single day in summer, an acre of turf will lose about 2,400 gallons of water by transpiration and evaporation.[27] The transpiration of water by plants helps to control and regulate humidity and temperature. A single tree can transpire 100 gallons of water a day. This is equivalent to 230,000 K calories of energy in evaporation, which is rendered unavailable to heat surfaces or raise air temperature.[28] Federer has compared the effectiveness of this evaporation by a tree to air conditioning. The mechanical equivalent to the tree transpiring 100 gallons a day is 5 average room air conditioners, each at 2,500 K calories per hour running 19 hours a day.[29] He also points out the important fact that the air conditioner only shifts heat from indoors to outdoors and also uses electric power. The heat is, therefore, still available to increase air temperatures. But with the tree, transpiration renders it unavailable. Thus it is clear that a tree shading a house is more effective. It produces no unwanted waste products from the process of cooling, uses no electric power and continues to work better and better over a long period of time. A numerical simulation of urban climate has suggested that where at least 20 per cent of an urban area in mid-latitudes is covered by plants, more incoming solar radiation is used to evaporate water than to warm the air.[30]

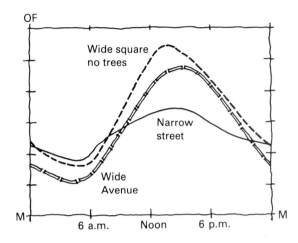

Diurnal temperature variations in Vienna, 4-5 August 1931. The graph shows the differences in temperature for a wide square with no trees, a wide avenue with trees and a narrow street (From Robinette, 1977)

Air Pollution Control

As I mentioned earlier, the only satisfactory controls for the solid particles, gases and other airborne contaminants are institutional and technical. Much improved air conditions have been achieved over the last twenty years in Great Britain due to tight air pollution control laws and regulations. At the same time it is evident that a return to the use of coal would again aggravate the air pollution problem. There can be little doubt that air pollution in some form will continue to exist for many years as a reality of urban climate. Where air pollution is dilute, however, an important environmental resource is plants. It has long been known that plants filter dust in cities. Current research in plant physiology suggests that they do more than act as filters. The surface area of a tree has evolved to maximise light and gas exchange. Trees have ten times the surface area of the soil on which they stand. A hundred-year-old beech, for instance, has been estimated to have some 800,000 leaves; a leaf surface area of 16,000 square metres per 160 square metres of tree base. Calculations show that the intercellular spaces of leaves (the sum of cell walls) increase the total leaf area to roughly 160,000 square metres.[31] Leaves can take up or absorb pollutants such as ozone and sulphur dioxide to significant levels. One calculation has demonstrated that a 15-inch diameter Douglas fir can remove 43.5 lb of sulphur dioxide per year, without injury from an atmospheric concentration of 0.25 parts per million (p.p.m.). By way of illustration of the effectiveness of trees in removing sulphur dioxide, it shows that to take up the 455,000 tons of sulphur dioxide released annually in St Louis, Missouri, it would require 50 million trees. These would occupy about 5 per cent of the city's land area.[32] Measurements taken in 1962 in Hyde Park, London, indicated

43

that concentrations of sulphur dioxide were reduced due, in part, to local circulation of air generated by the vegetation and in part by the uptake of gas by the leaves.[33]

Soil micro-organisms are more effective than vegetation in removing carbon monoxide and assist in the conversion of carbon monoxide to carbon dioxide. It is believed that oxygen released by roadside plants may help in lowering carbon monoxide level along heavy traffic routes. Nitrogen oxide combining with gases such as oxygen produces nitrogen dioxide, which is then readily absorbed by vegetation.[34]

Vegetation also collects heavy metals. In New Haven, Connecticut, one researcher found that a sugar maple 12 inches in diameter removed from the atmosphere during one growing season 60 mg of cadmium and 140 mg of lead.[35] This suggests that vegetated spaces can provide areas where dust can settle out and where air pollutants are diluted.

However, it is evident that plant damage occurs when pollutants are excessive. Schmid points out that the severity of plant damage is complicated by many factors, such as the age of the plant, its state of nutrition, moisture when exposed, and other factors. Plant species also vary in their tolerance to air pollution and their effectiveness in improving air quality. A 1973 report by the US Environmental Protection Agency estimates costs of air pollution at $16.1 billion for 1968, of which $0.1 billion was in damage to vegetation.[36] In effect, plants cannot be regarded as the panacea for air pollution, but they do assist air purity and serve one other important climatic function; as indicators of air pollution and thus of the health of the people who live in cities. There are, therefore, highly valid reasons for the reforestation of urban areas in the planning and design of urban open space.

Wind

Of all the influences the city has on weather it is the presence or the absence of wind that has the greatest impact on the comfort of the local climate, as anyone who has walked the streets of a Midwestern Canadian city in winter will agree. There is less wind on average in cities than in the open countryside. Miess states that within a town, wind velocity may be half of what it is over open water.[37] On the other hand, the existence of free-standing towers separated by large open areas and the general layout of streets speed up winds locally, creating the unpleasant gusty windswept conditions and snow drifting which are typical of a winter's day. It has been found that some winds associated with buildings can be increased up to three times. Wind affects temperatures, evaporation, the rate of moisture loss and transpiration from vegetation, and snow drifting, all of which are particularly important to local microclimatic conditions.

A building research station digest of 1972[38] shows the impact of the wind environment around building complexes, such as shopping centres, that have become typical of many redevelopment projects in the post-war years. The generally uniform low building layout of older towns, arranged along curved and twisting streets, provides shelter — the result of lower wind gradients at ground level. When winds meet a building that is considerably taller than its neighbours, the flow pattern changes. Air currents divide at about two-thirds or three-quarters of the building height, creating a downdraught on the windward face and highly turbulent conditions at ground level. Reduced air pressure on the lee side creates suction and high wind speeds around corners and through passageways under the building. Tests on a shopping complex with a 45-metre building flanking one side showed that prevailing westerly winds were deflected into the pedestrian precinct with velocities 2.2 times wind speed.[39]

Many studies of the effects of forest cover and shelter belts on winds have been made with respect to the speed of air movement, the protection afforded and the effect of wind barriers on heat loss from buildings. Tree stands are effective in slowing wind; the greater the roughness of the ground surface the more wind velocities are reduced. The smaller an open forest clearing, the less turbulence at ground level there will be. Shelter belts may reduce winds by 50 per cent, the sharpest

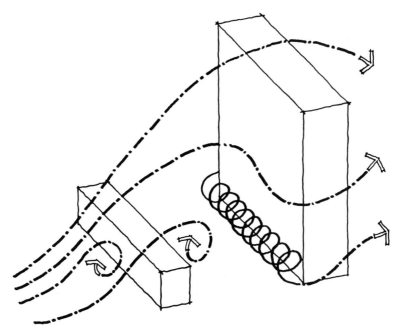

Patterns of wind caused by a building considerably taller than its neighbours (from Building Research Digest, UK, 1972)

reduction in wind velocity extending 10 to 15 times the height of the trees on the lee side.[40] According to Olgay a 20 m.p.h. wind can double the heat load of a house normally exposed to 5 m.p.h. winds.[41] The agricultural experiment station at Kansas State University has shown that the heating load on a house can be greatly reduced with the use of wind breaks.[42] A study of residential site design and energy conservation by the Ontario Ministry of Housing has calculated that landscaping is capable of producing energy savings in excess of 5 per cent.[43]

The relationship of buildings to open space in cities is therefore crucial to the problem of wind control. In cool climates where wind creates discomfort or danger either from its increased strength or cold (wind-chill factor) the problem is one of modifying building heights and siting in new development, or providing shelter by overhead structural or plant canopies and screens at ground level.

Implications for Design

Green Lungs

We have found that water and plants are the important natural elements of climate control in the city. But what is their sphere of influence? How much vegetation or surface area of water is needed to have a marked effect on the climate of the city? Where should these be located? These are questions that are important for design. Answers to them depend on the climate of the region, the nature and variations of climate between one place and another, the characteristics of the site and the nature of the built-up area. At a small scale, experience tells us that a sheltered, well treed open space is a cooler and more pleasant place on a hot day. The sphere of influence of its elements, tree canopy, shrubs and water, may well be local, however, particularly if it is an isolated place in the general fabric of streets and buildings. The walled gardens of old European towns create a sphere of influence within them that are considerably cooler than outside. The impact of major open spaces, the 'green lungs' of the city, that have long been the ideal of landscape planning, may well be limited in the overall urban climate. Jane Jacobs has observed that the term 'green lung' is only applicable to the park spaces themselves and has little effect on the overall quality of the air in the city.[44] There have been claims that the oxygen produced by vegetation can affect the balance of oxygen in the air. These have evolved from the fact that much more oxygen is produced in photosynthesis than is used up in respiration. There is, however, as much oxygen used up in plant decay and the metabolism of animals that feed on plants as there is released by photosynthesis. The concept of the 'green lung' may be inaccurate in describing the effect of parks on the oxygen content of the city overall, but research has established definite connections between forest vegetation cover, open space distribution and urban climate control. The concept of open space systems has been integrated into the planning of many new towns. The new town of Redditch is an example, in the United Kingdom, where small nucleated neighbourhoods are surrounded by an open space system that incorporates streams and natural drainage ponds, woven into the fabric of the town. But we are concerned more in this inquiry with the renewal of existing cities and the potential of their open space resources to create better environments.

Miess observes that the necessary amount of open space in an urban area and its optimum distribution cannot be stated quantitatively.[45] But from a climatic point of view, a fine mesh of open spaces, distributed evenly over the whole city, is more effective than reliance on a few large ones. These latter spaces need to be supplemented by a large number of small parks throughout the built-up area. 'Such a mesh facilitates horizontal exchange of air bodies of varying temperatures and consequently a balance is reached more quickly and with less resistance.'[46] A study of Dallas and Fort Worth found that the heat island reached its peak not in central areas of tall buildings, but along the fringes of the downtown area that contained low buildings and parking lots.[47] This suggests that effort to ameliorate climate should be emphasised in these areas. Bernatzky suggests that the effect of the heat island can be partially counteracted by concentric rings of open space to filter and oxygenate the air as it moves inward to the city centre.[48] In summer the heat from urban build-up in the city centre heats air which rises, creating a low air pressure situation. This in turn draws cooler air in from the edges of the city. The quality of the air as it moves into the city is increasingly degraded, accumulating gases and particulate matter and being progressively deoxygenated. Parks and vegetated spaces located in the path of this moving air will alter wind flow, ameliorate air quality and reduce temperature. In Chicago, air flow modelling has concluded that a finger plan with corridors of development and wedges of open space would have the most positive effect on air quality.[49]

Some Design Principles

There is still much to be learned about the effect of plants on city-wide climate and how the scientific data that have been accumulated may be applied in determining optimum patterns of open space. Researchers in the field have varying views on what those patterns might be. We must, however, be careful to avoid the trap that often awaits those seeking answers to such problems; the temptation to create cookie-pattern solutions for every urban situation. This, in fact, is precisely the criticism that has been levelled at many planning theories in the past that attempted to seek standard solutions to cities. They ignored the

47

individuality and uniqueness of each city and each place. Thus, while there can be no final or definitive solution to questions that have been explored here, certain general principles do emerge that are both pertinent and useful to this inquiry.

(1) The natural patterns of the land, its hills and valleys, rivers, streams, open water and plants, determine local climatic patterns and affect, in some measure, the environment of the city. Although the extent of this influence may be local, the retention and enhancement of natural features for climatic reasons are essential parts of open space planning. An example of where climatic patterns, conditioned by topography and vegetation, have had a major impact on city form is the case of Stuttgart, West Germany, described later in this chapter.

(2) Vegetation and water have a major effect on the maintenance of an equable micro-climate within cities. Since the large areas of paved and hard vertical surfaces in the city generate the greatest heat in summer, establishing canopy vegetation such as trees, trellises, wall climbing vines, etc. wherever possible will reduce the adverse effects of the urban heat island. It will also remove dust and purify toxic gases and other chemicals. Dense canopies that provide maximum shade are much more effective than current practice often allows, where trees are seen as individual specimens. The maintenance of vegetation and forest planting in both parks and non-recreational spaces throughout the city also increases the amount of overall surface area available for cooling and purifying the air. In Davis, California, it has been found that trees lower street temperatures by 10° F in summer, reducing electricity used for air conditioning by half. A city ordinance requires all paved parking lots, in shopping centres, schoolyards, etc. to be 50 per cent shaded by tree canopies within 15 years of the issuing of a building permit.[50] The retention of water and natural ponds in parks and other locations is also critical to restoring the energy balance by direct evaporation.

(3) The large roofscape areas of downtown and industrial sites contribute to heat build-up. The development of rooftop planting serves a similarly important role in climate amelioration. There is a need for basic research into lightweight low-maintenance techniques for establishing plants on existing rooftops similar to the experiment described earlier in this chapter. The use of naturalised urban vegetation that can survive with little or no care under the most severe conditions has important implications for climatic control.

(4) In most successful examples of climate manipulation in extreme environments, the emphasis has been on an urban texture of small spaces and low buildings. In hot summer climates, small living spaces increase areas of shade and reduce the build-up of solar radiation. They are, in addition, easier to control artificially through plants, water and ventila-

tion. In cold climates they are less subject to cold winds, snow drifting and extremes of temperature. Organisation of space can create suntraps by orientation of buildings to the south and exclusion of winter winds. In most existing cities where built form has evolved with little regard for climatic considerations, the materials of the landscape must serve a climatic role. Groundform and plants must be used to create small spaces, suntraps, sheltered places, shelter belts, to counteract prevailing winds, canopies to modify downdraughts and so on.

The response to climate is the first step in the establishment of a vernacular; of regionality, linking built form with the place in which it occurs. Without this response the designed landscape may be as clearly identified with the International Style as was the architectural fashion that gave rise to the name. Several contemporary examples of form evolving from climatic determinants are illustrated in the following pages.

Example one — A Northern University

In the late 1960s and early 1970s the University of Alberta underwent a major expansion programme to accommodate almost a doubling of its student population. Located within the city of Edmonton, Alberta, the university is very much a part of an urban environment that has had one of the fastest growth rates in Canada. One of the most critical objectives of the development plan was to create an appropriate campus environment for living and working, since the period of greatest activity during the academic year takes place during the severe winter months.

Over the years the evolution of the campus had been dictated by conventional planning. Buildings were placed formally in the landscape, isolated from each other by large open areas and reflecting prevailing attitudes and nostalgias for wide open spaces and a rural setting. The inappropriateness of this model of urban development to the climate and environment of the prairies was expressed in the way people moved around the campus; cutting through buildings not designed for the purpose in an effort to avoid the unpleasant conditions created by unimpeded winds, gusting around tall structures and permanent shade cast by ill placed buildings. An examination of building coverage revealed that less than 15 per cent of the campus was occupied by buildings. The remaining 85 per cent was taken up by parking lots, roads, service areas, manicured turf and residual space that made much of the campus unusable and inhospitable.[51] An examination of climatic data indicated that Edmonton is situated at latitude 53.35° North in a region of cold temperate climate.

The coldest time of the year and the period of least sunshine (100 hours and less per month between November and January) occurs during the academic year. While prevailing winds are from the south, the highest

Location of University of Alberta campus, c. 1969

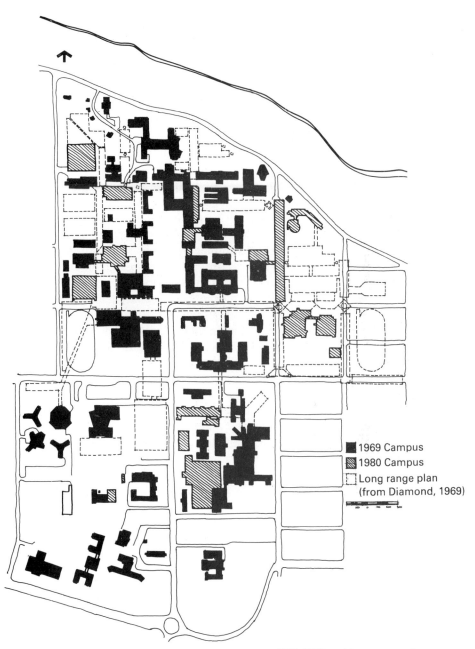

1969 Campus
1980 Campus
Long range plan
(from Diamond, 1969)

University of Alberta campus 1969-1980 and long range plan

velocities occur from the north-west. During these periods the combination of wind and cold temperatures creates, on occasion, a wind-chill factor of more than $-50°$ F, enough to freeze exposed flesh in less than one minute. In addition sun angles at the winter solstice (22 December) are only 13° to 15° at noon.

The two most critical design factors in cold climates, then, are wind and sun. The absence of wind and the presence of sunshine in the shaping of spaces can make the outdoors a very pleasant experience even when temperatures are very low. The development plan for the university, therefore, incorporated the following climatic criteria which became the guiding principles for its growth.

(1) The acquisition of additional land for campus expansion along conventional lines was rejected in favour of a policy of infilling within existing campus boundaries. This increased land coverage by buildings from 15 per cent to 34 per cent greatly increased the efficiency and economy of land use. Part of the increased coverage took the form of parking structures on many levels to reduce the area taken up by surface parking and to increase usable and contained open spaces. Infill buildings incorporated interior pedestrian streets linking academic departments, housing, food, recreation functions that provided alternative sheltered pedestrian routes during the winter months. The concept of infill and linkages also reinforced the notion of a high mix of uses, accessibility to services and social integration, that isolated university buildings tend to discourage.[52]

(2) Since the greatest need was to maintain maximum winter sunlight, development was designed to avoid tall structures on the south side of open spaces. Alternatively indoor/outdoor activity areas could be located on the south side of buildings.

(3) A limit of four to six storeys was recommended for most new building to reduce wind downdraught and gusting and increase available sunlight in winter.

These planning principles set a framework for open spaces that could respond to basic design principles for climatic control at a micro-climatic scale. These included:

— the creation of small well defined protected courtyards and places of passive use;
— the use of raised landforms, screens and planting around entrances, sitting and meeting places, to reduce wind chill and create sun traps;
— the use of coniferous wind breaks along pedestrian routes and associated with large spaces such as athletics areas;
— dense planting and screens at narrow building openings and

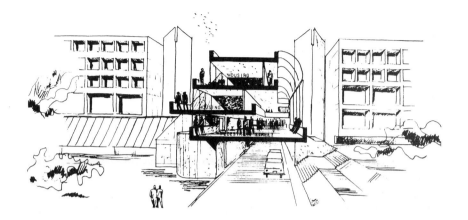

Design principles Connecting interior street and vehicular/pedestrian separation with housing over (from Diamond, 1969)

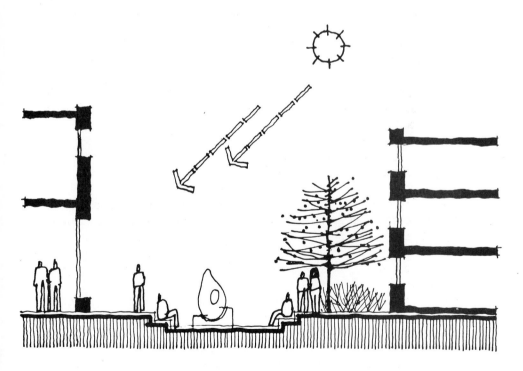

Small, well defined protected courts

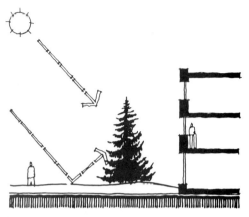

Walkways protected by windbreaks in large open areas

Snow glare and intense light from low sun may be reduced by use of coniferous or dense deciduous plants

One of the enclosed courts with land shaping and dense planting. It provides summer shade, and sunny protected spaces. Note the connecting pedestrian link built into a student housing block. The link provides alternative interior access in winter

connecting spaces where venturi winds are normally generated;

— reduction of glare from snow and creation of visual interest by plants and sculptural elements in the winter landscape when seen from indoors;

— deciduous tree canopies that provide shade and temperature reduction over paved surfaces in the heat of the summer while allowing full exposure to the winter sun. Dense deciduous canopies also contribute to the filtering of wind from above where a tall building creates downdraught.[53]

Example two — A Lake Front Park

The University of Alberta campus is an example of design with climate in the context of an essentially built environment. The development of the urban park, however, described here, is a case where landscape rather than architectural forms has controlled the climatic environment. Called Ontario Place, it is a series of man-made islands, canals, bays and exhibit buildings located off the Lake Ontario shoreline in downtown Toronto. Opened in 1971, its purpose was to promote the culture and history of Ontario and its people and focus attention on the great potential of a long neglected urban water front for renewal and recreation.

Building a park from landfill in the water on the edge of a major lake involves numerous physical and environmental problems, not the least of which is the impact of prevailing winds and wave action on a totally created landscape. A body of water as large as Lake Ontario has little value as a recreational resource as it stands. To make it usable, it requires quiet water and land protected from the elements. While there were many social, recreational and technical factors influencing the design of the complex, a dominant influence was the climatic environment created by its orientation to the water.[54]

Studies showed that protection from strong prevailing south-west winds blowing off the lake and consequent wave action was essential to the initial construction of pavilions. Protection from the elements was also critical to the stability of earth fill that made up the islands and the viability of recreation in an exposed island environment. Recreation facilities included a marina, clusters of boutiques and restaurants, open air forum, children's village, quiet water recreational boating and casual activities. These all required wind-protected micro-environments. This was particularly critical to the park's potential winter use for skating and cold weather festivities. The island forms that evolved, therefore, were a response to these requirements, particularly on the west island which took the brunt of prevailing south-west winds. A heavily armoured sea wall (constructed from three lake freighters) and a series of armoured points with connecting beaches (responding to marine engineering determinants), protect the marina and interior edges from wave erosion.

(a) **Ontario Place** Aerial view from south-west (b) Lakeside view, showing hard edge protecting land. Protective landform and planting is on the left (c) Interior waterway (Architects Craig Zeidler and Strong; landscape architects Hough Stansbury and Associates)

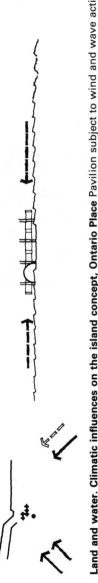

Land and water. Climatic influences on the island concept, Ontario Place Pavilion subject to wind and wave action. Costly construction in exposed waters. No usable water or land for recreation activities

Wave energy absorbed and redirected by edge. Pavilion remains exposed to wind. Usable water surface only partly calmed and remains inaccessible

Landform moderates and redirects wind. Pavilion sheltered yet strongly water oriented

A continuous raised landform and dense coniferous planting buffer parallel to south-west winds shelter water and land activities on the lee side and provide essential winter protection. Two contrasting physical environments have been thus created; a windward side facing the main body of the lake and buffeted by the weather, and a sheltered side that exploits quiet bays, canals and waterways and a wind-free landscape for social and recreational activities.

To determine the validity of the design, it was necessary to investigate the interaction of landscaped land forms with the wind profile. This would assess potential problems, reveal weaknesses in the design and indicate where changes might be necessary. A series of tests were consequently carried out in which a 1/30-inch scale model was placed in the low-speed eight-foot wind tunnel at the University of Toronto. The model was rotated through various wind directions and two types of tests were carried out. First, a smoke visualisation technique was used to define the stream lines of the flow across the model and outline the effects of the land forms and planting on the mean wind profile. Second, fine plastic particles were distributed evenly over the model surface and subsequently

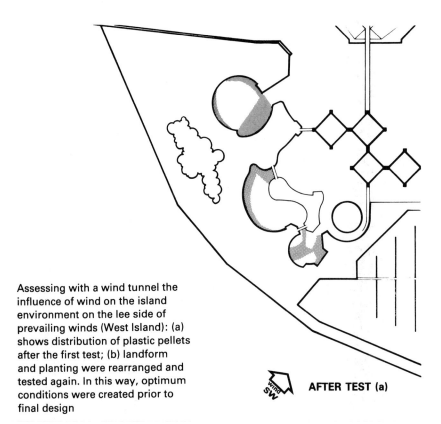

Assessing with a wind tunnel the influence of wind on the island environment on the lee side of prevailing winds (West Island): (a) shows distribution of plastic pellets after the first test; (b) landform and planting were rearranged and tested again. In this way, optimum conditions were created prior to final design

WIND SW

AFTER TEST (a)

wind tested to reveal areas of scour in places exposed to high wind and areas unaffected by wind. These showed clearly the relative protection afforded by the various land forms, buildings and plants and provided a basis for the final shaping of the landscape. Subsequent evaluation of the completed park has verified that these forms are effective in providing climatic protection in the areas where it is required. The continuing growth and density of plant material over time have served to heighten the contrast between sheltered and windy environments in the park and provide a diversity of places.

Example three — City Form and Climate

The links between major landforms, vegetation and urban form are nowhere better seen than in the city of Stuttgart. Located in the centre of an industrial region of over 2 million people, the city was once plagued by air pollution, a situation greatly accentuated by frequent temperature inversions due to its location. The city occupies two valleys lying at right angles to each other. The main part of the city is located in a basin-like valley (the Nesenbach), which is surrounded on three sides by steep

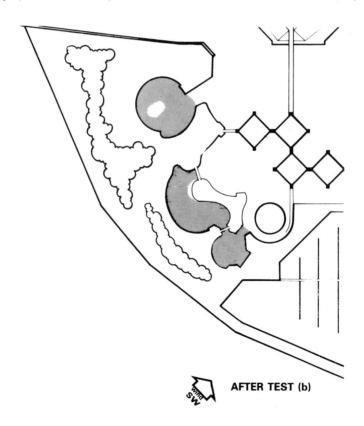

AFTER TEST (b)

slopes which extend on ridges into the centre of the city. The remainder is located along the open valley of the Neckar. The pollution problem became worse when urban expansion started to occupy the valley sides, replacing vineyards with building. These interrupted normal katabatic flows of air, associated with valley land formations, from the surrounding hill vegetation to the city. It became apparent that there were interrelated links between open space distribution, climatic phenomena generated by topography and a healthy city environment.

A network of parks and open spaces has now been established in the city, linking parks to each other, to the river, forests and vineyards on the slopes of the valleys. The forests, productive commercial resources, the vineyards and other arable lands account for about two-thirds of the total municipal area of 20,723 hectares.[55] The vineyards climatically tend to be more efficient than recreational open space since the vertical rows of vines permit uninterrupted air flow down valley sides. The function and character of the parks is highly varied. Stuttgart's natural topography is such that the city's central parks are flat and those further out are located on steep valley sides, providing a dramatic setting within the urban area. Within the parks themselves (which include some 490 hectares), the use of plants, lakes and water sculpture has been exploited to provide places full of refreshing and varied sights and sounds. Green spaces are on the average 3° C cooler than surrounding built-up areas.[56] On both a city-wide and human scale the parks and working landscapes within and surrounding Stuttgart are among the most climatically functional, socially useful and aesthetically pleasing of any modern park in the Western world.

One may be tempted to comment that the value of plants, landform and water to create beneficial micro-environments has been 'redis-covered' by contemporary science. It has begun to measure something that people knew by trial and error and have made use of for generations in traditional built environments. Applying traditional methods of climate control, in effect, now has the blessing of the scientific method. But there are climatic phenomena that the old vernacular urban landscapes were rarely, if ever, faced with. Atmospheric pollution, urban heat islands and downdraughts, drainage systems and hydrological imbalances are a creation of large industrial cities. Creating favourable habitats by natural means combines traditional wisdom, modern science and intelligent planning. The application of plants and water to the walls, floor and roof surfaces of the city can create a natural climatic control and can in large measure restore the energy balance through evaporation of water into the air, and the metabolic processes of plants. The arrangement of built and landscape elements can reduce the impact of wind, take advantage of sun and create favourable micro-climatic environments. Following the principle of economy of means, the natural patterns and materials of the

View to Stuttgart from forested slopes

Connections link park system together

Water forms a major element in the parks

Plants and shade over paved surfaces are distributed everywhere in Stuttgart

landscape can be made to work for the city environment in new ways and at less cost, compared to the energy costs currently incurred to maintain highly inhospitable conditions. It is evident that water and plants are interconnected elements of natural process playing a vital role in urban climate. It will also be evident that in our search for an ecological basis for urban design an understanding of their essential nature will reveal other opportunities and benefits. It is to these, therefore, that we must now turn.

Notes

1. Harry Graham, *Ruthless Rhymes for Heartless Homes* (Edward Arnold, London, reissued 1974).
2. Michael Miess, 'The Climate of Cities' in Ian C. Laurie (ed.), *Nature in Cities* (John Wiley, New York, 1979).
3. T. J. Chandler, *The Climate of London* (Hutchinson, London, 1975).
4. Miess, 'The Climate of Cities'.
5. Ford Foundation, *Exploring Energy Choices*, a preliminary report of the Ford Foundation's Energy Policy Project (The Ford Foundation, Washington, DC, 1974).
6. Miess, 'The Climate of Cities'.
7. Ibid.
8. H. E. Landsburg, 'The Climate of Towns' in William L. Thomas Jr. (ed.), *Man's Role in Changing the Face of the Earth* (University of Chicago Press, Chicago, 1956), vol. 2.
9. William P. Lowry, 'The Climate of Cities', *Scientific American* (Aug. 1967).
10. James Burke, *Connections* (Macmillan, London, 1978).
11. Melvin M. Rotsch, 'The Home Environment' in Melvin Kranzberg and Carroll W. Pursell Jr. (eds.), *Technology in Western Civilization* (Oxford University Press, Oxford, 1967), vol. 2.
12. Bernard Rudofsky, *Architecture without Architects* (The Museum of Modern Art, New York, 1964).
13. George F. Carter, *Man and the Land, a Cultural Geography* (Holt, Reinhart and Winston, New York, 1966).
14. Allan Cain, Farroukh Afshar, *et al.*, 'Traditional Cooling Systems in the Third World', *Ecologist*, vol. 6, no. 2 (1976).
15. Ibid.
16. Ibid.
17. Rudofsky, *Architecture without Architects*.
18. Mehdi N. Bahadori, 'Passive Cooling Systems in Iranian Architecture', *Scientific American (Feb. 1978)*.
19. T. H. D. Turner, 'The Design of Open Space', in Timothy Cochrane and Jane Brown (eds.), *Landscape Design for the Middle East* (RIBA Publications, London, 1978).
20. Gary O. Robinette (ed.), *Landscape Planning for Energy Conservation* (Environmental Design Press for American Society of Landscape Architects Foundation, Reston Va., 1977).
21. Ibid.
22. Miess, *The Climate of Cities*.
23. Rudolf Doernach, 'Uber den Nutzen von biotektonischen Grünsystemen', *Garten + Landschaft*, no. 6 (1979).
24. Ibid.
25. Falk Trillitzsch, 'Anregungen zum Thema Dachgarten', *Garten + Landschaft*, no. 6 (1979).
26. Hough, Stansbury and Associates, Practical roof-top experiment 1977-9, no compiled data.
27. Robinette, *Landscape Planning*.

28.　C. A. Federer, 'Effect of Trees in Modifying Urban Microclimate' in *Trees and Forests in an Urbanizing Environment Symposium* (Co-operative Extension Service, University of Massachusetts, Amherst, 1970).

29.　Ibid.

30.　James A. Schmid, *Urban Vegetation* (University of Chicago, Department of Geography, Research Paper no. 161, 1975).

31.　Fidenzio Salvatore, *The Potential Role of Vegetation in Improving the Urban Air Quality, a Study of Preventative Medicine* (York-Toronto Lung Assocation, Willowdale, Ontario, 1982).

32.　Schmid, *Urban Vegetation.*

33.　C. W. K. Wainwright and M. J. G. Wilson, 'Atmospheric Pollution in a London Park', *International Journal of Air and Water Pollution*, vol. 6 (1962).

34.　Salvatore, *The Potential Role.*

35.　Schmid, *Urban Vegetation.*

36.　Ford Foundation, *Exploring Energy Choices.*

37.　Miess, *The Climate of Cities.*

38.　Building Research Station Digest, 'Wind Environment around Tall Buildings', *RIBA Journal Digest*, no. 141 (May 1972).

39.　Ibid.

40.　Robinette, *Landscape Planning.*

41.　Victor G. Olgyay, *Design with Climate* (Princeton University Press, Princeton, 1963).

42.　Robinette, *Landscape Planning.*

43.　Ontario Ministry of Housing, *Residential Site Design and Energy Conservation, Part 1, General Report* (Government of Ontario, Toronto, 1980).

44.　Jane Jacobs, *The Life and Death of Great American Cities* (Random House, New York, 1961).

45.　Miess, *The Climate of Cities.*

46.　Ibid.

47.　Schmid, *Urban Vegetation*

48.　Aloys Bernatzky, 'The Effect of Trees on the Climate of Towns' in Shirley E. Wright *et al.* (eds.), *Tree Growth in the Landscape* (Dept. of Horticulture, Wye College, University of London, 1974).

49.　Salvatore, *The Potential Role.*

50.　Reg Lang and Audrey Armour, *New Directions in Municipal Energy Conservation, the California Experience* (Ontario Ministry of Energy, Toronto, 1980).

51.　A. J. Diamond and Barton Myers, 'University of Alberta, Long Range Development Plan', consultant report, June 1969.

52.　Ibid.

53.　Hough, Stansbury and Associates, 'University of Alberta, Long Range Landscape Development Plan', consultant report, July 1971.

54.　Hough, Stansbury and Associates, 'Ontario Place', unpublished report, 1971.

55.　International Federation of Landscape Architects, *10 Kongress der Internationalen Federation der Landschaftsarchitekten* (Stuttgart, 1966).

56.　Jenny Cox, 'The Green Ways of Stuttgart', *Landscape Design*, no. 110 (1975).

WATER

Wherever you walk in Venice, not far beneath your overheated feet is one of over 22 million wooden stakes, the majority of which are as sound as the day they were driven into the soft silts of the lagoon. The reason for their long lasting service is that the lagoon muds are, and presumably always have been, deficient in oxygen . . . tourists and local inhabitants should rejoice in the fact that the waters of Venice are polluted. All the time there is excess organic matter pouring through the canals, the water will be bung full of bacteria thriving on the products of decay and in so doing using up the oxygen dissolved in the water and that helps protect the all important piles.[1]

Introduction

It may seem to be a contradiction in terms to be suggesting, as the botanist David Bellamy does, that 'pollution is a good thing'. Everyone knows, of course, that 'pollution is a bad thing'. Yet in many ways the knee-jerk reaction to pollution inhibits a creative approach to the problem. Conventional wisdom needs to be challenged. While it is ironic that Venice should be standing thanks to its polluted water, this fact reflects a need to explore the interaction between natural process and urbanism. So this chapter explores the physical and biological properties of water, the way its natural cycles are affected by the city and the implications for urban design when alternatives to its current uses and management are examined.

Natural Processes

Hydrological Cycles
The vast, never ending cycle of distillation and circulation known as the hydrological cycle is a well known phenomenon. The most important feature is its dynamic quality. Water is constantly being replenished. Evaporating off the oceans, it circulates over land masses, falls as rain or

snow, percolates below the surface and is returned to the ocean via rivers and lakes. At every point in this movement some water is constantly being returned to the atmosphere as water vapour, to circulate round the earth and fall again as rain or snow. As a result the atmospheric water content remains practically constant. Annual precipitation of the earth's land surfaces averages about 27 inches (or 24,000 cubic miles of water).[2] At the same time distribution varies enormously. There are vast desert areas where rain falls only rarely and areas where annual rainfall is as much as 400 inches. The amount of water evaporating from oceans is on average 9 per cent more than what falls back to the oceans as rain. The 9 per cent represents the amount of rain falling over land areas and produces the flow of all the world's rivers.[3] The water which falls over the land as precipitation may follow a number of directions. Some of it is evaporated back to the atmosphere before it reaches the earth; some is intercepted by vegetation and is either evaporated, or transpired back to the atmosphere; some filters into the soil and underground reservoirs, and some runs off to enter streams, rivers, lakes and marshes on its way back to the ocean.

Forests and Watersheds

Forests protect watersheds. They stabilise slopes, minimise erosion, reduce sediment inputs to streams and maintain the quality and temperature of the water. In the hilly uplands of a watershed, where water sources originate, forest vegetation greatly influences the movement of water from the atmosphere to the earth and back again. It performs a vital function of maintaining stream flows; reducing peaks and potential flooding, but sustaining flow in dry periods. About 30 per cent of the rain falling on the forest is intercepted by the canopy and evaporates back to the atmosphere.[4] Some of the water that does reach the ground percolates through the soil into streams. The root activity and decaying matter of the forest floor act as a sponge holding and gradually releasing a great deal of water. Winter snows trapped in the forest are also gradually released to the streams and rivers in the spring, because the ground beneath the forest is less deeply frozen than in open ground and thawing takes longer in the shade of trees. Some is returned to the atmosphere by the biological processes of transpiration through the leaves of plants. So the forest has a great effect on the movement of water from the atmosphere to the earth and back to the atmosphere. Together with surface and underground water bodies it performs an important role as storage.

Human Impacts on Watersheds

Measurements of water movement in some watersheds have been made for many years. The Canadian Forestry Service has reported on experiments on the eastern slopes of the Rocky Mountains showing the effect of logging on stream flow. After logging, stream flows may increase by as much as 50 per cent, diminishing gradually as the forest regenerates. In one study 35 years elapsed before the stream was back to its natural flow level.[5] The flow regime, or the timing of flow, also changes. Peak or maximum flow after logging may increase by as much as 21 per cent and low flow by 90 per cent. Erosion increases due to higher run-off and peak flows remove soils and damage productive land. One study of sedimentation from erosional processes showed a sediment concentration 1,000 times greater in streams running through cultivated lands than in streams from a pine forest. Sediment concentrations were 17 times the prelogging rate in another study.[6] Thus, forests play a vital role in sustaining both the supply and the quality of water.

Biology and Transition[7]

Lakes contain practically all the fresh water in existence and maintain the rivers and streams of most watersheds. An understanding of their biological and evolutionary processes is, therefore, useful to this study of urban ecology.

Water Biology. Lakes can be classified on the basis of biological productivity. Productivity is a measure of the quantity of life in all forms supported by an ecosystem. At the base of an aquatic food chain green plants convert the energy of sunlight into food calories. The abundance and rate of growth of the algae depend particularly on the supply of dissolved nutrients which ultimately determines productivity at all higher levels of the food chain. Productivity can also be considered to be a measure of the organic matter produced by a system. Each stage of a food chain uses some of the production of the preceding stage, but much decomposes. In a lake decaying organic matter falls to the deeper water, where oxygen is consumed in the process of decomposition. Thus, increased productivity will lead to increased use, reducing the exchange of oxygen between the surface and bottom layers of the lake. Oxygen depletion may proceed to the point at which there is not enough oxygen for various species of fish to survive.

Oligotrophic lakes are nutrient poor. The supply of plant nutrients to the lake is small in relation to the volume of water to which these are added. Productivity is, therefore, low. Usually oligotrophic lakes are deep, often with a mean depth of more than 15 metres. The paucity of nutrients limits the amount of algal growth. The water is usually very clear, and what algal production occurs can take place through much of the water column as light can penetrate to a considerable depth. As productivity is low, decomposing organic matter may not consume a large proportion of the dissolved oxygen in the bottom layers. Fish such as lake

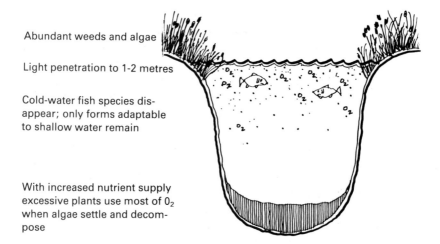

Weeds and algae scarce

Light penetration to 6-10 metres

Cold and warm-water fish species

Deep, cold, clear lake. Scarce algae, using little O_2 when they settle and decompose

Balanced production

Oligotrophic Lake

Abundant weeds and algae

Light penetration to 1-2 metres

Cold-water fish species disappear; only forms adaptable to shallow water remain

With increased nutrient supply excessive plants use most of O_2 when algae settle and decompose

Lake productivity The differences of biological productivity in oligotrophic and eutrophic lakes (from Hough Stansbury & Associates, 1977)

trout which have a requirement for oxygen-rich, cool, deep water habitats, are frequently found in oligotrophic lakes.

Eutrophic lakes are those which are rich in plant nutrients. They are frequently shallow, with a mean depth of less than 35 feet, so they may contain a small volume of water in relation to the supply of nutrients. The abundant supply of nutrients leads to a large algal population, which causes turbidity of the water. As algae require light for photosynthesis, the algal population tends to be concentrated near the water surface, preventing the passage of light to deeper water. In eutrophic lakes scums of algae on the very surface of the water are not uncommon, and beds of rooted plants or filamentous algae may cover the bottom of shallow-water areas or bays. High productivity greatly increases oxygen consumption in the deeper water, by decomposition of organic material. In periods of minimal water circulation, either during the summer when the water separates into warm and cold layers (thermal stratification), or during winter ice cover, oxygen concentrations in the lower layers may be severely depleted. This creates conditions in which deep-water fish cannot survive. Warm-water species such as bass, sunfish and pike are found in eutrophic lakes.

Lake Transition. Lakes are but a temporary feature of the landscape. Even the largest and deepest of lakes are transitory, undergoing a gradual process of change from youth, to maturity, to old age. Progressing even further, the death of a lake can be equated as the onset of a swamp or marshland condition. Thus, the ultimate fate of a lake is to become filled with sediment and eventually be supplanted by grass or forested land. Average natural sedimentation rates for lakes have been estimated at 1 millimetre per year. This means that approximately 35 to 50 feet of sediments have accumulated in most lakes since the recession of the last Ice Age some 10,000 to 150,000 years ago. It is not well recognised that changes occurring as a result of natural eutrophication are more complex and subtle and proceed much more slowly than was earlier anticipated. In fact, because many deep lakes, such as Superior, have continued to remain in an oligotrophic state since the last continental glacier receded, natural eutrophication is really an immeasurably slow process. In general, then, healthy bodies of water are self-perpetuating biological communities that purify themselves through the interaction of aquatic plants, fish and micro-organisms.

Human Impact on Lake Transition

In contrast to the slow natural evolution of lakes from an oligotrophic to a eutrophic condition, cultural, or man-made, eutrophication can create conditions in decades or less which would take tens of thousands of years in the absence of man. The deterioration of Lake Erie is a classic example. Induced fertilisation in thermally stratified lakes of the Canadian Pre-Cambrian shield leads to increased level of phytoplankton, the onset of high levels of blue-green algae in late summer, reduced pH and dissolved oxygen in the deeper waters. Consequently, numerous lakes accumulate growths of planktonic blue-green algae along shore lines that create unpleasant odours when they decompose. Cold-water fish die off owing to reduced oxygen in the lake's deeper waters.

In shallow, naturally eutrophic lakes, increased enrichment resulting from agricultural run-off, urbanisation along the system and inadequate sewage treatment increases stresses on already productive environments. When induced enrichment reaches critical volumes their self-purification capacity is surpassed and rapid deterioration occurs. However, Vallentyne points out that natural and man-made eutrophication differ in two respects — rate and reversibility.

> Natural eutrophication is slow and for all practical purposes, irreversible, under a given set of climatic conditions. It is caused by changes in the form and depth of a basin as it gradually fills with sediment. To reverse natural eutrophication in this sense, one would have to scour out the basin again — a rather formidable task in any man's terms . . . Man-made eutrophication, on the other hand, is rapid and reversible. It is caused by an increase in the rate of supply of nutrients to an essentially constant volume of water, without any appreciable change in the depth or form of a basin. As a result, man-made eutrophication can be reversed by eliminating man-made sources of supply. Reversed, however, should not be interpreted to mean anything other than return to what there was before the advent of man.[8]

Urban Processes

General

It will be clear from the previous discussion that the biophysical processes of water, land and forests are an interacting system, profoundly influenced by man. Since water is a crucial component of the city's support systems, an understanding of these processes is essential to its wise use and management. This is true not only with respect to the larger context of regional watershed, but to the city itself. Many of the pollution problems that affect the water system as a whole begin in the city, so it is here that we must focus attention. My primary purpose, with this knowledge as a base, is to examine how aquatic processes are altered in cities and what implications for urban design arise from these changes.

There are a number of problems that deserve our attention in an urban context. One is the problem of water supply: another is its disposal. Supply involves the problem of moving water from where it is plentiful — the rivers, lakes and underground reservoirs, to where it is needed — the cities. The natural hydrological cycle is short-circuited by water diversions, artificial storage in reservoirs and urban piped supply systems. Disposal involves the problem of removing it from where it has been used back to the rivers, lakes and oceans via urban drainage systems.

The Urban Hydrological Cycle

Urbanisation creates a new hydrological environment. Asphalt and concrete replace the soil, buildings replace trees and the catchbasin and storm sewer have replaced the streams of the natural watershed. The amount of water run-off is governed by the filtration characteristics of the land and is related to slope, soil type and vegetation. It is directly related to the percentage of impervious surfaces. In forested land, run-off is generally absent, as a glance at the undisturbed litter of the forest floor, even on sloping ground, will show. It has been estimated that run-off from urban areas that are completely paved or roofed might constitute 85 per cent of the precipitation. Fifteen per cent is intercepted by streets, buildings, roofs and walls and other paved and soft surfaces.[9] Piped drainage, designed to carry excess water away from urban surfaces, has two major effects, particularly in those climates that suffer from sudden storms.

Flooding and Erosion. There is a tendency for flash floods and erosion. These are caused by large areas of impervious paving and the concentration of water flows to specific points. The greater the run-off from a storm the more swollen are the streams and the size of flood peaks. Conversely, the greater the volume from run-off, the less there is to replenish groundwater and streams. So, rainfall is accompanied by extremes of flood and low flow. Discharge velocities are also higher than in natural conditions. This is well illustrated in the forested ravine lands that follow a meandering course through densely built-up parts of some cities. In the sudden storms typical of the summer season, streams will rise from a sluggish trickle to a raging torrent in a matter of minutes, carving into already eroded banks and undercutting stone retaining walls. The damaging effects of erosion from water in river courses are much greater when urbanisation seals ground surfaces. They increase substantially with the number of urban centres in upstream locations. Downstream solutions to problems caused upstream become more difficult and costly, requiring larger culverts, protection of urbanised flood plains, straightening and stabilisation of stream banks. There is consequently wholesale destruction of natural ponds, marshes, plants and wildlife habitat. The effects of urbanisation on the water cycle become

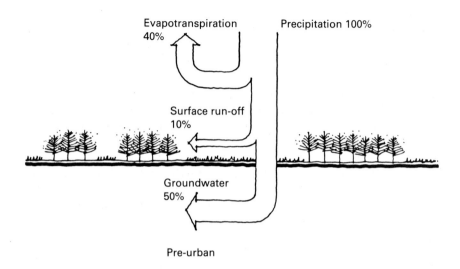

Evapotranspiration
40%

Precipitation 100%

Surface run-off
10%

Groundwater
50%

Pre-urban

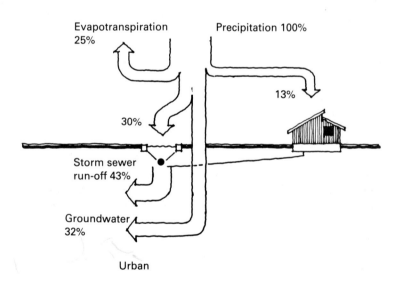

Evapotranspiration
25%

Precipitation 100%

13%

30%

Storm sewer
run-off 43%

Groundwater
32%

Urban

Hydrological changes resulting from urbanisation (from Ministry of the Environment, Ontario, 1978)

clear when we see that on average 28.6 inches of water per year leaves Ontario cities, of which 12.5 inches are from storm run-off. Annual storm-water volumes can exceed sewage flows in low-density urban areas.[10] Calculations show that with an urbanised area that has 50 per cent impervious surfaces and is 50 per cent sewered, the number of stream flows that equal or exceed the capacity of its banks would, over a period of years, be increased nearly fourfold.[11]

Water Quality. Storm drainage systems impair water quality and disrupt aquatic life. Water pollution of lakes and streams results from combined sanitary and storm sewer systems that still serve many cities. The provision of overflows permits mixed sewage and stormwater to bypass sewage treatment plants in major storms and enter rivers and streams. The wet-weather loads from combined systems may be many times larger than loads discharged from treatment plants during storms and can equal or exceed total annual discharges from treatment plants.[12] Water quality is also affected drastically by sedimentation. Surface run-off from land cleared of forest increases overland flow and consequently the amount of sediments and nutrients carried to streams from agricultural land uses. The result includes loss of soil, turbidity and accumulation of sediments in water bodies which makes them highly eutrophic. The rate at which urbanisation can change rates of soil loss (in lb per acre per year) from previously undeveloped land can be seen in the following table:[13]

Forest land	30—600
Cultivated agricultural land	600—40,000
Exposed construction sites	3,000—450,000
Developing urban areas	500—12,000
Developed urban areas	170—860

It has been estimated that in the state of New Jersey the sediment yields that can be expected on flat lands for forested areas are 10 to 40 tons per square mile annually; while moderately heavily urbanised areas are 25 to 100 tons.[14] In addition to sediments a wide variety of chemical pollutants, salts, heavy metals and debris add other contaminants to the water. They are carried through storm sewer systems and contribute to higher temperatures, BOD (biological oxygen demand) and a marked depletion of aquatic life in rivers, streams and lakes.

Some Problems and Perceptions

The development of a reliable water supply has been a primary determinant in the growth of large and densely populated cities. It has provided the means for controlling disease, raising public health standards and effectively fighting fire. At the same time, abundance and security of supply lead to the perception of water as a free good, and result in misuse, wastage and environmental pollution. A review of how water systems in the city have evolved and how they have influenced urban life is, therefore, appropriate here.

Keeping Clean

Whole cultures have evolved around the ritual of washing. Superb monuments in engineering, architecture and art have been its product. The best known historically are, of course, the Roman baths that were built in many of the cities the Romans occupied. As the great engineers of antiquity, they were concerned with hygiene and public health. Indeed, life in large cities such as Rome would have been impossible without a water supply and sewers. Although the first recorded water-supply system was built in 591 BC to water the fields and palace gardens near the city of Nineveh,[15] it was the Romans who recognised the need for clean water and secured their supplies from distant mountain streams via aqueducts, rather than from the river Tiber. The first was built in 312 BC by the censor Appius Claudius. These supplied the baths and city water. The Cloaca Maxima, Rome's famous sewer, was built about 600 BC and emptied into the Tiber. It is interesting to note that from that time no one bathed in the river or drank from it. By 226 AD no less than eleven aqueducts carried water to the city.[16]

In the centuries that followed, towns in the medieval and Renaissance eras were notorious for their lack of sanitary facilities. The streets acted as the dumping ground for the refuse of the town. Mumford observes, however, that in spite of these practices the smallness of medieval towns, their accessibility to fresh air and open countryside, and the importance of the ritual bath maintained greater health than might normally be expected. But this could not be maintained as cities grew larger.[17] Water was supplied via the public fountain which served three purposes: for drinking, as a work of art, and as a centre of social life. The tradition of the ritual bath declined in the sixteenth century, which was marked by poor personal hygiene, and was re-introduced into England in the seventeenth century as a luxury. Bathing was seen as a curative rather than a cleansing process.[18] The extensive use of perfumes by royalty in the Court of Versailles, which became known as 'Le Cour Parfumé',[19] undoubtedly had a functional role to play. While important suites in the palace were equipped with bathrooms, these were dismantled in the reign of Louis XV, the age of reason.[20] Most of the palace's water supply was directed to the great fountains, whose waterworks are said to have developed 100 horsepower with a capability of raising a million gallons of water a day 502 feet.[21] In effect, the traditional role of the fountain as

The ancient well in the Piazza Cavour, San Gimignano, Italy

The fountains of Versailles, France The traditional role of water in cities – for drinking and social focus – became subjugated to its purpose as art, serving the extravagant tastes of the nobility. It is said that when the King walked in the gardens, each sector of the Versailles waterworks was turned on just before the King arrived. There was never enough water to keep all the fountains running at the same time

75

a supplier of water for drinking, and as a centre of social life, became subjected to its purpose as a work of art in the pedigree landscapes created by nobility.

The private bathroom and the health standard of a WC for every family were made possible by the introduction of sanitary sewers in the nineteenth century. The sewer, introduced into many cities in the eighteenth century, was built to carry away rain water, so it antedated the development of the sanitary sewer. Until this time human wastes were emptied by 'night soil men' hired for this purpose. The relationship of this practice to farming has been described by Tarr.[22] The waste, collected from households, restaurants and markets, was sold to neighbouring farmers for use on their land. The law often stipulated that cesspools could only be emptied at night, hence the name 'night soil'. The practice was widely followed in the New England and Midatlantic states of America, where wastes were collected in 74 cities. Baltimore fertilised garden crops with urban night soil as late as 1910. Tarr reports that 70,000 cesspools and privy vaults were emptied and sold to a contractor for 25 cents per load of 200 gallons. The waste was shipped by barge to a depot 10 miles below the city and sold to farmers. Virginia and Maryland farmers bought over 12 million gallons a year to grow crops such as potatoes, cabbage and tomatoes, which were subsequently sold in the Baltimore market.[23]

As cities became more densely populated, the cesspools proved incapable of handling the increased load of human waste. The introduction of piped water vastly increased consumption. The estimated 3 gallons a day consumption that was used before piped supplies were introduced rose to 40 to 60 gallons. Also, the consequent health hazards from cholera and yellow fever epidemics that periodically swept the nineteenth-century cities brought about the crusade that forced the cities to build the sewage systems.[24] When connected to every household, they removed raw wastes directly to the rivers and lakes. Thus, public health in the cities improved. In London prior to 1850, the old tributaries to the Thames were used only for surface drainage. By the middle of the nineteenth century, largely as a result of the widespread use of WCs and a rapid expansion of the population, the river Thames received the untreated sewage of 4 million people. It is reported that in 1858, 'the year of the great stink', it became necessary to hang sheets soaked in disinfectant at the windows of the Houses of Parliament to counteract the smell.[25]

The problem of water use in cities has several facets. The first is the continued growth and improvement of technology. Today consumption of water for domestic purposes is estimated, on average, in North America to be 100 gallons per person per day. It takes 20 gallons to take a bath, 10 gallons to do the dishes, 5 to 6 gallons to flush the WC. The largest consumer of water is the bathroom, at 75 gallons per person per day. The requirement that water must be pure, regardless of its use, increases pressure on natural resources. The same quality of water services fire fighting, car washing, irrigation, domestic and industrial uses.

With this kind of use come the immense physical and biological problems associated with the return of used water to the natural system. The sewage treatment plant has provided a technological solution to the immediate problem of contaminated urban water. The increasing quantities of pure water taken out of the natural system and returned contaminated are perceived as a problem requiring engineering, rather than biological, solutions. The effect of removing the problem of disposal away from the city, which, while undoubtedly improving health and eradicating epidemics in Western cities, has also delayed solutions to the ultimate, large problem of wasted resources. On 1 August 1976 the *New York Times*, commenting on the sewage sludge washed up along 80 miles of ocean front on Long Island that closed down all beaches, noted 'the catch-22 of water pollution control is that as the city's rivers get cleaner, the oceans get dirtier, because new sewage treatment plants produce sludge — and the sludge is then dumped in the ocean'.[26] Jerome Goldstein notes that 'the Federal water pollution control act of 1972 [US] requires that towns stop sending raw sludge into waterways . . . At the same time the act does not provide any federal funds for upgrading septic tanks, or developing compost toilets — only for central treatment plants.'[27]

Keeping your Shoes Dry

The storm sewer and catchbasin as the conventional method of solving the problem of drainage and water disposal have, until recently, been unquestioned. As the established dictum of design, the rules have been simple — water drains to the catchbasin. It is here that the problem stops, and connections with larger environmental problems are not made. But, as we have seen, the benefits of well drained streets and civic spaces are paid for by the costs of eroded stream banks, flooding, impaired water quality and the disappearance of aquatic life. There are numerous examples of the problem of discontinuity. One is the effect of urban pets on water quality. It was estimated in 1974 that more than half of the $\frac{3}{4}$ million dogs owned in the United States reside in cities.[28] The products of animal defecation in public open space, washed untreated into urban storm sewers, create a potentially dangerous health hazard that would be intolerable in human terms. Another example is provided by municipal attitudes to the question of quality versus quantity of run-off. A survey of urban drainage practices across Canada showed that municipalities tend to see quantity as their business and quality as the responsibility of higher levels of government. There is also a failure to grasp fully the hidden environmental and economic costs of local practice, such as connecting downspouts to the sewer rather than discharging roof water directly to the ground.[29] Conventional design, in fact, contributes to the general deterioration of the environment by shifting an urban problem on to the larger landscape. The annual costs in erosion control, channelisation of stream banks, larger sewers and water treatment facilities are the technological consequences of the need to keep one's shoes dry. The impacts on natural landscapes are the ecological consequences.

There are several ways of approaching these problems that differ from current practice. The first is the obvious and well established conservation measure of using less — one that becomes more pressing with scarcity and rising costs. The second is related to the perceptions and values that have evolved from urban life. The traditional role of the fountain as a vernacular expression of water supply, social interaction and art became subjugated to an expression of art alone in the pedigree gardens created by nobility. The preoccupation with the expression of water as display or status symbol, defying gravity with extraordinary feats of engineering, is reflected in the modern city. The sparkling fountain gracing the civic square, symbolic of mountain streams, cascading falls and unspoiled places, is made possible by the city's filtration plant, hydraulic equipment and heavy doses of chlorine. While accepting the validity of its aesthetic purpose, one may well question some other assumptions and values that it represents. The dichotomy between the euphoric image of nature and the realities of the hydrological cycle in cities emphasises in another way the isolation of urban life from natural processes. It is difficult to reconcile the image of sparkling fountains and children's play pools with the debris-clogged and muddy urban streams, or the blackened snow that piles up along city streets over the winter. One may question, too, the design implications of water features that have little connection with the genius of the place; fountains and waterfalls that rely on high-powered machinery to simulate steep topographic terrain in places that are absolutely flat. The third way of approaching the question of water is to consider the opportunities for urban design that arise when the city's waste products are perceived as resources. The task is to redefine design values to permit a vernacular expression of water to develop that is in tune with natural process. These alternatives will be examined later in this chapter.

Some Alternative Values and Opportunities

The Thames Revival

The continuing deterioration of rivers and lakes from urban pollution is a fact that is attributed to the costs of progress. But one of the most dramatic examples of the process of deterioration and the seemingly impossible feat of bringing a river back to health is the story of the rehabilitation of the Thames in London.[30] The 25 miles of tidal river within London are subjected to daily fluctuations and have been subjected to two periods of gross pollution: once in the 1850s and again in the 1950s. As an ecological entity the Inner Thames was a wilderness of marshes and reed beds, harbouring vast populations of birds. It is reported that spoonbills nested in the area of Putney Bridge up to the sixteenth century and montague and marsh harriers hunted in the marshes of south London. The water supported a thriving fish industry including salmon and sea trout. By the middle of the nineteenth century the widespread use of WCs and the rapid expansion of the population created such polluted conditions that all fish were eradicated, together with the birds that fed on them. The construction of docklands aided the destruction of habitat. The first effort to build a sewage system was completed in 1874. Its main feature was the construction of intercepting sewers that discharged into the Thames at the extreme east end of London at Beckton and Crossness, avoiding the central areas.

By 1900, some of the river's quality had been restored by this work, but it gradually deteriorated again during the first half of the twentieth century due to increased discharges of effluent from both domestic and industrial sources. During the 1940s and 1950s the health of the Thames was at its low ebb, little better than an open sewer, containing no oxygen, and permitting the survival of only specialised forms of life adapted to anaerobic conditions.

The crisis conditions of the 1950s led to the creation of several government committees which surveyed the Thames and examined the effects of pollutants. As a result of these investigations the problems of large pollutant loads in an enclosed tidal system were better understood, and a programme of improvements was drawn up. It was recognised that the effect of pollutants on dissolved oxygen in the river was a critical factor. As we saw earlier in this chapter with the induced eutrophication of lakes, when the oxygen content is entirely removed, oxidation of wastes cannot occur and anaerobic conditions are created. In this situation hydrogen sulphide is formed, giving off the familiar smell of rotten eggs. The problem of fluctuating tides exacerbated the problem on the Thames since it may take up to 80 days for water to be flushed to sea in periods of low rainfall. In 1964 greatly enlarged and improved sewage works were begun, and were completed in 1974. The most up-to-date filtration, treatment and aeration equipment was installed so that the fluid discharged to the Thames would be pure water.

Two criteria for estuarine quality have become the basis for control. First, quality must be good enough to allow the passage of migratory fish at all stages of the tide. Second, it must support fauna on the mud

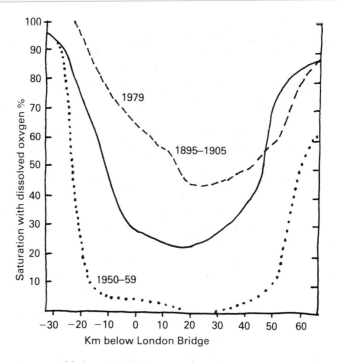

Oxygen sag curves, third quarter The improvement in the quality of the River Thames since the last century can be seen in this graph showing the percentage dissolved oxygen for the summer quarters of the three periods 1895-1905, 1950-1959 and 1979. The river is now healthier than before records began and represents a return to the quality which was last shown in the mid-eighteenth century (from L.B. Wood, n.d.)

bottom, essential for sustaining sea fisheries. The concept of 'pollution budgets' was introduced: these set the maximum quantity of pollution load for treatment plants that can be tolerated if the desirable water quality is to be secured. A goal of 30 per cent dissolved oxygen was set to reach the desired quality. A third criteria was that toxic and non-biodegradable substances such as heavy metals should be excluded from industrial effluent. Records of oxygen sag curves for the Thames have shown that objectives have been met. The curve for the third quarter of 1979 showed that despite low fresh-water flows, the average minimum dissolved oxygen was above 44 per cent. The results have been spectacular. The Thames that had been devoid of fish for 30 miles between 1920 and 1964 now supports aquatic life. By 1975 no less than 86 species of fresh-water and marine fish had been identified. Large flocks of wildfowl have now returned to the Inner Thames and as a wintering area it attracts at peak times 10,000 birds or more.

Wastes as Resources

The rehabilitation of the Thames shows that the problem of pollution can be solved by sophisticated treatment technology where other alternatives are impractical or not available. But does the problem stop there? What are the products of the treatment plant, and what does one do with them? What alternative ways of looking at the problem can provide opportunities for design?

It is a fact that sewage treatment technology becomes progressively more complex the more elements that are removed from the water. Primary treatment is a mechanical process of separating used water from the materials that have been added to it. The product is sludge, the total organic waste and waste water generated by residential and commercial establishments. It is made up of the settled sewage solids combined with varying amounts of water and dissolved material that are removed by screening, sedimentation, chemical precipitation, or bacterial digestion. Raw, it is very high in moisture and biologically unstable. When subjected to secondary treatment it is anaerobically digested and produces methane gas and carbon dioxide. The digested material has a higher degree of biological stability, and is rich in phosphates, nitrates, potassium and trace elements. Tertiary treatment aims to remove 95 per cent of all remaining substances and chemicals, leaving the water in a drinkable form which is then ready to be returned to the natural water system. The technology involved is, however, very costly and few communities are able to afford tertiary treatment.

When the products of the treatment plant are seen to be valuable, rather than as wastes to be disposed of, the current practice of dumping, by landfill, dumping at sea or incineration, can be regarded as the misuse of resources. In almost all countries where resources are limited, or expensive to buy, they tend to be productively used. It is simply a question of pragmatic long-term investment in a healthy environment. Modern China has demonstrated the importance of human wastes to agricultural development and has provided practical approaches for treating them to minimise health hazards. In spite of the introduction of artificial fertilisers, natural fertilisers brought from the cities remain today by far the most important source of nutrients.[31] It has also shown that 'night soil' is far more effective in returning available nutrients to soils and plants than animal manures.

Government agencies in Europe and North America are taking a keen interest in composting of waste and its application to land as an alternative to dumping. More will be said in a later chapter on the relationship of organic urban wastes to the land, particularly its relevance to urban agriculture and the reclamation of urban waste lands. The significance of this concept lies primarily in the solutions it provides to the practical realities of waste-disposal problems in urban areas. It makes ecological as well as economic sense and by establishing a potential connection between urban man and the land it has educational value. Both the waste water and the nutrients that it contains when it leaves the urban environment are products of natural processes. The task is to recycle these resources back into the system so that they may again be available for use. There are various practical alternatives within cities that provide the opportunity of implementing this principle.

Land as a Filter

The advanced treatment and disposal of effluent may be accomplished by returning water and the nutrients it contains to the environment. The soil's micro-biological and chemical capacities are used to filter out nurients for re-use by plants, and return pure water to ground reserves. Studies at Pennsylvania State University have shown that given the right soil types, agricultural crop yields are usually increased as a result of land application of waste water. Secondary treated domestic waste water has considerable fertiliser value. As an example, the application of waste water at 5 cm per week during the growing season at the Penn State project provided the equivalent of 232 kg of nitrogen, 245 kg of phosphate and 254 kg of potash per hectare. This would be equal to applying 2.2 metric tons per hectare of a 10-10-11 fertiliser. Over a ten-year period the 5 cm per week waste-water application resulted in annual yield increase ranging from −8 to 346 per cent for corn grain, 85 to 191 per cent for red clover and 79 to 139 per cent for alfalfa.[32]

There are a number of examples of this alternative in operation. One of the best known is the Muskegon County Project Michigan.[33] Begun in 1973, the Muskegon system recycles 43 million gallons per day on to formerly sandy unproductive lands totalling 10,300 acres. Its purpose was to reclaim the land for productive purposes and to reduce costs of standard sewage treatment. The waste water is collected via connecting sewers which deliver it via a pumping station to the site. Here it is aerated in three 8-acre cells, each with a capacity of 42 million gallons. Following aeration, the water flows into storage lagoons, is chlorinated and then pumped on to the land through an irrigation system. During the 1975 season 4,500 acres were planted to corn and irrigated with 4 inches per week of waste water. The average yield for the year was 60 bushels per acre which nearly equalled the 65 bushel per acre average yield on operating farmland. The total cost of this treatment system, which includes the land itself, was $1 for each gallon treatment capacity, which is reported to be about a sixth of the cost of similarly sized waste treatment plants.

Penn State research has also demonstrated the value of forest land as 'living filters'. Advanced treatment of sewage effluent is provided by natural biological and chemical processes as it moves through the living

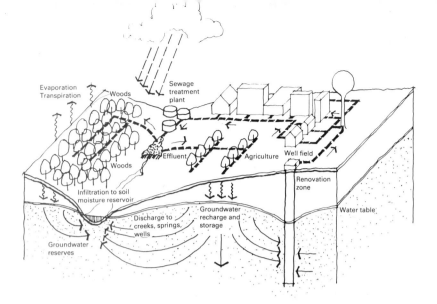

The waste-water renovation and conservation cycle Land application of waste water, after secondary treatment, is an advanced treatment method. This approach (the 'living filter') considers effluent and nutrients as resources rather than as a product for treatment and disposal. Treatment is provided by natural biological and chemical processes as the water moves through the living filter provided by soil, plants, micro-organisms and related ecosystems. The renovated water then percolates to recharge the groundwater reservoir (from Sopper, 1979)

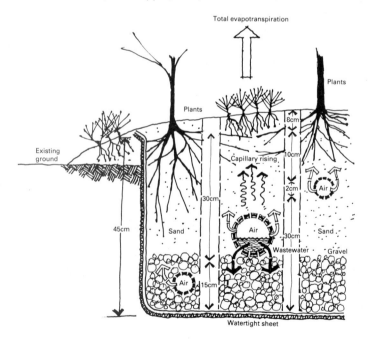

The evapotranspiration bed In this system all waste water evaporates since soil infiltration is prevented by a watertight plastic sheet. This may be particularly important for development on shallow soils with underlying bedrock. The heat and energy created by aerobic micro-organisms increases evapotranspiration rate by 50 to 70 per cent (from Bernhart, 1974)

filter provided by the soil, plants and micro-organisms. Purified water then percolates to recharge water reservoirs. In ten years groundwater has been raised by 14 feet despite the fact that 2 million gallons a day are pumped by the University from wells that must also supply the rest of the town.[34] In some areas waste water can be applied to the forest all the year round, the sheltered humus of the forest floor preventing the freezing that is characteristic of open lands in winter.

Since the early 1960s waste water has been irrigated in several forest stands consisting of eastern mixed hardwood and red pine. It has been found that satisfactory water purification was obtained in all forests where waste water was applied at a rate of 2.5 cm per week during the growing season, with total annual nitrogen loadings of 150 kg per hectare.[35] The studies have found that the rate of application is critical to the sustainability of the existing forest ecosystem. Overloading may cause collapse of the system's water renovation capacity. However, they also found that new developing forest stands composed of pioneer species are very efficient and have a much greater renovation capacity than mature stands. Tree growth and wood fibre production may also be considerably increased. After 16 years of waste water irrigation the average diameter of white spruce was 20.3 cm in comparison to 10.1 in the unirrigated control forest. The average height of trees in the control forest was 4.5 metres, whereas irrigated trees had an average height of 9.2 metres.[36]

Other studies on waste water in Canada have shown that the evapotranspiration capability of plants is considerable. Experiments with specially designed aerobic seepage beds planted with vegetation showed a measurement of 0.1 gallons per square foot per day. Apple trees were found to transpire about 18 gallons per summer day, going down to 3 gallons per day in winter.[37] An installation by the Department of Landscape Architecture at the University of Toronto for a provincial park visitor centre aims to test the feasibility of recycling nutrient effluent waste by applying the principle of soil aeration and evapotranspiration.[38]

Aquatic Plants as a Filter

Biologists have known for some years that marshes have very high capacities for recycling wastes. The highly productive nature of marshland ecology promotes the uptake of nitrates and phosphates by aquatic plants. Research in Mississippi has shown that 1 acre of water hyacinths absorbs annually 3,500 lb of nitrogen, 800 lb of phosphorus, 27,000 lb of phenols, and 96 lb of highly toxic trace metals.[39] An experimental sewage treatment plant in California has been built to provide tertiary treatment using biological processes rather than chemical ones. Using solar heated lagoons that support water hyacinth, duckweed and fresh-water inverte-brates, the process is a large stable aquatic ecosystem that metabolises the sewage and produces clean water that can be used for irrigation or groundwater recharge. It requires little maintenance or electricity and no chemicals. The methane gas produced in the initial anaerobic process provides sufficient energy to supply power for the facility. Thus energy requirements are reduced from one-third to one-sixth of conventional high-technology systems. While this example has greater applicability in warm climates such as California, a similar process designed for cities in colder climates was proposed in 1979 in a Canadian national competition for the design of a low-energy building complex in a Midwestern city.[40] The winning design demonstrated the practical application of established biological techniques to the recycling and productive use of waste water within the confined area of a city block. It included a building housing a hotel, market and restaurant that would do more than simply save fossil fuel energy in heating and cooling, but create a biologically integrated structure that would contribute to the environment from which it drew its support. Opportunities arising from programme requirements — the food market and restaurant, heating, lighting and utilities — suggested a cycle of glasshouse market gardening and fish production: consumption of produce in the restaurant, sale of produce in the market, sewage processing in a mini-utility, waste-water use for growing food and fish production. In this system waste water from kitchens, sewage and organic market wastes was the basis for fish production and hydroponic market gardening (soilless agriculture) permitting concentrated plant production under glass in a confined area, which in turn would supply the hotel and markets.

Growing trout is a relatively low-intensive management occupation. Natural potholes in the prairies provide sufficient nutrients to feed the fish, which are harvested periodically. However, large areas are needed. It was calculated for this project that to supply enough fish for 150 people for a year a pond 3.5 to 4 hectares in size would be required under natural conditions. However, in constricted urban conditions another solution had to be found. Biological productivity can be greatly enhanced with high-intensive management techniques in which temperatures, nutrients, oxygen, water and fish production are controlled. Nutrients such as waste water enhance production, as we saw in the discussion on lake biology. Polyculture (growing a number of species having different biological requirements) is also more energy efficient and more productive. On this basis fish can be produced in the much more confined areas of the city. One system has produced 20,000 trout at a total weight of 2,720 kg in a tank 5 metres high and 2.3 metres in diameter.[41]

Fish production, therefore, included a 2- to 3-acre outdoor pond integrated into the building site. Nutrients, fed to the pond from the mini-utility, are transformed into algae by photosynthesis and piped to fish tanks inside the building designed as balanced aquatic communities of algae, insects, crustaceans and fish feeding at different trophic levels.

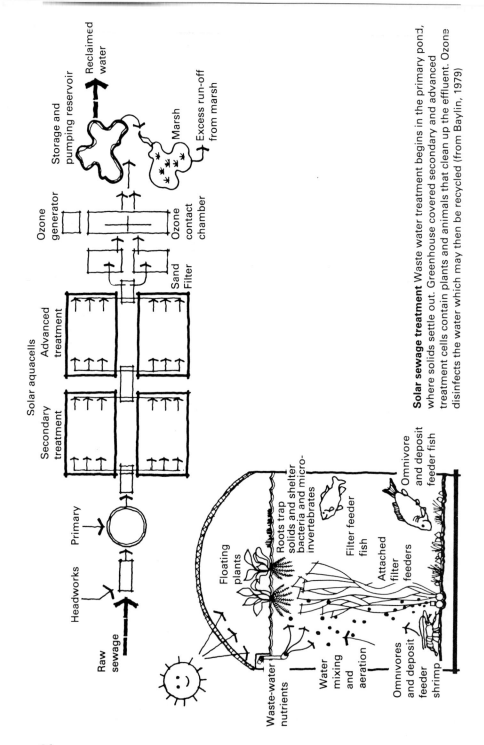

Solar sewage treatment Waste water treatment begins in the primary pond, where solids settle out. Greenhouse covered secondary and advanced treatment cells contain plants and animals that clean up the effluent. Ozone disinfects the water which may then be recycled (from Baylin, 1979)

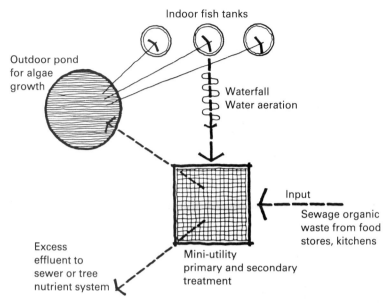

Low energy office, hotel retail project, Regina Diagram showing the year-round production of fresh vegetables, soft fruits and fish, based on the recycling of nutrient energy produced by the building. The by-products of hotel, market and restaurant operations are recycled through the mini-utility to production areas (from Robbie, 1980)

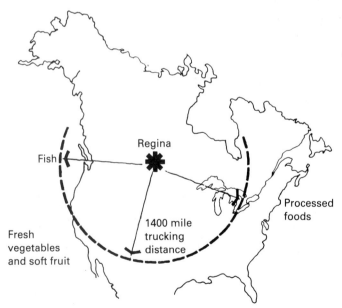

The location map shows the trucking distances required to supply Regina with foodstuffs. The production of food within the building could therefore reduce this dependency on remote production areas in the US and Mexico (from Robbie, 1980)

87

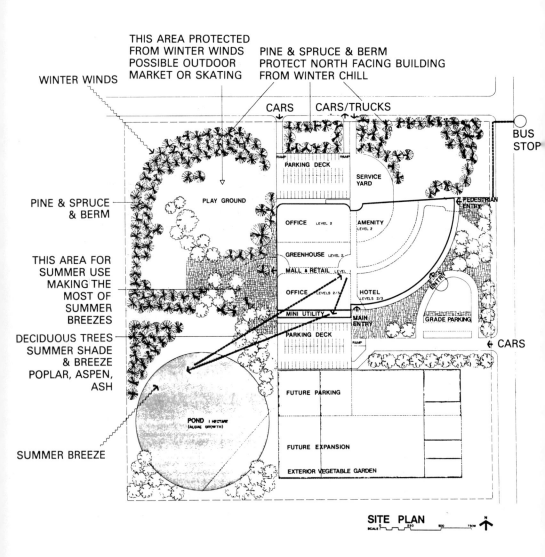

THIS AREA PROTECTED
FROM WINTER WINDS
POSSIBLE OUTDOOR
MARKET OR SKATING

PINE & SPRUCE & BERM
PROTECT NORTH FACING BUILDING
FROM WINTER CHILL

WINTER WINDS

CARS   CARS/TRUCKS

BUS
STOP

PARKING DECK

SERVICE
YARD

PLAY GROUND

PINE & SPRUCE
& BERM

PEDESTRIAN
ENTRY

OFFICE   LEVEL 2

AMENITY
LEVEL 2

THIS AREA FOR
SUMMER USE
MAKING THE
MOST OF
SUMMER
BREEZES

GREENHOUSE   LEVEL 2

MALL & RETAIL   LEVEL

OFFICE   LEVELS 2/3

HOTEL
LEVELS 2/3

MINI UTILITY

MAIN
ENTRY

GRADE PARKING

DECIDUOUS TREES
SUMMER SHADE
& BREEZE
POPLAR, ASPEN,
ASH

PARKING DECK

CARS

RAMP

FUTURE PARKING

POND   1 HECTARE
(ALGAE GROWTH)

SUMMER BREEZE

FUTURE EXPANSION

EXTERIOR VEGETABLE GARDEN

SITE PLAN

N

Winning submission for the Low Energy Building Design Awards Competition, 1980
(Public Works, Canada; Energy, Mines and Resources, Canada)

88

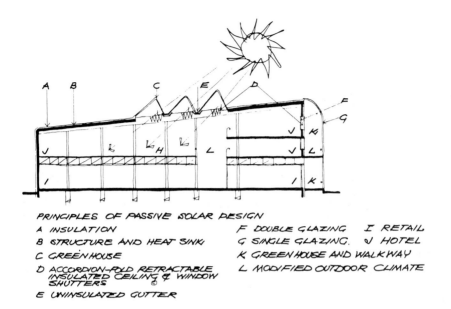

PRINCIPLES OF PASSIVE SOLAR DESIGN

A INSULATION
B STRUCTURE AND HEAT SINK
C GREENHOUSE
D ACCORDION-FOLD RETRACTABLE INSULATED CEILING & WINDOW SHUTTERS
E UNINSULATED GUTTER

F DOUBLE GLAZING
G SINGLE GLAZING.
K GREENHOUSE AND WALKWAY
L MODIFIED OUTDOOR CLIMATE

I RETAIL
J HOTEL

The section (above) and plan details (below) show the solar greenhouse system used for hydroponic vegetable and fish production

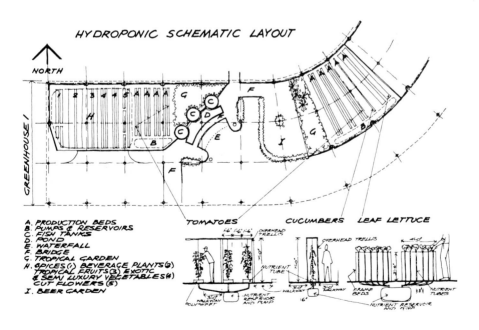

HYDROPONIC SCHEMATIC LAYOUT

NORTH

GREENHOUSE 1

A. PRODUCTION BEDS
B. PUMPS & RESERVOIRS
C. FISH TANKS
D. POND
E. WATERFALL
F. BRIDGE
G. TROPICAL GARDEN
H. SPICES (1) BEVERAGE PLANTS (2) TROPICAL FRUITS (3) EXOTIC & SEMI LUXURY VEGETABLES (4) CUT FLOWERS (5)
I. BEER GARDEN

TOMATOES   CUCUMBERS   LEAF LETTUCE

89

The relevance of these developments to urban areas is apparent when one considers that sewage treatment plants are located on the outskirts of the cities adjacent to open land. There are possibilities for maintaining urban woodlands whose function would be to recharge groundwater, purify effluent, protect wildlife and other relevant environmental uses. The fact that sewage effluent is particularly applicable to the development and growth of young or new forests provides alternative connections. Current research in Canada at provincial and federal levels aims to produce pulpwood from fast-growing hybrid poplars. These trees require well drained soils and high inputs of fertiliser for vigorous growth. Such plantations could best be associated with urban areas, given the appropriate soils, where the nutrients of treatment plants could benefit pulpwood production, soils, groundwater and amenity values. Some work of this nature is being undertaken near Warsaw, where growing poplar for paper-making is irrigated from primary treated sewage throughout the year. The system enables poplar to be grown on poor soil at a profit.

In summary, although advanced treatment technology may in some situations be the only solution to pure water, it is expensive and fails if the resources it produces are not integrated with natural processes. The application of biological solutions to water use is not only cheaper, as much practical work throughout the world is demonstrating, but provides opportunities for alternative approaches to urban design.

Rainwater — the Principle of Storage

The basic lesson that nature provides in the water cycle is one of storage. Natural floodplains and lakes are the storage reservoirs of rivers that reduce the magnitude of peaks downstream, by spreading and equalising flows over a longer period of time. Vegetated soils and woodlands provide storage by trapping and percolating water through the ground with minimum run-off and maximum benefit to groundwater recharge. Water quality is enhanced by vegetation and storage which in turn will contribute to the diversity of natural and human habitat. Thus storm drainage must be designed to correspond as closely as possible to natural patterns, allowing water to be retained and absorbed into the soil at a similar rate to natural conditions. This principle is beginning to be recognised among the planning and engineering professions as the realistic alternative to current practice. A discussion of a few of these alternatives is appropriate here.

Groundwater Recharge. Rainwater applied direct to the land helps to replenish groundwater reserves. Natural drainage over turfed or vegetated land is very useful in controlling and managing stormwater. Functionally it aids natural infiltration into the ground and controls the velocity of water flow, which is essential to control erosion and sedimentation. The objective is to achieve a rate of water run-off that is equivalent to the predevelopment levels, helping to minimise flood and erosion damage. Some low to medium housing developments in North America have adopted the practice of overland flow from developed surfaces over turfed areas and channels as an alternative to traditional storm sewers, since it has been shown to be a great deal cheaper. Vegetation is the crucial factor that ensures that water is recycled back to the natural system. Natural drainage, woodlands, rough grass, small streams and marshes preserved for this purpose provide the functional basis for determining open space patterns as the new town of Woodlands in Texas had demonstrated. This example will be examined later in this chapter.

Retention Ponds and Lakes. Retention ponds are, when modelled after nature, a means of controlling water run-off by modifying flows, smoothing out peak loads by releasing water slowly to lessen the danger of downstream flooding and improving the quality by allowing sediments to settle. They also help to replenish natural groundwater. Storage of water is created naturally as lakes, ponds and marshes and often occurs by accident in many urban places that do not come under the label of parks and playgrounds. The wealth of abandoned industrial or mining lands, vacant lots, waterfront sites and highway interchanges perform, quite fortuitously, a valuable hydrological function by retaining and storing water. It is often lost when development occurs and sites are 'improved'. Storage of water on low-density development is becoming an accepted alternative in certain areas as a cheap solution to urban drainage. The Ministry of the Environment for Ontario has concluded, for instance, that maximum use should be made of water-retention facilities to control run-off in large paved urban areas.[42] Many alternatives are possible, each depending on the nature of the place, its rainfall, topography, drainage patterns, soils and type of development, viz.:

(1) *Permanent storage.* This is appropriate where a continuous supply is available and where inflow and outflow and soils permit a stable condition. Ponds that can be maintained at some minimum water level offer multi-purpose potential for community uses. Balanced ecosystems of plants, animals, fish and other aquatic organisms maintain stability, provide places for nature study, education and fish management. Open water provides places for boating and recreation and visual enhancement. Examples of the concept have been implemented in a variety of housing developments in the US and elsewhere.

(2) *Temporary storage.* It might well be assumed that densely urbanised areas do not have the capability to cope with rainfall storage. It was for this reason, in fact, that storm drainage was introduced in the

nineteenth century. Where space is at a premium, or where permanent ponds are inappropriate, or where an existing storm drainage system is subjected to additional loads, the principle of delayed return to the receiving body may be put into practice. Flood plains of rivers and streams work on this principle, releasing excess water slowly and smoothing out peak loads. In the city temporary storage is useful in situations where various functions must be accommodated on the same area of ground. It can be designed to accumulate water during rainstorms and drain completely after the storm over a period of time. The land thus serves dual purposes; assisting hydrological functions, but still providing space for urban uses. Golf courses, playing fields, cemeteries and parks are situations where management could accommodate compatible uses. In fact, they often do by default rather than by design, as the flooded fields and lawns of many urban parks after a sudden rain will testify.

Where non-paved areas are insufficient or unable to cope with natural storage there are many other open space resources that are potentially available and can fulfil hydrological roles. A study in 1971 showed that the amount of open space of all kinds in the downtown area of Toronto was over 57 per cent.[43] Built-up space and rooftops made up the remaining 43 per cent. Thus a major proportion of the city's paved or impervious space is, in fact, available and may be designed for temporary storage. Water may be held long enough to reduce peak flows, then released slowly into storm systems. For instance, parking lots take up a large proportion of most downtown areas. If designed with a hydrological function in mind, such spaces can provide a storage resource which would not significantly interfere with their parking uses. As an example, it is accepted practice to design lots in cold climates for snow storage. A similar practice could be extended into summer months for rainwater.

Streets, which may take up to 27 per cent of downtown space, may also act as temporary storage, as may storm sewers themselves. An illustration of storage alternatives and water quality management was given in a report for the city of St Thomas, Ontario, in 1978 to demonstrate how new stormwater technology can effectively reduce problems of flooding and water pollution and the costs of traditional methods.[44] Among the many alternatives proposed, the report suggests a number of realistic methods as part of its total plan for the city:

— disconnection of rainwater leaders from residential roofs and discharge of rainwater on to lawns;
— water storage in small ponds in upstream areas of catchments;
— creating temporary storage of stormwater on streets by controlling catchbasin inlets;
— creating temporary storage of stormwater conduits by control gates or dams;

— improved street cleaning to remove the major sources of pollutants;
— reduction of de-icing salts on streets by more frequent snow ploughing, application only to sloped and curved sections of roads and control of volumes applied.

Roof Run-off Storage. Flat roofs and basement storage are other resources that can be used to serve a storage purpose on the principle that buildings should take care of their own rainwater rather than throwing the problem on to public space. Flat roofs performed this function until the introduction of the 'upside down' roof which in modern building is designed to remain free of water at all times. Many older roofs do still pond considerable amounts of water, by default rather than by design. Collecting water from domestic rooftops was common practice in most places until mains water was introduced. Again, the universal acceptance of the storm sewer has in most cities replaced this conservation-minded practice. In country areas rainwater is pure and can be used for most purposes. In the city rain falling through the haze of urban pollution picks up impurities that make it unsuitable for some things, unless it is treated first. It is quite acceptable, however, for uses such as washing cars and windows and watering the garden. Its main advantage in a storage tank is the fact that it can conserve domestic water supplies that are currently used at 100 gallons per person per day for every activity.

Some Considerations of Design

The Basis for Design Form

In this review of water I have tried to make connections between urban and natural processes. It becomes apparent that if we examine these connections in the context of the urban environment, the city's open space resources become a fundamental factor in re-establishing a hydrological balance. Urban land has a significance beyond the transportation, economic or recreational assets that we normally ascribe to it. The notion of investment in the land now begins to acquire conservation and health values. An ecological basis for urban design suggests that when the city's water resources are recycled back into the system there are reduced costs and increased benefits. Urban development becomes a participant in the operation of natural systems. The major land resources associated with sewage treatment plants that are currently underused or unproductive can, where land resources permit, be made to function as groundwater recharge areas and purification of the city's waste water. Urban forests and market gardens acting to purify waste water and recharge groundwater can also become the valued resources that the city needs when they provide food, timber and wildlife reserves close to

93

home. The value of urban forests to the city is immense and provides the basis for useful, productive and low-maintenance landscapes. Similarly, allotment and market gardens, within and on the edges of the city, provide the basis for commercial and recreational land uses that serve productive and environmental functions and increase landscape diversity. These will be discussed more fully in later chapters.

The city's residential parks, open spaces and waste lands, parking lots, playgrounds and roofs could be adapted where appropriate to serve a hydrological function by creating temporary or permanent storage areas and wetlands, thereby helping to redress the problems of erosion and pollution that present practice perpetuates. In places where water conservation is imperative, rainwater storage has traditionally been, or has become, accepted practice. One example is the Denver Urban Renewal Authority, which took action in 1970 to require developers to detain rainfall directly falling on their properties in an urban renewal project, so as to reduce surcharge of storm drainage systems in the downtown area.[45] Such measures are becoming imperative everywhere as environmental and economic costs begin to dictate the adoption of an environmentally sensitive technology to improve the quality of the city. The principles of urban ecology require, first, that environmental problems must be resolved *internally* within a development; and, second, that the products of urban processes must be passed on to the larger environment as benefits rather than costly liabilities.

Design and the New Symbolism

Thus far I have dealt with the ecological and functional basis for design. It will be obvious, however, that water, perhaps more than any other element of the landscape, has deep-rooted spiritual and symbolic meaning to which design must respond. As a design element water has historically been manipulated and shaped to create places of delight and beauty. It has reflected cultural attitudes towards nature. The exuberant splendour of the Italian water garden, created by the volume, light and sound of its fountains, exploited the hillsides and streams around Florence and Rome by natural gravity. The symbolism of the Japanese miniature garden was the oneness of man and nature. The placid lakes of the English landscape garden expressed the romantic qualities of a benign natural landscape. The task today is to create a new design symbolism for water that reflects the hydrological processes of the city; one that re-establishes its identity with life processes. The opportunity for this to occur lies in the establishment of a vernacular landscape whose aesthetic rests, first, on its ecological and functional basis for form, and, second, on the *integration* of design objectives. Design must be multi-faceted. Single-purpose solutions to problems tend to create other problems. So when the design and management of the urban water system are integrated with other

The symbolism of the great gardens of history As an element of design, water was manipulated to create places of delight and beauty. Operating without electricity, their form tended to be an expression of the place, gravity and the natural opportunities available

objectives — the improvement of climate, creation of wildlife habitats, consideration of social and aesthetic needs — it leads to valid design solutions.

The permanent storage pond, functioning like its counterpart in nature as a floodplain, releases water slowly to the river, the atmosphere and to groundwater. It must also be concerned with its potential for enriching social objectives. There may be increased productivity resulting from an enriched water supply or potential stagnation from insufficient flow-through. Permanent storage requires a diverse biological community of plants and aquatic fauna to maintain health and stability. For instance, the control of mosquitoes requires fish to feed on the larvae, which provides opportunity for managing the pond for fish. Plants associated with water edges provide opportunity for creating aquatic habitats for a variety of birds and animals. The design of edges themselves is related to such problems as public access, protection from encroachment and recreational uses of the water.

The city's paved areas within its parks, playgrounds, plazas and other places should be conceived as multi-functional landscapes of wet and dry

95

surfaces, where the ground is designed to control and retain water. Water can be removed quickly in some places and allowed to pond in others. Doubling as water storage for rain, the urban floorscapes can provide other values by improving local climate through evaporation and by enriching the potential for social uses. The design of edges, depths, paving and control of the quality and character of run-off from roofs and ground surfaces can be made to shape constantly changing places for use and enjoyment in wet, dry or winter weather.

Practical problems must be overcome, however. The eutrophic condition and chemical impurities of some urban stormwater, particularly during development of a watershed, may invalidate the recreational and aesthetic basis for many an urban storage lake or pond. Reduction of de-icing salts used in the maintenance of roads, greater frequency of street cleaning, silt traps and holding ponds for sediment control, the separation of pure water from contaminated water with respect to use, community responsibility in releasing impurities to the drainage system are all measures that may be necessary to ensure the practical application of design principles.

The engineering functionalism of the sewage treatment plant can also be brought into harmony with form and symbolised in unexpected ways, as in the flowform sculptures at Järne, Sweden.[46] Here sewage water cascades down various sculptured basins and is aerated as it drops. Porous paving materials that permit water to penetrate through to the soil and ground vegetation to grow while maintaining a hard surface offer other opportunities for integrating design with hydrology. The variety and pattern of ground surfacing and the beauty it adds to the city floorscape are matched by the hydrological and climatic functions it performs; a welcome relief from the visual tyranny of asphalt surfaces.

Hydrology and the Prairie Landscape

The city of Winnipeg, located on low-lying land in the prairies, is an example of where the high costs of conventional underground storm sewers prompted the development of storm retention ponds in the city's new suburban areas. Begun in 1965, Winnipeg has both temporary and permanent lakes and there are now some 37 of these in the city. The basins were developed to provide intermediate storage areas for heavy rainfall which cannot be immediately absorbed by the storm sewer system. In addition, they have a water quality function as settlement ponds. By settling out most of the pollution load from incoming urban storm water run-off before it reaches natural water courses, they improve water quality.

A number of residential areas in the city have been laid out around open greens that contain the retention lakes. There has consequently been an attempt to include recreational and amenity benefits that include

Sculpture and sewage works The flowform cascades at the Rudolf Steiner Seminariat. Järne, Sweden. The cascades aerate effluent from a community of more than 200 people (from Bunyard, 1978)

water-based activities such as canoeing, fishing, sailing, skating and curling. Guidelines have been developed to provide information for new developments on slopes, depths and shoreline construction for new lakes and the maintenance and operation of existing ones,[47] viz.:

X   — Storm water impoundments, being nutrient rich, tend to propagate algae and submergent plants which, in the process of decay, create unpleasant odours and visual conditions. Design that incorporates a bi-annual turnover generates enough movement to avoid stagnation. Deep ponds have a pronounced wave action that inhibits plant growth.

— Mosquitoes, a major problem in Winnipeg, may be controlled by stocking deep ponds with fish which feed on the larvae.

X — The use of fountains helps keep water aerated and in motion. This has been incorporated into several lakes.

— Shoreline slopes should be 7-10:1, extending at least 30 feet into the water for reasons of safety.

There are both positive and negative aspects to the system as it has been applied to the Winnipeg situation. On the positive side, the environmental benefits are undeniable, and as an engineering solution there are significant economic benefits. A report by the city of Winnipeg and detailed research findings for several impoundment installations concluded that the city and developers would save as much as 79 per cent in capital costs when impoundments are used in lieu of undergroud sewers for developments of 100 acres or more. The average saving would be 36 per cent.[48] On the negative side, the public outcry that has from time to time followed occasional accidents and drownings in the lakes is an indication that a truly integrated design approach to the retention pond system is lacking. The opportunities to create the physical conditions conducive to waterside use and balanced communities of plants and animals that could contribute to safety and social opportunity have not been exploited. The lakes, in effect, have been seen as an engineering problem with aesthetics and recreation as an incidental benefit.

Woodlands and Hydrology

While we are concerned here with existing cities and their rehabilitation, the new city of Woodlands, a mixed-use community 25 miles north of Houston, Texas,[49] provides an excellent example of urban form adapting

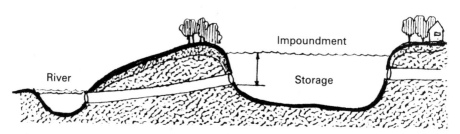

The diagram shows the principle of the impoundment system in suburban Winnipeg (from 'The Pipeline', City of Winnipeg Waterworks, Waste and Disposal Division, 1980)

to hydrological processes.[50] It is relevant particularly to low-density suburban areas where it is possible to adapt the natural conditions of a site to urban development. Located in a subtropical region having mild winters and warm, humid summers, the key features of the site are its extensive mixed woodland, flat topography and imperfectly drained soils. Heavy seasonal rains result in frequent flooding of streams. The problem facing the designers was how to preserve the woodland environment while permitting land drainage for urban development. Much of the site is poorly drained and there is standing water after rains. Streams have very low base flows and shallow floodplains in the flat topography. Thus the environmental analysis carried out in the initial stages of the general plan showed clearly that the maintenance of the hydrological balance was a key planning factor in which the preservation of permeable soils played a major role. It also became apparent that the introduction of conventional piped storm drainage would destroy much of the forest landscape. Run-off had to be retarded to ensure maximum recharge. So, the development was shaped to respond to hydrological determinants. Planning objectives included design for maximum recharge, protection of permeable soils, retardation of erosion and siltation, increase of stream baseflow, protection of vegetation and wildlife habitats. Roads were sited on ridges away from drainage areas; intensive development was located on impermeable soils; minor residential streets were oriented perpendicular to slopes and used as berms to impede flow over very permeable soils; porous paving was recommended for paved areas to increase water storage; the existing natural drainage system of streams, natural draws and ponds was used and artificial impoundments and settlement ponds were used to enhance this network. The open space network was related to the drainage system and vegetation. At the town scale, primary open spaces were conceived as a conservation zone, incorporating areas performing valuable hydrological vegetation and wildlife functions. They included the 25-, 50- and portions of the 100-year floodplains of existing streams. Secondary open space included other components of the natural drainage system, secondary draws, impoundment sites and recharge areas. Tertiary open space at the scale of individual development areas included vegetation not cleared for building, small green spaces among detached houses, vegetation buffers along roads, and so on.

Analysis of soil types resulted in the designation of a 'permissible coverage' factor. This defined the percentage of an area that may be made impervious without affecting the absorption capability of the soil after a high frequency storm (i.e. 1 inch in 6 hours). For instance, highly permeable 'A' type soils that cannot be used to drain upslope less permeable soils have a high permissible coverage factor; less permeable 'B' soils have a lower factor. The permissible coverage factor provides a simple indication of the maximum density of allowable development, based on soil performance characteristics.

A similar performance measure, 'permissible clearance', was formulated for different categories of site vegetation. It provided an indication of the percentage of an area that may be cleared without serious environmental disruption. Determination of the clearance factor was based on the role of various types of vegetation in maintaining hydrological balance, tolerance of species to disturbance and their value as wildlife habitat. From the combination of these two sets of factors a 'landscape tolerance' was derived which was an indicator of development potential.

Following the development of a general plan, site planning guidelines were prepared which provided a means of communicating ecological principles to planners and designers. Their purpose was to permit identification of areas intrinsically suited to specific land uses — residential circulation, open space — in the context of a natural drainage system and the maintenance of a woodland environment.

As construction phases proceeded it was evident that the natural drainage system was effective. It was reported that despite 13 inches of rain in three days and 4 inches in one hour, no surface water remained after six hours. Ponds filled and returned to normal within the same period of time. While estimates have shown that the effective costs of the natural drainage system are, in fact, equivalent to, or only slightly less than, conventional piped systems, they none the less represent other kinds of economies. It has been pointed out that conventional developers who show little concern for environmental values can realise a greater return on investment than the Woodlands new town is obtaining.[51] Part of this profit is gained, however, at public expense, the costs of solving flooding, erosion and water-quality problems being transferred to public authorities. With the Woodlands Project, however, the cost of initial prevention is substantially less than the costs of corrective measures after development.

Hydrology and the Inner City

An attempt to give physical form to the inherent potential of rainwater has been made in a housing project in central Ottawa. Called the LeBreton Flats Demonstration Project, it is a joint undertaking by the National Capital Commission, Canada Mortgage and Housing Corporation and the city of Ottawa. The overall project undertaken aimed to demonstrate innovation in housing, responding first to the social and economic realities of the city, and second to the need for conserving energy in housing design. Located on the edges of an established neighbourhood in the densely populated inner city, the project was concerned with the rehabilitation of derelict urban land within an existing

Retention pond and golf course (photo: Tom Coyle)

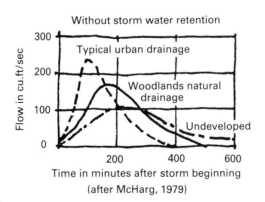

Without storm water retention

Time in minutes after storm beginning

(after McHarg, 1979)

Site Planning Principles

Hydrology. Removal of forest cover and the addition of impervious surfaces will increase frequency of flooding and change stream characteristics. However, the use of a natural drainage system would increase water table recharge and increase lag times for run-off entering the stream. Protection of floodplains and drainage swales is imperative for flood control, for regulating stream flow and for maintaining water quality.

101

Objectives	Adaptations
Reduce flooding.	Ensure ability of existing primary and secondary drainage channels to handle storm run-off by defining drainage easements. These drainage easements will be determined by the 25 year floodplain, however, a minimum vegetation easement of undisturbed forest and understory must be respected: 300' for primary drainage channels and 100' for secondary drainage channels.
Minimise erosion and siltation.	Prohibit clearing of ground cover, shrub understory, or trees within drainage easements.
	Enhance existing channels where necessary with berms and 'create' natural swales by introducing layered plantings of native vegetation.
Contribute no increase in off-site discharge during the Design Storm.	Provide adequate storage of run-off generated by Design Storm in impoundments or temporary water storage ponds.
Retard run-off and maximise recharge to even base flow of streams.	Use check dams in swales and on lots to slow flow over permeable soils to enhance recharge. Install trickle tubes in impounded areas to permit even flow.

100'+

300'+

easement

easement

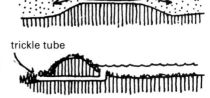

trickle tube

(From Wallace, McHarg, Roberts and Todd, **Woodlands New Community, Guidelines for Site Planning Report,** 1973)

AB soils (LA,EU,BL,BOH,AL,WI) which receive no
run-off from other soils

These soils have a high storage capacity for
excess run-off, but when located upslope from
less permeable soils, they cannot be used to drain
them. In this condition, the excess storage
capacity should be used to recharge run-off from
higher density development on the AB soils
themselves.

A soils have more excess storage capacity than B
soils. Therefore, less area of A soils is required to
recharge a given amount of run-off.

Excess
storage
capacity

A soils   B soils

Management Guidelines

A soils may be cleared up to 90% and still achieve
local recharge of the 1″ storm.

B soils may be cleared up to 75% and still achieve
local recharge of the 1″ storm.

Areas used for recharge should remain wooded.

A soils   B soils
Up to 90%   Up to 75%
cleared and   cleared and
rendered   rendered
impermeable   impermeable

Housing Suitability

On A soils all types and densities are suitable.

On B soils most types and densities are suitable.
Housing types and densities which require more
than 75% clearance cannot be accommodated
without additional uncleared A or B soils. This
would result in decreased gross density.

Siting Considerations

Situate buildings and impervious surfaces on
higher elevations so that run-off will drain to lower
elevations where it can be recharged.

Situate buildings and impervious surfaces so that
they drain to the uncleared area.

(From Wallace et al., 1973)

medium-density ethnic community. Part of the new housing is grouped around a small 1¼ acre park, the focus of the entire neighbourhood. It became apparent, after evaluating local community concerns and interests, reviewing the conserver philosophy of the project and the resources of the site, that the conserver concept, a prime housing objective, must be extended to the park itself. It was apparent that the concept of stormwater retention should be explored in high-density residential areas. Since the rainfall of the Ottawa region typically falls as sudden summer storms, the environmental problems of conventional urban drainage are equal to, if not more severe than, those of outlying suburban areas. The potential opportunities were twofold.[52]

— to demonstrate on a small scale the creative and practical alternatives to traditional site development practice in storm drainage in an inner-city park;
— to create a resource that would integrate environmental with educational and recreational objectives, i.e. storage and slow release of urban drainage to create temporary ponds for play and recreation that are dynamically tied to the hydrological cycle.

Several important considerations dictated the design solution. The first was the smallness of the park in relation to the size of the community using it. The second was the volume of water that could be accommodated during a storm while not interfering with other essential park functions and the maintenance of safety. The third was the community's perception of the kind of park they needed. There was a strong desire for a 'green' park with grass and flowers, places for sitting and strolling, for meeting and informal games. This was understandable in view of the dearth of parks in the general neighbourhood. In addition it was evident that most active games requiring hard surfaces were played on local streets, which traditionally have been the social hub for both children and adults.

The way the hydrological function of the park was expressed as design form was directly affected by these considerations. The need for a green park permitted most of the park to be soft — grass, trees and planting beds. At the same time the need for socialising, gathering and informal hard-surface games resulted in a new approach to the street design bordering the south side of the park. The presence of children was recognised as a valid open space function for local streets. By incorporating safety measures to slow local traffic on the street, the park concept could integrate both the street and the park as one unit, the street providing hard surfaces, the park providing the soft ones. The ability of the park to serve a hydrological function was thus enhanced by absorbing run-off to the fullest extent over its planted surfaces and by the

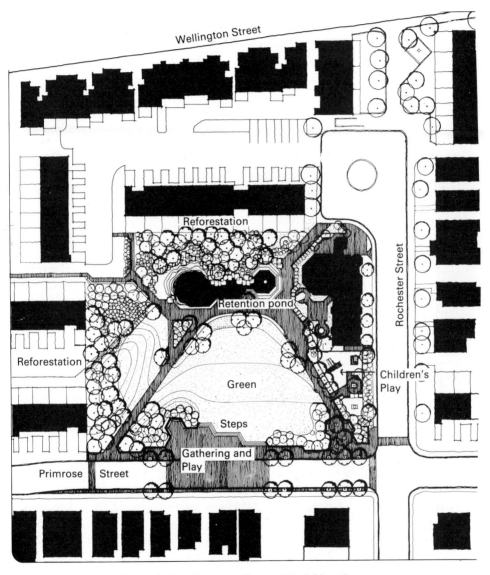

Lebreton Park and surrounding residential housing

The retention pond wet. During a rainstorm the pond fills to 18 inches and takes on a very different character inviting unstructured water-related play and visual variety

The retention pond dry. Flexipave surface provides a durable topcoat for a variety of dry-weather activities

inclusion of a stormwater retention pond. This was hard-surfaced, since the notion of a naturalised impoundment with a mud bottom and aquatic edge plants was rejected as impractical.

The pond was designed to hold 20,000 US gallons, which is the maximum amount of water that might occur in any one rainstorm in a two-year period. A peak rainfall of 15 minutes, amounting to 0.9 inches for the Ottawa region, was assumed for purposes of calculation. Roofwater obtained from adjacent housing and overland flow within the park is collected by a series of drainage channels which deliver the water to the storage basin. Water from parking areas and streets in the housing area was not collected to minimise the introduction of pollutants in a general play environment. A small weir and catchbasin inlet were designed to permit the pond to fill to a depth of 18 inches and drain out slowly to the storm sewer system over a period of time. The weir can be set to vary the flow, but an average of two to three days was regarded as a reasonable period for a temporary storage situation.

The character of the pond is, therefore, continually changing. During winter it may become an ice surface for skating. During the summer it is filled periodically after a rain and slowly drains away. The hard surfaced bottom is designed to take intensive use and contoured to permit many different activities, depending on whether it is wet or dry. Thus children's activities respond to the changing environment. After a rainstorm, activity focuses on water play; when the pond dries out it becomes a place for roller skating, skateboarding, or whatever activity is currently in vogue.

This is an experiment whose purpose is to integrate an urban natural process — water and its management — with social and educational values. It involves natural process and design in the familiar and daily routine of city living. A hydrological function is established for park settings which have traditionally been devoted to recreation alone. In this way it brings together solutions to environmental problems in the city with social needs and art. As design, it is intended to delight the senses, provide recreation and creative play, function practically and bring people closer to the continuum of natural events. As I remarked in the first chapter, children learn about life and their environment less by the occasional visit to the nature centre or the museum than by constant and direct experience in their daily surroundings. It becomes the building block on which discussion and learning are developed. The pond in the park after the rainstorm that one can splash through is the focus for play and learning while it lasts. It provides the best opportunity for understanding hydrology in cities. Through play children are brought more closely to the cycles of rain and sunshine. Water as the agelesss material of design can assume a new relevance. It is on this basis that an alternative design form will emerge.

Thus far, we have explored the role of water in nature under natural and urban conditions. We have seen how developments in supply and disposal technology, by improving human health, have been a central factor in urban growth. But the benefits of health and urban growth have been achieved at the expense of disturbed natural cycles and the creation of a general environmental deterioration with respect to a worsened climate, water pollution and diminished wildlife habitats. The technological remedies designed to mitigate some of these problems only shift them from one place to another — from the city where they begin to the larger environment. Urban design, operating in the ethical climate of a throwaway society and man-made design conventions, contributes to, rather than reverses, these trends. It views water from a single perspective — an image of nature supported by a technology that has no environmental basis for form. Thus the waterfall and fountain, as an expression of civic pride, owes its existence to hydraulic equipment and chemicals, which only serve to emphasise the isolation of urban life from the processes of nature.

It becomes clear that the opportunities for alternative solutions lie in a better understanding of the nature of the places we live in. Urban ecology provides the conceptual vehicle for urban design, whose principles invoke a basic shift in values. We begin to see wastes as resources that contribute to environmental health and diversity, drawing maximum benefits from the means available. Waste water returned to the land can enrich the soil, provide the nutrients for produce, crops and urban forests, giving biological, social and civic value to currently wasted urban land. Stormwater retained in the city's open spaces contributes to the restoration of the hydrological balance and can help ameliorate urban climate. It enriches the potential for integrating environmental, social and aesthetic benefits within parks and urban open space systems and brings nature's processes closer to everyday urban life.

It has also become clear in our discussions so far that water, being a part of the whole interconnected system of natural processes, affects every aspect of the subject at hand. It is central to the maintenance of biological communities — plants and animals — which are themselves vital to the city's environmental health. The last two chapters have shown how plants influence climate and how they are directly connected to the hydrological cycle. They have from time immemorial shared pride of place in civic design. It is now time to turn to plants themselves, since they reveal other issues that must be examined in our search for an ecological expression of urban design.

Notes

1. David Bellamy, *Bellamy's Europe* (British Broadcasting Corporation, London, 1976).
2. Environment Canada, *Water — Nature's Most Versatile Substance* (Inland Waters Directorate, Ottawa, 1976).
3. Ibid.
4. Petawawa Forest Experiment Station, *Water Trail* (Public Awareness Program, Canadian Forestry Service, Chalk River, Ontario, 1978).
5. D. L. Golding, *Forests and Water* (Fact Sheet, Department of Fisheries and Environment, Ottawa, n.d.).
6. Ibid.
7. Hough Stansbury and Associates, 'Water Quality and Recreational use of Inland Lakes', prepared for the Ontario Ministry of the Environment, SE Region, May 1977.
8. J. R. Vallentyne, *The Algal Bowl* (Department of the Environment, Fisheries and Marine Service, Ottawa; Miscellaneous Special Publication 22, 1974).
9. Howard W. Lull and William E. Sopper, *Hydrologic Effects from Urbanization of Forested Watersheds in the NE* (USDA Forest Service Research Paper NE 146, US Dept. of Agriculture, 1969).
10. Ontario Ministry of the Environment, *Evaluation of the Magnitude and Significance of Pollution Loadings from Urban Stormwater Run-off in Ontario*, Research Report no. 81.
11. Luna B. Leopold, *Hydrology for Urban Land Planning. A Guide Book on the Hydrologic Effects of Urban Land Use* (Geological Survey circular 554, US Dept. of the Interior, Washington, DC, 1968).
12. Ontario Ministry of the Environment, *Modern Concepts in Urban Drainage*, Conference Proceedings no. 5, A Canada, Ontario Agreement on Great Lakes Water Quality (Toronto, 1977).
13. Ibid.
14. Lull and Sopper, *Hydrologic Effects*.
15. R. J. Forbes, 'Mesopotamian and Egyptian Technology', in Melvin Kranzberg and Carroll W. Pursell Jr. (eds.), *Technology in Western Civilization* (Oxford University Press, Oxford, 1967), vol. 1.
16. A. G. Drachmann, 'The Classical Civilization', in Kranzberg and Pursell, *Technology in Western Civilization*, vol. 1.
17. Lewis Mumford, *The City in History* (Harcourt, Brace and World, New York, 1961).
18. Lawrence Wright, *Clean and Decent* (Routledge and Kegan Paul, London, 1960).
19. Leslie S. Mathews, *The Antiques of Perfume* (G. Bell, London, 1973).
20. Wright, *Clean and Decent*.
21. Mumford, *The City in History*.
22. Jerome Goldstein, *Sensible Sludge* (Rodale Press, Emmaus, Pa., 1977).
23. Ibid.
24. L. B. Wood, *The Rehabilitation of the Tidal River Thames*, unpublished Thames Water Authority Paper, n.d.
25. Ibid.
26. Goldstein, *Sensible Sludge*.
27. Ibid.
28. Alan M. Beck, 'The Ecology of Urban Dogs' in *Wildlife in an Urbanizing Environment* (Co-operative Extension Service, University of Massachusetts, Amherst, 1974).
29. Reg Lang and Audrey Armour, *Environmental Planning Resource Book* (Lands Directorate, Environment Canada, Montreal, 1980).
30. Wood, *Rehabilitation*.
31. Michael G. McGarry, 'The Taboo Resource', *Ecologist,* vol. 6, no. 4 (1976).
32. William E. Soper, *Surface Application of Sewage Effluent and Sludge* (ASA-CSSA-SSSA, Madison, Wi., 1979).
33. Goldstein, *Sensible Sludge*.
34. Lawrence K. Hills, 'Putting Waste Water to Work', *Ecologist*, vol. 5, no. 9 (1975).

109

35. Sopper, *Surface Application*.

36. Ibid.

37. A. P. Bernhart, 'Treatment and Disposal of Waste Water from Homes by Soil Infiltration and Evapotranspiration' in *Individual Onsite Wastewater Systems*, Conference Proceedings, National Sanitation Foundation, Ann Arbor, Mich., 1974.

38. F. Salvatori, *Recycling Nutrient Wastes by Onsite Sewage Disposal* (Research Proposal, Department of Landscape Architecture, University of Toronto, Toronto, 1981).

39. Frank Baylin, 'Solar Sewage Treatment', *Popular Science* (May 1979).

40. Robbie, Williams, Kassum Partnership; Hough Stansbury Assoc. *et al.*, *Low Energy Building Design Competition* (Public Works Canada and Department of Energy Mines and Resources, Ottawa, 1980).

41. J. E. Bardack, J. H. Ryther and W. O. McLarney, *Aquaculture, the Farming and Husbandry of Freshwater and Marine Organisms* (John Wiley, New York, 1972).

42. Ontario Ministry of the Environment, *Modern Concepts for Urban Drainage*.

43. Michael Hough, *The Urban Landscape* (Conservation Council of Ontario, Toronto, 1971).

44. James F. MacLaren Ltd, 'Stormwater Management Technology Systems Demonstration in the City of St Thomas', unpublished paper for the Central Mortgage and Housing Corporation and the City of St Thomas, Ontario, 1978.

45. Herbert G. Poertner, 'Drainage Plans with Environmental Benefits', *Landscape Architecture Yearbook* (1974).

46. Peter Bunyard, 'Sewage Treatment in a Swedish Sculpture Garden', *Ecologist*, no. 1 (Jan.-Feb. 1978).

47. A. Penman, 'Stormwater Management by Use of Impoundments', unpublished paper, City of Winnipeg Works and Operations Department, Waterworks, Waste and Disposal Division, n.d.

48. *Winnipeg Free Press*, 26 Feb. 1980.

49. Wallace, McHarg, Roberts and Todd were the environmental planning consultants in a multi-disciplinary team hired in 1971 to prepare plans for the site.

50. Ian L. McHarg and Jonathan Sutton, 'Ecological Plumbing for the Texas Coastal Plain' in Grady Clay (ed.), *Water and the Landscape* (McGraw-Hill, New York, 1979).

51. Tom M. Coyle, 'The Application of Ecological Planning to the Urban Planning and Development Process', unpublished student paper, Faculty of Environmental Studies, York University, Toronto, 1980.

52. Hough, Stansbury and Associates, LeBreton Flats Landscape Development. Report (LeBreton Flats Project Office, Central Mortgage and Housing Corporation, Ottawa, Jan. 1979).

Chapter FOUR

PLANTS

'I talked to the trees, that's why they put me away' — The Goon Show.

Introduction

The enquiring observer of plants in the city may be struck by the extent to which they depend on horticultural and technical props for their survival and health. He may wonder what motivates people to use plants the way they do and what purposes they serve; pollarded lindens at the base of 30-storey tower blocks; tropical plants crammed into the dark and unused recesses of an office interior; the unbroken turf and occasional tree of every city park. He may wonder why people put so much energy and effort into the nurture of cultivated and fragile landscapes that are usually far less diverse, vigorous and interesting than the 'weedy' landscapes that flourish in every unattended corner of the city. Why indeed is the one tended with such care and attention and the other ignored or vigorously suppressed?

My task here is not to provide another guide to design with plants in the conventional sense of discussing principles of form, space, colour, texture and so on. This has been done successfully many times. My intent is to examine plants from another perspective; to seek a valid basis for aesthetics that has its roots in urban ecology, and to explore functions and opportunities for urban plants that are consistent with the ideals of a conserver philosophy. To this end we must first review briefly some aspects of natural processes, how these are altered in the city environment, how attitudes and perceptions have shaped the city landscape, and what opportunities exist for alternative ways of using plants in cities.

Natural Processes

Plants are the basis of life on earth. They produce all the oxygen in the earth's atmosphere; they provide the food through photosynthesis and the habitat that supports all living creatures. Plants are environment specific, evolving different forms and communities that have adapted to specific climates, rainfall, soils and physiographic types. These major plant communities are grouped into general regions which range from arctic tundra, northern coniferous forests, temperate deciduous forests, tropical regions, savanna, the grasslands and desert. Our concern here is primarily with the temperate-zone deciduous forests of eastern North America, Britain and Europe. It is in these regions that the majority of industrialised cities have evolved.

Succession

Each forest type goes through a period of infancy, youth, maturity, old age and rebirth. In some forests such as the northern boreal regions, this process of succession is dependent on fire that reduces them to ashes, after which rebirth starts again immediately. In the deciduous regions the process is continuous under natural conditions. Parts of the community die and regenerate, but the forest as a whole remains. Odum describes this constantly evolving pattern of forest growth, starting with an empty field from which the forest has been cleared and abandoned.[1] The original forest that occupied the field will return, but only after a series of temporary plant communities have prepared the way. The successive stages of the new forest will each be different from that which ultimately develops. While subject to much discussion by ecologists today, Odum describes succession as being based on three parameters:

— it is the 'orderly' process of community changes which are 'predictable';
— it results from the modification of the physical environment by the community;
— it culminates in the establishment of as 'stable' an ecosystem as is biologically possible on the site in question. With each successive stage the insects, birds and animals change, giving way to other groups of creatures. Succession is rapid to begin with in early stages, and slows down in later ones. The diversity of animal and plant species tends to be greatest in early stages and subsequently becomes stable or declines.

Succession starts with the invasion of grasses and other colonising plants. Over time and depending on the degree of soil disturbance, these are replaced by shrubs and fast-growing pioneer tree species. These, in turn, are replaced by climax species, such as hemlock, oak, maple and beech. Once mature, a plant community is said to have reached a 'steady state'. The climax vegetation perpetuates and reproduces itself at the expense of other species that have been crowded out. Most ecologists consider this steady-state situation to be more of a theoretical concept than actual, however. Odum describes it in terms of bioenergetics; 'energy fixed tends to be balanced by the energy cost of maintenance'.[2]

Structure

Forest communities grow in a series of layers. The highest, forming the canopy, are the dominant species that control the environment for the rest of the forest. Beneath these are smaller understorey trees that are adapted to living in partial shade. At the lowest level on the forest floor are the ferns, mosses and herbaceous plants. Each basic group of plants is structured to take advantage of various conditions. The canopy species are exposed to maximum sunlight. They intercept much of the rain and evaporate a great deal of moisture back into the air. At the same time the canopy is an important modifying climatic agent for the life that exists beneath. The understorey plants growing in the shade of the canopy reproduce in the spring when it is bare and sunlight can reach the forest floor. At the level of the soil are the fungi, moulds, bacteria and other decomposers that recycle nutrients from rotting leaves and fallen trees and branches back into the system via the soil and roots. The number of layers varies depending on the forest type. Highly developed, northern deciduous forests usually consist of four strata. In southern communities the layers are more complex and some tropical rain forests may be arranged in as many as 27 groups.[3]

Urban Processes

Influences

As we have seen in Chapter Three, forests regulate the flow of water in streams and rivers and its storage underground maintains its purity and health. Forests have a great effect on the movement of water from the atmosphere to the earth and back again. They are thus interwoven with the physical and biological processes on which life processes depend. Cities have created modified environments to which natural plant communities have generally not had time to adapt. In terms of biological time, cities first appeared less than 10,000 years ago. Flowering plants are the product of an evolutionary process which began in the mesozoic era some 200 million years ago. Trees have been exposed to more than 100 million years of selective pressures to adapt to natural environments.[4] Their survival in the city on the other hand is subject to many

The natural progression to the 'ultimate tree' for the consumer society. A plastic lollipop stuck to a pole; no watering, no spraying, no pruning, permanent or throw away model

The ideal cultivated street tree The Norway maple – perfectly formed; even-aged; resistant to disease. The selection process has provided the landscape design industry with a small group of plants bred to withstand any kind of environmental condition and usable everywhere regardless of the site

114

environmental pressures to which they have not previously been subjected.

The city climate is warmer, which has had a marked effect on plant distribution and survival. The atmosphere of industrial cities contains chemical pollutants such as sulphur dioxide, from residential and industrial combustion, ozone from the photochemical breakdown of automobile exhausts, nitrogen oxides and fluorides, and fine particles emitted from industrial processes. These pollutants interfere with normal transpiration and respiration processes of plants. Their root systems, adapted to forest soil conditions, must cope with paved surfaces, disturbed and compacted soils. Such conditions reduce water penetration and supply of nutrients, lower groundwater levels and interfere with the transfer of air and gases. The soil is contaminated with salts that are applied to the streets of many cities to keep them clear of snow and ice. The attraction of trees for urban pets may also contribute to the concentration of salts beyond their level of tolerance. There are also other physical problems that plants must contend with in the city environment; for instance, confined soils and exposure to cold from restricted or raised planting areas; exposure to heating and cooling vents on buildings; exposure to high winds or extreme heat; waterlogging from old basement structures or excessive dryness; the altered structure of urban soils; continuous disturbance from construction and maintenance activities, and so on.

Urban Plant Communities

The impact of the city has been far reaching on plant communities. There are three general groups that deserve attention.

The Cultivated Plant Group. This is the group of plants that is the product of horticultural science — the cultivation and selective breeding of plants that will satisfy the environmental and cultural demands of urban conditions. Through cloning and grafting techniques a range of plant species has been, and continues to be, developed in response to increasingly stringent requirements. For example, a large portion of the seed and stock of Canadian shade trees is imported from the US and Western Europe.[5] These must be resistant to a growing number of diseases, leaf rusts and insects. They must withstand drought, restricted soil conditions and doses of road salts. Their branches must be resistant to breakage from high winds. Their leaves must tolerate poisonous gases and particulates in the urban atmosphere. They must also respond to rapidly changing mechanical constraints. For instance, roots cannot interfere with underground services; branching habit and height must not compete with overhead wires. In addition to a multitude of environmental and physical limitations imposed on trees, their selection and breeding has been dictated by prevailing aesthetic values and conventions. How should trees behave? What is their ideal form?: How profusely can they be made to flower?

The ideal tree must be fast-growing, but long-lived. It must be symmetrical and perfectly formed. Characteristics such as messy fruit or slippery leaves, thorns, peeling bark and other inconveniences are unacceptable. These requirements are built into every designer's specifications for planting and have helped set the aesthetic and cultural standards for plant nurseries. The physical conditions under which plants are grown in nurseries are geared to uniform standards of soil, resistance to disease and form. They are grown to be transplanted to equally uniform sites. The unwary designer attempting to select moisture-loving plants for a wet, poorly drained site may well find they succumb to these conditions. The nursery plant, grown on well drained loams, is no longer adapted to its original environment. The procedures necessary to ensure the survival of plants involve complex engineering and horticultural requirements for transplantation, moving, soil preparation, guying, irrigation systems and protection.

The success of this humanised landscape, then, involves a transformation of urban sites to suit a limited number of horticulturally bred and selected plant species. But it is achieved with large expenditures of energy and a radical reduction of diversity.

The Native Plant Community. In many cities one may still find native plant communities that have remained relatively unaltered. These remnants of natural forests or wetland have been surrounded by the advancing city, but still retain elements of the original ecosystems that once prevailed. In some North American cities they survive more by good fortune than by design. Topographical obstructions or, on occasion, planning regulations, have forced the city to move around them. Some have since been incorporated into urban parks systems. The Tinicum marsh and Fairmount Park in Philadelphia and the ravine lands in Toronto are examples. Others, such as the common lands of forest and heathland in British and European cities, have been kept open for public use since the first days of village settlement and have never been enclosed or cultivated.[6]

Many natural areas have been encroached on by transportation links and development. Changes in drainage patterns, erosion and human use have severely altered their original character. But they still retain something of the natural diversity of the original natural community. A study for one urban valley site in the metropolitan Toronto area identified eight distinct vegetation associations within an area of a few acres.[7] Among these was found old field, mixed forest, hemlock stands and wetland. Many woodland remnants still retain plants and animals that

116

The native plant community
Remnants of old forests that have somehow survived, even though they have, in many cases, been drastically altered. They provide the irreplaceable historic and educational links with nature in cities

have become locally rare due to their isolation in the urban region. It is here in the middle of the city that one can still find trout lilies flourishing on the forest floor, or observe the annual migration of birds. Such places are one of the irreplaceable links btween natural and urban processes. They are a small but vitally important historic and educational resource for nature in the city.

The Naturalised Urban Plant Community. These are the plants that have adapted to city conditions without the assistance of man. The evolution of civilisation has fundamentally altered the original ecosystems that once flourished in the absence of man. Pollen analysis has shown that from its earliest beginnings the disturbance of land has been associated with plants of the open ground such as the dandelion, chickweed and plantain. These

117

plants colonised the land following the Ice Age. Their habitat and distribution were subsequently restricted by the afforestation which followed, but expanded again when agriculture and cities again laid the soil bare.[8] Modern industrialised cities have had a profound influence on plant communities. Many have been lost or become extinct through the disappearance or changes to habitats in which they are able to grow. At the same time new associations have become established in man-made habitats as a result of species migrating from other climatic zones. While urbanisation reduces the amount of vegetation, it has been shown that in European cities there is a comparatively high number of species present compared to the surrounding agricultural countryside.[9] The types of association that have adopted the city are different from the native associations that the city displaced. Continual disturbance of the urban environment creates ecologically unstable conditions that are favourable to the invasion of numerous pioneer species typical of early succession stages of natural ecosystems. Ragweed, for example, migrated across Canada eastwards from the prairies where it originated as the railways, highways and settlements prepared the way.[10] The increasing number of alien species colonising the city has been shown in Europe to have originated from warmer areas of the world.[11] Their success is due to a warmer climatic environment. Their expansion and naturalisation have been greatly influenced, not only by direct introductions and environmental changes, but also by spontaneous hybridisation with cultivated plants. From these, new species are continually evolving, adapted to the special soil and climatic conditions of the city.

The city offers a wide range of sites for these naturalised urban communities. They include waste lands that have been created from the demolition of old buildings; abandoned waterfronts and industrial lands; railway embankments; road rights-of-way and similar places. It is here that associations of white poplar, Manitoba maple, dandelion, chickweed, yarrow and other species grow in vigorous profusion. Even in the most paved-over parts of the city, mosses and grasses colonise rooftops and walls of buildings, dandelions, thistles and docks push their way through corners and cracks in the pavement. Ailanthus finds a foothold in the foundations of buildings and appears through basement gratings, where the warmth and alkalinity of the soil give it places to flourish. Plants, in fact, are everywhere in the city, a testament to their extraordinary tenacity and ability to evolve and adapt to new conditions and envirionmental niches that the city provides. Venice provides an excellent example of the phenomenon of urban plants in an intense urban environment that has, over time, become almost devoid of 'green' space in the conventional sense. Within the city limits 147 vascular plants have been recorded growing wild, including seven ferns and twenty grass species. The delicate maidenhair fern may be found in shaded cool

a

b

Naturalised plants downtown
(a) a dense stand of ailanthus, crowded into a corner service station; (b) a regenerating vacant lot. In many parts of the city, dense stands of trees, regenerating on their own, provide essential summer shade where it's needed to buildings and paved areas. The compound leaves of the Tree of Heaven (*Ailanthus altissima*), a tree widespread in North American cities, sprout late and fall early, minimising obstruction to the winter sun

corners of the city's footbridges, a rare plant originally from the warmer wetter coasts of Britain. Rock samphire grows along the edges of the canals; ivy-leaved toadflax on the Bridge of Sighs; and many other plants take advantage of the special micro-climates created by the city's nooks and crannies.[12]

Perceptions and Cultural Values

Horticultural science and the aesthetic that has evolved with it is engrained in our urban tradition. The standard dictionary definition of horticulture — the art or science of cultivating or managing gardens — embodies the ideal of nature under control. Each tree, shrub and flower is a symbol of human ingenuity; an artefact in a humanised landscape. Like sculpture, they are moulded and shaped, admired for their form, flower, leaves, unusual character or uniform repetition. We no longer see plants as interdependent, related parts of a total natural community, but as individual specimens. Set in an unrelenting carpet of mown turf, the ornamental tree and shrub are as unchanging as the architectural setting in which they are placed. There is an unending human struggle to maintain order and control. It is evident in the formidable array of machines, fertilisers, herbicides and manpower, marshalled to maintain a landscape as close as possible to the form in which it was conceived. The dynamics of plant succession are subjugated to our expectations of how plants should perform and behave in the city. The city landscape is a product of conflicting values. It expresses a deep-seated affinity with natural things. The spring bulbs displayed in every civic space clearly demonstrate this emotion. But these expressions of nature take place on our own terms, subject to standards of order and tidiness imposed by public values. The diverse community of plants that flourish in profusion in the adjoining abandoned lot, in every crack in the pavement, and invade every well kept shrub border and lawn, represent, in the public mind, disorder, untidiness, neglect.

This state of affairs is perpetuated by the design professions. The nature of urban design, whose primary objective is to create environmental quality in cities, in reality perpetuates urban dereliction. Every landscape improvement, intended to 'rehabilitate' a neglected area of the city, replaces the natural diversity of regenerating nature with the uniform and technology-dependent landscape of established design tradition. Design sets its own limitations to diversity. It establishes landscapes by brute force, the site being adapted to a predetermined list of plants. This anomaly is an expression of the deep-seated aesthetic conventions that have been part of professional training for generations. While large-scale rural planning now embraces the discipline of ecology,

120

natural processes are simply not part of the urban design problem. Somewhere a line is drawn that divides the nature of problem-solving into two distinct and separate camps. An examination of the planting specification that sets out the technical requirements for plants in most construction contracts reflects these attitudes and perceptions. Requirements for form ensure that the plant is symmetrical, well shaped and grown free of competition. Planting requirements ensure an ideal growing medium for plant roots, irrespective of existing soil conditions. Topsoil and a variety of soil amendments are required to ensure optimum growth conditions for turf and groundcovers — a case of robbing Peter to pay Paul. Irrigation systems are often needed to ensure regular and systematic watering. Together with pruning, mulching, spraying and other established horticultural practices, the effect of technology is to create environmental conditions that are as insulated from the nature of the place as possible. It permits the development and use of plants that depend on the presence of horticultural technology for survival. In turn it helps mould and perpetuate the image of a universal, high-maintenance, gardenesque landscape, divested of its own intrinsic vitality, adaptability, self-sufficiency or diversity. If we look at the technology needed to sustain the increasingly fashionable tropical landscapes that grace the interiors of prestige office buildings, we find this dependence on man-made systems even more extreme. Landscape design convention, in fact, parallels the 'International Style' of building (getting the least results for the maximum effort) that has been so rightly condemned by architectural critics. The inbuilt conflicts between acceptable and unacceptable forms of nature that appear when man-made improvements replace naturally diverse and self-sustaining environments are clearly evident. As the case of the Outer Harbour Headland in the city of Toronto described in Chapter One demonstrates, many a splendid and rich environment could be added to the urban parks system for the minimum cost of leaving them alone.

The traditional values embodied in civic space — the manicured lawns, flowerbeds and specimen trees — quite obviously have their place in the city. Horticulture is for the landscape of the industrial city an essential technical science. How else could a street tree survive in the peculiarly hostile habitat of the city street? The problem is not with science but with its application and the assumptions that go with it. The preoccupations of research in developing plants that are more and more resistant to air pollution is a case in point. The picture of ultimate technological success where the air we breathe chokes us to death but our trees flourish unscathed is one of misplaced priorities. The current frame of reference perpetuates universal standards of design aesthetics and upkeep of urban open space. We are concerned more with a scientific interest in plants as individual phenomena than with their place in the economy of nature. Urban design values are adrift, dictated by artistic conventions that lack a firm foundation in process and function. Such values work in opposition to the principles of ecology and the conserver view and deny its fundamental principles of process, economy of means, diversity and social opportunity. The problem lies in the wasted energy of current practice; in a lack of a functional role for urban plants beyond that of marginal amenity values; in the idea that parks should serve only a single purpose; in the fact that plants with no economic or productive benefits are seen to have higher value than those that do, whereas in modern forestry the opposite holds true.

Some Alternative Values and Opportunities

A Functional Framework

Our task here is to establish an alternative functional framework for urban plants based on the insights of urban ecology. From this a new aesthetic can emerge. To do so requires two shifts in perceptual thinking. The first requires a frame of reference that embraces co-operation rather than confrontation with nature's processes. The second involves an approach to urban design that derives its inspiration from the functional landscapes of the countryside. Nan Fairbrother has eloquently shown how the visual appeal of agricultural landscapes is the product of a working environment.[13] Similarly, well managed, productive forest landscapes are attractive. Their aesthetic arises from the integration of many objectives — the production of timber, protection of soils, water and natural features, enhancement of wildlife, recreation. A study carried out in 1971 to develop design guidelines in forest management practices for those untrained in design makes the following observations on aesthetics.

> Most people who are unaccustomed to thinking in visual design terms tend to equate aesthetics with emotional appeal and personal preference. It becomes a matter of opinion whether one kind of forest landscape or another is attractive or otherwise . . . design considerations, if they are to become a useful tool in forest management, must be capable of more objective evaluation. Generally speaking the following principles are true.
> — Well managed forests that include factors of site protection, prevention of erosion . . . wildlife values and fast regeneration of cutover sites, look better than those ignoring such considerations.
> — The basic management objectives for optimum wildlife habitat are similar to those of aesthetics: (viz.) diversity of forest types and vegetative cover; maximization of forest edges; optimum relationship between forest cover and forest openings. The management practices that follow the requirements of wildlife habitat usually result in visually pleasing forest landscapes.[14]

It is the integration of objectives in forestry and other occupations concerned with the land that provides the underlying framework for design and aesthetic values. To the established principles of design and aesthetic uses of plants should be added multi-functional and ecological disciplines inherent in good forest management. Bringing rural occupations to the city and integrating a countryside management philosophy with urban design involves co-operation as opposed to confrontation with nature. We stand to gain from this approach in economy, educational values and overall benefits. A range of opportunities are made available for a richer, more diverse and more useful environment, and a framework for an investment in the land. These are explored in more detail in the following sections of this chapter.

The Naturalised Plant Resource — Fortuitous Succession

Most industrial cities are generously endowed with lands that are not officially classified as recreational open space. They occur along transportation routes and service corridors, empty building lots, old industrial workings and waterfronts that have been abandoned. Many areas have been sealed from public use by ownership rights, or simply left unreclaimed. Many of these places once destroyed and subsequently abandoned or neglected have over time evolved as naturalised urban plant communities. W. G. Teagle has described the conditions in the industrial Midlands of Britain, where over two and a half centuries of industrial activity have left an indelible mark on the region. The original native heath landscape was substituted for one of hills and valleys, created by coal mining and quarrying, which greatly influenced plant distribution. The proliferation of canals in the nineteenth century encouraged the spread of aquatic plants and invertebrates which were previously unable to become established in the fast-flowing streams that drained the surrounding uplands. The railways that followed played a significant role in the dispersal of plants such as the Oxford ragwort.[15] Their embankments and cuttings also provided a sanctuary for plants in the immediate surroundings that were being destroyed.

These naturally reclaimed industrial landscapes often have an ecological, historic and topographic diversity that is infinitely richer than the land reclamation programmes aimed at their rehabilitation have created. The 'green desert' monocultures of grass and trees are no match for the complex relationships of plants, soils, water, topography, micro-climate and wildlife that are found here. In many cities the sheer cost of effecting such improvements is an important factor that has saved many significant habitats. It is, maybe, the most telling argument for the thesis under discussion that the diversity, vigour, beauty and wonder of natural process is available at little cost to enrich urban design. Look behind the gas filling station, the forgotten space used as a junkyard, or the alley tucked away behind the city's main thoroughfares, or the backs of many abandoned buildings in the poorer parts of town and you will find magical places of dense forests and varied groundcovers that have appeared on their own. An examination of the city's residential areas will reveal connections between the types of plants found there and the relative prosperity of the various neighbourhoods. There is a marked tendency in well-to-do neighbourhoods for vegetation to be not only denser but to have a greater variety of exotic species. The less wealthy 'down-at-heel' neighbourhoods have less cultivated vegetation overall, but have a much higher proportion of native or naturalised species. Many of these places rely on such trees as Manitoba maple and Tree of Heaven that have become established on their own. These 'weed trees' often provide the only shade over streets and sidewalks, creating, in many cases, a quality environment that is rarely matched by conventional design. No self-respecting designer would plant Tree of Heaven (messy fruit and slippery leaves) smack up against a building wall (foundation planting); or Manitoba maple on a residential street (weed tree — roots get in the drains). A tree survey in 1972 in Edinburgh[16] showed that numbers, size-class distribution and composition of plants were affected appreciably in residential areas by a social factor, the percentage of home ownership. The number of trees per hectare increased progressively from 20 trees with 0-25 per cent owner-occupancy, to 115 trees with 26 per cent owner-occupancy. The percentage of elder and sycamore (two 'weed trees' in Britain) decreased with increasing home ownership.

Such observations reveal the value of naturalised plants to the city. The astonishing vigour of nature, with its ability to compete in and colonise the city against all odds and human intervention is clear. A comment by Sukopp is relevant here. 'Ecosystems which have developed in urban conditions may be the prevailing ecosystems of the future. Many of the most resistant plants in our industrial areas and in cities . . . are non natives.'[17] We cannot afford to rely entirely on technological systems to create urban landscapes, while ignoring the real nature of the places we live in. Recent research is raising many questions about established horticultural practices, such as the addition of soil amendments, pruning and mulching in new planting. Studies on tree-planting in a variety of soil types have shown that adding soil amendments such as peatmoss to the plant pit do not produce more root growth than no amendments.[18] Investigation of the accepted nursery practice of pruning back the crowns of newly planted trees revealed that the pruned trees showed no benefit from pruning over those left unpruned. It was concluded that the intact crown of the tree plays a more beneficial role in carbohydrate production, auxin release (a plant hormone regulating growth) and subsequent root regeneration than in transpiring water resulting in moisture stress.[19]

Some Design Alternatives

General Concerns

We must begin our search for alternative perspectives of the city landscape by accepting the premise that ecological processes operating in the city must form an indispensable basis for landscape design. The interrelationships of climate, geology and geomorphology, water, soils, plants and animals provide the fundamental ecological information on which the environmental planning and management of land are based. The application of this process to the design of the city landscape must logically follow. At the broad level of open space planning the naturalised plant communities that occur all over the city require inventory and evaluation. Those habitats for plants and animals, or those possessing rare or unusual species, should be integrated into the open space planning network. They provide, among other things, alternative opportunities for diverse and rich social and educational experiences. A biological classification and management approach to open space with respect to its sensitivity to human intrusion is required for cities. Dorney has proposed a method for rating environmentally sensitive areas where sites are ranked into five classes of sensitivity or significance. These are derived from an assessment of such factors as the presence of rare or endangered species, important plant or animal associations, size of the area, animal diversity and other factors.[20] Parallel examples are the International Biological Program, or various parks classification systems. A classification system for cities would include both remnant natural areas and naturalised plant communities. This might range from highly valued or unique reserves requiring restricted or carefully controlled access to those areas that can support diverse human activity and permit unrestricted access.

At a detailed level, ecological information on climate, soils, plant tolerance and succession creates opportunities for recognising and acknowledging the uniqueness and variety of urban places. A design philosophy inspired by urban ecology is based on the principle that design solutions must be adapted to the site. Many alternatives become available once this frame of reference is accepted. The naturalised plant community becomes a valued resource for establishing vegetation on poor sites and sterile soils. Plants may be seen as constantly evolving communities rather than individual phenomena. Colonising plants adapted to urban soils can enhance and modify them and provide alternatives to importing fertility to the city. Landscape maintenance can become a process of integrated management based on ecological parameters, and assures us of the practical tools for maintaining productive and self-sustaining landscapes.

(c)

Some general categories of habitat type in urban open space

Wetlands
(a) Wetlands and open bodies of water contain rich associations of wetland species and are susceptible to damage through groundwater depletion and water pollution
(b) Abandoned industrial sites may also support rich communities that have occurred through a combination of water impoundment and natural succession. Being enclosed or off limits, they survive as precious natural reserves. Abandoned industrial sites are often durable features in the city landscape
(c) As man-made marshes, sewage lagoons are rich in nutrients and support diverse associations of plants, invertebrates and birds

127

(d)

(e)

(f)

Woodlands
(d) Remnant mature woodlands often contain locally rare trees, shrubs and ground vegetation as well as birds and other animals
(e) Naturally occurring regenerating woodlands, for instance on vacant lots, lanes, etc., are tough and resilient and provide climatic and social benefits to less favoured parts of the city
(f) Ravines and valleylands. Those that contain steep banks and remnant native vegetation that are highly susceptible to erosion and destruction, often contain highly diverse groupings of plants. Valley floors in many ravines are often disturbed by the removal of the original vegetation for reasons of access, park development, and so on. Many of these are resilient and can withstand considerable use

(g)

(h)

(i)

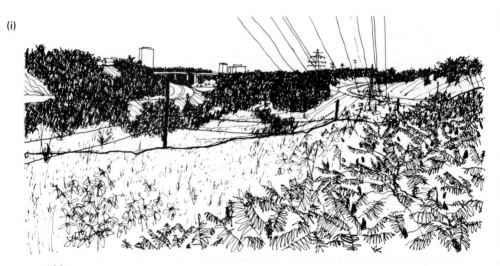

Regenerating landscapes
(g) Many landscapes have been completely changed ecologically, hydrologically and topographically due to mining or similar operations. These regenerating landscapes can often sustain high pressures of use from children and adults. As changed but none the less vital natural environments they are of priceless educational and ecological value
(h) Former wastelands recolonised by early succession plants are ecologically diverse, resilient and of considerable educational and social benefit in residential areas. Their preservation and inclusion into new developments would do much to enrich these places
(i)(j) Power line rights-of-way railways are the connecting links through the city, support a diverse group of pioneer plants and are valuable wildlife habitats.

131

Design and Plant Succession: an Alternative to the Green Lollipop

There is an aesthetic appeal to old trees rising clear from an open grassed sward uninterrupted by obstructions. It is the landscape that is encouraged in urban parks because it permits maximum use of the ground plane for human activity. It is achieved all at once and is easily maintained. But this is a landscape without a future; the ultimate death of the old trees leaves nothing in their place. New trees planted will take years before the original environment can be recreated. The countless streets that were changed overnight by Dutch elm disease are evidence of this fact. The propensity for creating static landscapes from climax species (what has been called the 'international urban tree community')[21] derives from an aesthetic perception of nature that sees beauty in decay rather than in the vitality of continuing life. This problem is admirably expressed by Guldemond.

> Our grandchildren will want to see old trees, so we will have to plant them. That means we cannot just wait and let the old tree stands die out . . . We have to [consider] natural principles, which implies a normal distribution of age classes . . . I always have a rather uncomfortable feeling when I see a park full of wonderful old trees, splendid to look at, but without any young material for the future and so without the permanence we all wish.[22]

A wood without a future The classical woodland stereotype when translated into reality; nothing to replace the grand old trees

As we have seen, the forest environment performs many functions. From the point of view of human use, forests have throughout history provided the natural resources essential to the growth of cities. The care of forests is evolving towards a concept of management that has many objectives; economic, social and environmental. Harvesting of wood, recreation and amenity values, education, preservation and maintenance of forest diversity, all have their place in an integrated management process. The planning and upkeep of urban parks are, however, limited primarily to amenity and aesthetic objectives. While this may be relevant to the pedigree parks and civic spaces, it is quite inadequate for the management of natural or naturalised forest areas. It is also incapable of fulfilling the multiple functions that plants must play in cities in the future.

The task of design, supported by ongoing management, is to reinstate natural process. Another approach to planting is needed that will provide a perpetuating adaptive landscape in many areas where traditional horticultural approaches are inappropriate. This may be defined as the process of naturalisation which brings an ecological view to the design and maintenance of the urban landscape. Natural process rather than horticultural technology forms its underlying framework. It involves the introduction of natural landscape elements into the city that include the re-establishment of woodlands through the reforestation of some lands, the creation of wetlands where hydrological conditions are appropriate, the development of meadow communities through modified turf management and the establishment of varied wildlife habitats. These are inherently productive self-regulating communities achieved through ecologically sensitive management rather than total maintenance control. When this approach is placed in context with areas requiring higher levels of upkeep, it achieves benefits in environmental, social and aesthetic diversity and in overall economy in energy, materials and manpower.

Urban Woodlands

Urban forestry, a concept new to North America, involves the transfer of ecologically sound forest management practices from the rural forest to the urban setting. Its objectives are based on the premiss that forests, existing or introduced into cities, function to create low-cost and self-sustaining landscapes. Urban forestry requires a management philosophy that integrates aspects of horticulture with ecology and provides environmental and social benefits. An integrated management policy of this kind may also produce direct economic benefits in the form of forest products.

Urban reforestation also involves land that has often not supported trees for a long period of time. Its intent is to create diverse plant associations that are in harmony with the nature of the site, i.e. with its soils, topography, climate and related environmental conditions. In addition, its long-term objective is to rehabilitate sites that have degenerated over time through soil compaction, removal of topsoil, reduction of productivity and nutrients. The philosophy of woodland establishment under discussion is based on the principle of natural succession speeded up and assisted by management. It follows three general phases: (1) an initial planting of fast-growing, light-demanding pioneer species that quickly provide vegetative cover, ameliorate soil drainage, fix nitrogen and stimulate soil micro-organisms and create favourable micro-climatic conditions for more long-lived species; (2) an intermediate phase of plants that ultimately replace the pioneers; (3) a climax phase of slow-growing, shade-tolerant species that are the long-lived plants. In practice the planting of these phases may be done all at one time, or introduced at intervals in the development of the woodland. The initial and final composition, character and uses of woodlands will be quite different as they evolve. They provide varying and useful places from the beginning. Initially they become socially useful and durable in a short time, something conventional climax-oriented planting design does not do. Later the landscape will evolve to a different character, responding to changing uses and environmental conditions. The approach obviates the current problems that occur when whole sections of urban plant material die from disease. It also maintains a dynamic sense of process and diversity that gives us a realistic view of nature and a valid basis for design with plants. Various examples of the approach have been put into practice.

A Self-sustaining Residential Landscape. The landscape of many housing developments and parks in the Netherlands has been brought to a high level of sophistication and design. They are based on the conviction that plants are functionally and aesthetically essential to urban life. In the high-density apartment developments at Delft, courtyards have been planted as urban woodlands in addition to providing open space for nursery schools, play areas and sports facilities. Design is based on certain fundamental ecological and social objectives.

— There must be freedom of movement and play by children and adults. In these woodland landscapes the sheer vigour of early plant associations and their density provide a tough and highly varied environment. They withstand the pressures of play and other activities, even in high-density housing environments. The Dutch believe that it is unrealistic to attempt to confine children to specific play areas. While these are provided, the whole environment is available for play. The complexity and ruggedness of the woodland landscape can accommodate pressures that would soon reduce conventional design layouts to ruins.

Housing at Delft, the Netherlands The creation of urban forests based on the principle of managed succession has been pioneered by the Dutch and has since been developed in Britain for housing and land reclamation. The now famous Delft experiment has demonstrated how this approach to the landscape enhances environmental and social values. Wooded landscapes maintain equitable micro-climate through absorption of solar radiation evapotranspiration and reduction of winds. Socially they provide a diverse environment of open and closed space that has immediate and long-term benefits in forest cover, diversity of wildlife, tough and creative play environments and amenity.

(a) Minor pathways are left to be made by residents. Once established as links they are paved. This organic functional approach to the use of the landscape has a somewhat untidy appearance by conventional standards, but the plant associations are rugged and low-maintenance and develop their own innate aesthetic

b

c

(b) Turf is left to grow under trees at the interface between wooded and open landscape. Such practice minimises upkeep

(c) A playground space surrounded by woods. A basic difference between this kind of design and conventional planting design is in initial perceptions. Convention assumes the addition of plants to open areas to make spaces. The urban forestry approach assumes a totally forested landscape from which the necessary open spaces are cut out

— Maintenance and upkeep must be low. The advantage of woodlands is that they require considerably less upkeep than do conventional landscapes. Maintenance responds to use patterns and circulation over time. For instance, secondary paths are created in response to natural desire lines. They are gravelled and left as pedestrian and cycle routes once they have been established as permanent patterns of movement. Turf and vegetation under trees is only minimally maintained, and is generally left to take care of itself. As the woodland matures and responds to use, a self-perpetuating stable vegetation develops that requires little upkeep. The objects of design and management are not based on aesthetics, but rather to produce a usable indigenous vegetation with a character of its own.[23]

The quality of these housing landscapes is, therefore, radically different from conventional design. They have the natural, informal, somewhat untidy, yet functional character of a heavily used landscape. It is an aesthetic derived from the interaction of vegetation and human activity. A study of one apartment complex in Delft concluded that the landscape design and its use by children resulted in a greater attraction and more efficient use of the available space compared to the more conventional planning of open spaces.[24]

A Rehabilitation Programme for an Urban Park System. The parks, parkways and waterways that form a comprehensive open space network in Canada's capital city are a part of its long-range development plan initiated in 1950 by the French planner Greber. Both in its planning and design quality it compares favourably with the best urban tradition to be found in North America and Europe. Its overall image as a landscape of beautifully manicured lawns, well maintained shrub borbers, and banks of flowers and cultivated trees has over the years come to be regarded as the ideal of civic open space design. The image represents a period of history when this kind of intensive maintenance was considered an appropriate and proper expression of national pride and commitment to good design. Today it poses serious questions for the National Capital Commission, the agency responsible for the implementation of the plan. How can a programme of development and ongoing maintenance be sustained in the face of escalating costs in energy, equipment and manpower? With over thirty open space corridors comprising an area of some 2,748 hectares to be developed and 3,000 hectares of turf requiring weekly maintenance, the financial burden becomes increasingly difficult to bear.[25] Are the accepted quality standards for landscape development and upkeep appropriate for all the city's lands? These standards have, apart from being costly, resulted in a large-scale landscape that provides little variety or diversity from one place to another and creates an alternative image of

137

Managed Succession	Natural Regeneration
Stage 1. Establishment – pioneer and climax species mixed Typical Plant Species: Poplar Alder, Maple Basswood Hemlock	Stage 1. Existing conditions mown turf / existing woodland
Stage 2. Canopy closure and thinning	Stage 2. Abandon mowing / prevailing wind
Stage 3 onward. Mature climax woodland development understorey planting	Stage 3. Regeneration / edge regeneration meadow community development / woodland regeneration

General reforestation categories

Plantation involves the planting of predominantly similar species where the final woodland composition is determined by the initial planting. This is the normal procedure of forestry practice and is based primarily on commercial objectives.

Managed succession developed in the Netherlands and Britain is based on the principle of natural succession and assisted through management. The initial and final composition, character and uses of the woodland will be quite different as it evolves. The nurse crop functions to ameliorate soil drainage, fix nitrogen, stimulate soil micro-organisms and create a micro-climatic environment suited to the development of climax species. This approach is, therefore, concerned primarily with the rehabilitation of derelict landscapes, rather than with commercial objectives. Arguments on the advantages and disadvantages of native versus non-native plant species may be less important than considerations of structure, wildlife habitat, adaptability to soils, local climate, air pollution, drainage, and so on.

Natural regeneration involves discontinuing mowing regimes in areas where a woodland seed source is available. In the absence of disturbance a woodland landscape is re-established naturally over time.

monotony. These questions posed together make a cogent argument for seeking alternative ways of developing and maintaining the capital city's landscape.

With these considerations in mind, the National Capital Commission initiated in 1981 a naturalisation programme for its parkway corridors that includes the creation of meadow lands through a modified mowing regime and an experimental reforestation study programme designed to gain long-term knowledge of the most appropriate methods for establishing new woodlands in the urban region. This radical departure from conventional practice on the part of a major public organisation represents the beginnings of a new approach to the urban landscape that over time will become low-maintenance, economical and self-sustaining. The project includes layout of a number of test plots in one of the city's parkways designed to evaluate specific planting techiques, management procedures and public acceptance of the idea. The lack of experience in the approach made it essential to test out alternatives before launching a full-scale programme. While in general terms the approach taken was based on managed succession, there were many questions that required answers and which dictated the test plot design, i.e.:

— the proportions of various species through the successional range of plants suited to the soils and climate of the region. Four relatively simple groupings of plants were selected related to well and poorly drained sites;
— the most effective types of site preparation techniques relative to cost factors, manpower, competition and speed of plant establishment;
— the most effective planting techniques with respect to spacing, initial maintenance and speed of establishment;
— the best methods of controlling competing plants such as grasses and damage by rodents;
— the types of management required up to the establishment of woodland (canopy closure) and subsequent management of the evolving woodland (thinning of stands in relation to long-range objectives).

Monitoring and evaluation of the test plots will be ongoing over the next five years and will provide the necessary practical experience for the future. The following diagrams illustrate some of the principles on which the experiment is based.

An Urban Ecological Park. The naturalised vegetation of the city, be it a fortuitously reclaimed site, or spontaneous herbs colonising a small space in a parking lot or old wall, is a resource for play and environmental learning. Such places are rich in opportunity for adventure and discovery.

Prescription	Planting Procedure	Comments
Alternative 1 Mechanical/manual cultivation – cultivation of planting area prior to planting (fall) to kill ground vegetation – manual cultivation regularly during growing season (monthly)	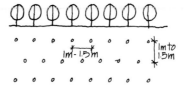	– labour intensive – application to small or awkwardly sheltered are – application to closely sp planting where fast can closure is a high priority – constant maintenance required during growin seasons
Alternative 2 Chemical treatment – application of Round-up or equivalent herbicide to kill ground vegetation (fall) – mechanical/manual cultivation of area 7-10 days following chemical application – application of Simazine or equivalent herbicide (spring, prior to planting) in doughnut pattern around tree locations	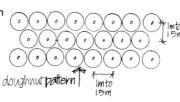	– greatly reduced labour requirements, since onl application required per (depending on rate of ap cation) – applicable in small or aw wardly shaped areas an closely spaced planting – chemical treatment in u areas may present probl of health and public acceptance
		Note: Simazine is register use only for white pine a balsam fir plantations; v Simazine is also applied hardwoods, many specie sensitive to chemical herbicides
Alternative 3 All mechanical cultivation – mechanical cultivation of area prior to planting (fall) to kill ground vegetation – mechanical cultivation between rows done regularly during growing season		– greatly reduced labour requirements – suitable for large areas v machinery may be econc ally used – growing season cultivati still requires ongoing ma tenance (monthly) until canopy closure
Alternative 4 – application of Round-up or equivalent herbicide to kill ground vegetation (fall) – mechanical cultivation of area 7-10 days following chemical application, between rows – application of Simazine or equivalent herbicide (spring, prior to planting) by mechanical spray between rows	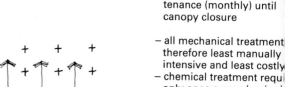	– all mechanical treatment therefore least manually intensive and least costly – chemical treatment requ only once a year (spring) depending on rate of app tion, until canopy closure – requires large areas whe machinery can be econor ally used – chemical treatment in url areas may present proble of health and public acce ance

Site preparation is a crucial factor in woodland establishment. It is necessary to reduce competition from herbaceous plants and rodent damage until the tree canopy closes and competing ground flora are naturally suppressed. The table shows a number of alternative approaches under study by the National Capital Commission.

Planting techniques

Prescription	Year		Procedure	Comments
Alternative 1 100% pioneer species planted, followed by climax species after canopy closure (managed succession category)	1		– species planted at random or in rows – pioneer species mixture: aspen, alder, poplar, etc.	– pioneer mixture can vary and include pine, black locust, etc. – spacing may be close, 1.0-1.5m for quick closure or in rows 3.0 m apart for mechanical cultivation
	3-5		– after canopy closure, thin proportion of pioneer species	– slower canopy closure involves less thinning later
			– plant intermediate/climax species, maple, birch, basswood, hemlock, etc.	– plant mixture varies relative to site type
Alternative 2 Pioneer and climax species planted at the same time (managed succession category)	1		– pioneer species planted at random or in rows: poplar, aspen, alder, white pine, etc., with intermediate and climax species of red maple, birch, basswood, hemlock, sugar maple, etc.	– spacing as in Alternative 1
	3		– after canopy closure, thin competing pioneer species but retain partial shade	

The layout and spacing of plant materials depends on a number of interrelated factors that require investigation, for instance the balance between closely spaced plants that achieve fast canopy closure but involve costly hand cultivation, versus widely spaced plants that achieve slower closure but involve cheaper mechanical cultivation; the relative merits of an initial 100 per cent pioneer planting versus mixing fast- and slow-growing species together.

Edge planting criteria

Prescription	Year	Procedure	Comments
Edge treatment along walks and adjacent to housing	1	– + range incorporate edge treatment to reforestation areas, shrubs, small trees – leave mown area between planting and activity Objectives: – protection from casual access – spring and fall colour – attraction to wildlife – maintenance of visual quality – mown turf creates planting islands and aids rodent control	– woodland edge planting for woodland protection may become part of management plan – after canopy closure meadow community may be allowed to develop in association with shrub edge – some mown turf adjacent to walks and housing should be maintained for visual and recreational purposes

pathway
mown strip
reforestation
edge planting
mown strip
housing

| Introduction of man-made design elements | | = incorporate viewing areas where appropriate | |

mown turf

142

Introduction of interpretive
panels

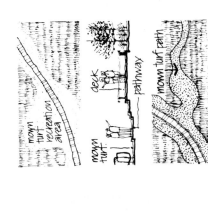

– incorporate picnic, sitting and
sunning places or recreation
areas requiring mown turf

– under certain conditions
mown turf pathways may be
included where traffic is light

– explanation of naturalisation
interest

Design Considerations

Public involvement and acceptance of urban forestry are critical to its successful establishment. The design and layout of woodlands require very careful consideration to emphasise the fact that this alternative landscape may be as representative of quality and care and civic pride as the horticultural landscape it replaces. The object is to give a sense of purpose and intent when man-made elements are placed in association with naturalised areas. Design criteria include some of the following.

Variety. A variety of plants is required for different site types (poorly drained, well drained, slopes, flat areas, etc.). These relate to the characteristics of the location. In addition the aim should be ultimately to achieve an uneven-aged woodland that is diverse in species composition.

Turf edges. The image of neglect is nowhere more apparent than where edges are poorly considered. Turf left to grow long adjacent to human

143

144

activity tends to represent abandonment of responsibility. Naturalised turf or new planting close to walks and housing collects litter, which involves higher maintenance costs. The opportunity is lost for passive activities (sitting, walking, sunbathing, etc.) that require short turf. Naturalised turf encourages immigration of rodents in initial stages of woodland establishment. Thus, the establishment of well maintained turf edges is important in functional and visual terms.

Planting edges. The development of woodland edges over time creates a more natural woodland, encourages wildlife such as songbirds, adds colour with flowering trees and shrubs, and could, in initial establishment stages, provide buffering and physical protection to the new plantings in public areas that may be vulnerable to damage.

Structural elements. Integrating man-made elements into existing forest or wetland habitats is an accepted design practice that both protects and enhances natural places. The same holds true for naturalisation objectives in urban areas.

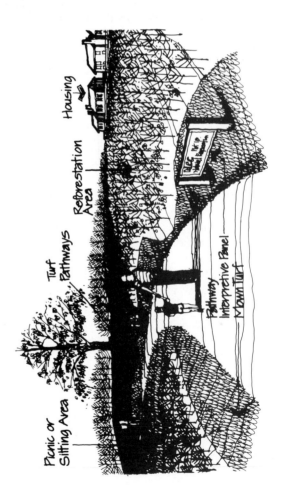

Community reforestation The creation and rehabilitation of urban woodland are closely linked to community involvement and action. Students at the faculty of Environmental Studies, York University, Toronto, initiated a woodland rehabilitation programme in 1981 to expand the remnant patches of natural woods on the campus. Classes from the local schools planted a variety of tree seedlings over a period of a week in plots that were demarcated and measured for future study. Variables under consideration include species mix, soil conditions, rodent damage, survival and growth rates. Research aims to identify suitable and low-cost methods of revegetating the campus. For the children the experience provided valuable lessons about the importance of trees for shade, shelter, wildlife and group participation

Hawthorns, brambles, wild flowers and wild grasses; ponds that harbour tadpoles and small fish; landform and rubble outcrops that provide varied habitats; these are the essential alternative places to football pitches and passive recreational landscapes.

The William Curtis Ecological Park is an experimental prototype of a new kind of urban park. Located on a 2-acre plot in a run-down industrial area of central London, it was created in 1977 to show how some of London's large stock of unused land might economically be put to creative use.[26] It was conceived as a study centre for London schools, for research and study in urban ecology and urban wildlife conservation. Over several years a plant cover of numerous naturalised and native plant communities has been established on 350 truckloads of mixed fill that were brought from demolition and excavation sites. These were dumped over the original hardcore of the site. A pond, dug and fed by rainwater from a nearby roof, has been established with aquatic flora and fauna. Paths and a look-out point have been laid out. The plant communities are evolving under permanent management and monitoring by a trained

145

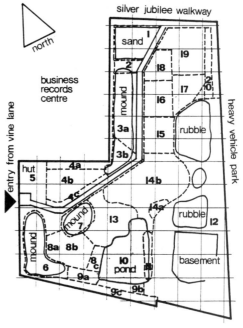

Plan of William Curtis Ecological Park management compartments, 10m² recording grid superimposed (© Ecological Parks Trust, 1977-78)

The William Curtis Ecological Park, London This park was the first to be established by the Ecological Parks Trust. Its formation arose from the Queen's Silver Jubilee in 1977. Its object is to advance public education and further knowledge of the ecology of urban areas. The experience and success of this park has provided ample evidence that urban man's need for contact with nature can be met, not only with occasional field trips to remote areas, but by study in the inner city (photo: Lyndis Cole)

Key to management compartments

Plant Community or Habitat
1. Sand dune (school project)
2. Gorse scrub
3a. Birch/pine woodland
3b. Birch/oak woodland
4a. London pioneer species, screening
    4b from reflected heat from building
4b. Species-poor deciduous woodland
4c. Hedgerow
5. Hut compartment – primary school
   gardens, annual weeds, etc.
6. Species-rich deciduous woodland
7. Copse
8a. Perennial wayside weeds
8b. Wet peat meadow
8c. Tall sedge community
9a. Alder carr
9b. Willow bed
9c. Pre-existing stand of sycamore,
   sallow, etc.
10. Pond with marginal vegetation
11. Gravel pond margin
12. Area of natural succession on a
    variety of substrates
13. Wet clay meadow
14a. Copse
14b. Sown grassland: not cultivated: control for compartments 15, 16, 17, 18
15. Short pasture grassland: cultivated
    January 1978
16. Dry meadow: cultivated January
    1978
17. Cornfield: cultivated March 1979 –
    mainly barley, plus school experi-
    mental wheat plot
18. As 16, allocated for chalk grassland
19. Self-sown meadow and scrub: not
    cultivated: control for compart-
    ments, 15, 16, 17, 18
20. Hedge to act as windbreak

ecologist. They include a planted woodland of native trees and shrubs and creepers on suitable walls. The fresh-water pond supports submergent and emergent plants and aquatic life. There are plant communities representative of particular types of soil conditions, and a central grass meadow.

As the park evolved, problems had to be faced and resolved. One was soil compaction. The solution was to reproduce soil processes of the vegetation type as closely as possible; for instance, by spreading leaves over the emerging woodland area; spreading sedge peat on the wet meadow area. Another was unchecked growth of the weed cladophera in the pond, stimulated by high-nutrient London tap water. It required competition from other organisms and a replacement of mains supply with relatively sterile rainwater.

As an experiment in environmental education and an ecological approach to the use of derelict urban sites, this interesting project is a practical example at little cost, but much effort and enthusiasm, of one creative alternative to urban landscape.

Woodland Parks and Integrated Management. The remnants of natural forest communities that have somehow survived in cities are an irreplaceable, though often neglected, resource. They stand as a classic example of the need for ecologically based management. Many have deteriorated from urban pressures. The urbanisation of surrounding watersheds alters stream erosion processes, sedimentation patterns, nutrient flows and water quality. It creates changes to drainage patterns, soil chemistry, vegetation and animal communities. The need to preserve locally rare ecosystems, preserve wildlife and scenic quality is, therefore, crucial. Management objectives that integrate the influences of the surrounding city with the dynamics of a changed but evolving ecosystem under urban conditions provide irreplaceable opportunity for education.

Urban natural areas are the field study centres of the city, where plants and animals can be observed; where community dynamics can be studied; where the interactions of urban and natural processes may be measured. They can demonstrate the role of forests in the maintenance of the water regime and the modification of climate. They are outdoor laboratories for teaching reforestation and silvicultural techniques. This may include shelterwood, group selection and other cutting methods appropriate to the forest type. It is here that different management objectives must be integrated in the light of many and sometimes conflicting demands. They provide the essential links to the care and management of forests in rural areas beyond the city. Understanding the processes of nature and human intervention in the familiar surroundings of the city is, maybe, the most effective way of ensuring a knowledgeable and informed concern for the larger environment.

In countries where significant rural timber resources are lacking, the city may play a role in producing timber to offset the costs of recreational facilities and park maintenance. Although wood is relatively abundant in North America, escalating transport costs and increasing interest in wood as an alternative source of fuel may well make urban timber production economically attractive. At the same time there are indirect economic reasons for using city-grown trees that also relate to ecologically sound management practices. The removal and disposal of old trees is a continuing and ever increasing cost that must be borne by city authorities. These can provide a return if the wasteful practice of chipping and disposal at the city dump is changed. In Philadelphia, for instance, half a million board feet of sawlogs and 2,000 cords of pulpwood were disposed of in 1960, which could have kept a small sawmill in operation all year.[27]

Zurich, a city of a half million people, has a major proportion of its park space (nearly a quarter of the urban area) in forest and common land. These lands, some 2,200 hectares in extent, are within a half hour's street-car ride from the city centre and lie within or on the edges of the city. They have for many years been maintained on an integrated management basis, providing timber, recreation and athletic facilities, wildlife, agriculture, visual amenity and education. The forests are a mixture of deciduous beech, oak and maple stands and conifers. Forestry practice is carried out by the City Department of Forestry. It involves a variety of silvicultural techniques including shelterwood, seed tree and patch cutting systems, depending on the forest type. The aim is to produce an unevenly aged forest of young and mature stands with a major emphasis on an aesthetic forest quality. Great care is taken in cutting, therefore, to ensure that this quality is maintained. Cutting occurs in the winter and the logs are stored along an extensive system of forest roads for shipping to various sawmills outside the city. Forest roads are also designed and used for walking, nature trails, cross-country skiing and exercise by the citizens of Zurich. Fitness tracks and exercise stops are also integrated into the forest setting. The forest supports deer which are managed by city authorities.

The basic aim of forestry is to produce commercial timber for sawlogs and pulp. These products bring a return and help support increasingly extensive and sophisticated recreational facilities that the city provides. In 1979 the balance sheet for the city's operations showed the costs of all recreation and forestry operations to be Fr. 4.5 million. This also included financial assistance to private clubs. Income from forest products amounted to nearly Fr. 2.5 million. Income, therefore, amounted to approximately 55 per cent of the total costs of the park system. An interesting sidelight on the economics of the operation is demonstrated in the sale of beechwood to Italy for fruit boxes. These arrive back from Italy with fruit, bought by the Swiss. The cost of the fruit is paid for by

Zurich's forest parks Integrated urban forest management including forest products, wildlife, small-scale farming and recreation. Sophisticated silviculture maintains the productivity of these woodlands and their aesthetic appeal. It shows how a parks system can be, at least partially, economically self-sustaining, contributing in ways other than recreation to the public good. As a multi-functional, self-sustaining landscape it provides social, economic and environmental benefits and calls in question the assumption that parks are exclusively places for leisure

the sale of the boxes.[28]

It is apparent, therefore, that the concept of bringing rural occupations to the city in the form of urban forest resources provides numerous benefits that conventional parks operations are unable to do. As we saw in Chapter Two, vegetation has a marked influence on climate and the urban environment generally. As well as the social benefits of a more varied and useful landscape, the urban forest provides the basis for education in forest practice. Its presence as a part of the life of the city and under the scrutiny of its citizens ensures that high standards of forestry are maintained. It thus helps close the perceptual gap between urban and rural areas by creating a better understanding of their ultimate interdependence. In addition, it makes potential economic sense, a fact that has relevance for many municipalities trying to meet increasing demands for public amenities with diminishing budgets.

Management and the Evolving Urban Landscape

Management and Maintenance

The alternative ways of approaching plants that we have been examining offer design opportunities that provide a valid functional and ecological basis for form. They are also allied to the concept of continuous evolving management. The implementation of design, from paper planning to layout on the ground, is only the start of the design process. It presents a different picture, condition and usefulness at different stages, guided by a management process that determines its form over time. Conventional maintenance deals with landscape inorganically, as static form. Its object is to keep the design as close to the sketches the client accepted as possible — the fixed picture. It brings with it a formidable arsenal of mowing equipment, leaf vacuums, fertiliser spreaders, herbicide and pesticide sprayers to keep plants under control. The maintenance regime is high in energy and resources and aims to achieve standardised results. Obviously some types of urban landscape need this kind of careful maintenance. Those subjected to intense human pressure, or those with intended gardenesque or prestige objectives, are evident examples. But others don't. The role of management in cities must be to provide the greatest diversity possible, fitting a great many situations and needs.

The Green Carpet

Perhaps the most pervasive element of the cultivated landscape is the lawn. Instant wall-to-wall grass appears everywhere, in hot climates and cold, in prestige projects and in run-of-the-mill ones, in large landscapes and small. Turf depends on standardised requirements for topsoil, fertilisers, herbicides, watering and cutting heights that challenge its credibility as a living material. The lawn, maintained everywhere at 2-$2\frac{1}{2}$ inches in height, is the product of the mowing mchine which dictates the appearance and design form of much of the urban scene. Slopes greater than 33 per cent are difficult to mow. Less than 2 per cent they won't drain properly. Edges must be trimmed and defined. The mowing regime continues uninterrupted around and under other elements in the landscape, defying the variations of environment that occur under trees, in and around groups of shrubs, on slopes and in odd corners. Plants in the maintained lawn are thus restricted to the lollipop on a stick varieties, since the growth and spread by suckering of many species is inhibited.

A high level of turf maintenance is appropriate, as I have remarked, in the carefully controlled prestige places of the city centre and other situations where use specifically requires it. It is, however, self-defeating when universally applied and where it is not required. As a high-cost, high-energy floor covering, it produces the least diversity for the most effort. As a product of a pervasive cultural aesthetic, it defies logic.

There are simpler ways of producing a diverse landscape through a broader-based ecological approach to management processes. One alternative is a more intelligent and less intensive use of mowers to permit plant diversity and wildlife habitat to become management objectives. In several western Canadian provinces, farmers mow road verges for hay, thereby obtaining a hay crop while keeping the verge tidy. This practice could well be applied to many parts of the city. A study for the National Capital Commission in Ottawa on the implications of modified mowing regimes on the city's maintained grasslands showed the value of such an alternative. By cutting only those areas that were necessary for recreation, fire hazard, etc., and leaving remaining grasslands unmown during the summer months, a far greater diversity of bird species was created in a very short space of time. The number of exotic 'nuisance' species such as starling and house sparrows was reduced and the number of grassland species such as bobolinks rose dramatically as the appropriate habitat became available.[29] This illustrates the need for grassland management objectives that take into account the recreational, visual and functional aspects of parkland that require areas of short turf and the encouragement of habitat diversity.

If the maintenance of grassland as opposed to woodland regeneration is the objective, then cutting of unmown areas is periodically required. In order to preserve optimum grassland bird habitat, mowing should be limited to the late fall, after breeding is over and after migrating birds have taken advantage of grassland seed sources.

Visually, the combination of rough and fine turf can create a complexity and variety to the landscape in large grass areas that universal mowing can never achieve. The problems that often arise when grass is left unmown are to a great extent perceptual. The image of neglect is nowhere more apparent than where the interface between mown and unmown turf is poorly considered. Turf left to grow long adjacent to human activity tends to represent neglect and abandonment of responsibility. There are also practical aspects to the perceptual problem. Naturalised turf close to walks, roads or housing collects litter which involves higher maintenance costs, and there is always the risk of fire. The creation of well designed edges that accommodate mown areas for recreational and functional use and at the same time maintain graceful lines, flowing through the landscape, establish a sense of purpose and design intent. There are numerous opportunities for creating herbaceous groundcovers that are extensively used in Dutch parks and open spaces. They are also being used experimentally to rehabilitate industrial spoil heaps in Britain and elsewhere. Many of these occur in urban areas on sites for future urban renewal. A survey made of metalliferous mine wastes in Britain included field experiments which suggested that with the high concentration of toxic metals, rehabilitation could be more effectively achieved with naturally occurring grasses than with commercial varieties. Naturally occurring populations grew faster and persisted longer. They provided excellent stabilising cover, provided adequate fertiliser was applied, and they have persisted for many years. Three

Alternatives to mowing The creation of diverse meadow plant communities

a

b

(a) the fixed picture. Inorganic maintenance at work: acres of grass at 2 in. and maximum input for minimum output; (b) an alternative mowing regime: cutting where it's needed, along the road edge and leaving a natural edge where mowing is unnecessary

153

cultivars are now commercially available that are tolerant of various pH and metal concentrations.[30]

The options available and their relevance to different situations are discussed in a report for the Nature Conservancy Council in Britain.[31] They include the introduction of native herbaceous flora and meadow communities. The conditions under which these thrive in the nutrient-deficient soils are typical of much derelict urban land. This, in fact, is the opposite condition demanded by cultivated turf grasses. The elimination of imported topsoil and fertilisers makes their installation a great deal cheaper. Their floral diversity and low long-term maintenance are ideally suited to large-scale reclamation. They are applicable in such places as roadsides, vacant lots and similar areas where pressures of human activity are low. The Dutch, however, have adopted another approach for such areas. Their high-resilient wild areas are based on high-nutrient input and acceptance of weeds. These communities are seen as a constantly evolving system that adapts to wear and tear. This kind of ground surface is fortuitously created when turf along pedestrian routes is replaced with colonising weeds, resistant to wear and often covering the ground more effectively than the original turf.

Another alternative for managing many of the city's grasslands is to replace machinery with livestock. The uniform green carpet quality of the lawn is a product of modern technology, which could not exist before the age of fossil fuel. Grass meadows were maintained by grazing animals. The eighteenth-century English landscape garden was conceived as an extension of the pastoral, agricultural landscape of a livestock economy and it used agricultural methods for the maintenance of its grounds. Sheep are remarkably effective as mowing machines. They graze close to the surface, nibbling at the grass shoots to produce a low, even turf that is both appropriate to many recreational uses and visually attractive. Sheep also encourage species diversity by selective grazing, something mowing machines cannot do. They require few physical facilities or personal attention, barring enclosure, access to water and shelter from the wind. Anyone who has visited the upland sheep country in the north of England will attest to their hardiness and ability to keep precipitous slopes in almost immaculate condition. Mechanical mowers are unable to maintain steep slopes economically.

Sheep and other grazing animals are extensively used as an alternative to mechanical mowing in many country parks in Britain.[32] In some towns and villages, places such as the churchyard and meadows are kept down through arrangements with local farmers. This practice, which was once common in cities, has now all but disappeared. But its advantages as an economic and practical alternative to modern machinery are consider-able, as the occasional example reveals. Laurie points out that many urban commons that are kept in a fairly natural, or unmanicured state,

a

b

a Newcastle common grazing, which is extensively used by Newcastle residents for recreation and a green link between neighbourhoods in the city. Cattle keep the turf of the common short, and grazing animals are therefore a part of its life

b An alternative to mowing behind fences: sheep in an oil tank farm in Toronto. Here short turf is needed to prevent fire and sheep do the job admirably for little or no cost

are maintained at an extraordinary low cost in relation to the use made of them and their size.[33] Some urban commons are still grazed today, as at Newcastle, England. A petroleum company in Toronto has used sheep to mow the raised berms surrounding its fuel storage tanks for over ten years. It has applied this technique to its holdings in other Ontario cities. Sheep are bought from the local stockyards in the spring and sold back in the autumn. Ten sheep maintain 3 to 4 acres of steeply sloping grassed banks in a close-cropped and fertilised condition. The cost from the stockyards of each animal in 1977 was $50 per head.[34] Even without taking into account the resale value of the animals, $500 per season for grass cutting is considerably cheaper than mowing mechanically; and mowers don't fertilise the grass, either. In addition, the company has no need for equipment, or outlay, barring an occasional bale of hay in very dry periods and a water supply.

There are various factors to be considered if such a practice is to be applied to the city. The major limitation is domestic dogs. Dogs worry sheep and can cause grave injury. So the need for fencing is critical. In the absence of basic research into effective means of keeping dogs and sheep separated, or of enforceable laws to keep dogs under control (as in country areas), this strategy has practical applications to those urban open spaces that are fenced, or can be adequately supervised. Industrial areas, high-security installations, private or quasi-public land and cemeteries are examples.

The establishment of rural grazing management adapted to urban areas is needed. For instance, adaptation of rotation grazing and paddocks where sheep progressively graze an area may be appropriate to large sites. Continuous grazing, where animals roam the whole area, may work best for smaller sites. Reverting back to mechanical mowing in some areas every second or third year may be required to minimise build-up of parasites. There are also animal husbandry factors, such as shearing, dipping and vaccination for parasite control, that requires arrangements with agriculture and health authorities. The practical economies of using grazing animals on urban grasslands is illustrated by the fact that the University of Manitoba mowed its lawns with a herd of thirty sheep in the late 1940s and early 1950s. The reason for this was a tight maintenance budget. The sheep were guided by a herdsman throughout the campus area. Moveable fences were set up to assist him in controlling the movement of animals. It is reported that this practice was terminated due to criticism by campus horticulturalists, who wanted to see more flowers planted as well as a more attractive turf.[35] This is particularly interesting since it points to the strength of prevailing aesthetic values at the time. It also points to the need, in a conserver social environment, for a return to economic and environmentally sound means of managing urban space that also provide educational opportunities. The British country parks use sheep, cows and deer, as much for education and enjoyment of visitors as for keeping the grass under control. The isolated zoo-like environment of the demonstration city farm that some parks provide for deprived city children has less educational relevance than functioning farm management situations which are part of the daily life of the city. The urban commons in Newcastle are continuously grazed by cattle through arrangements with local farmers. They are also in daily use for recreation and as a pedestrian link between different parts of the city. The presence of grazing animals is, therefore, an accepted part of urban life in Newcastle. The functional use of animals in urban open space management makes increasingly economic sense the higher the cost of maintenance becomes. For instance the maintenance of cemetery ground, where upkeep is tied to perpetual care agreements, is becoming prohibitive and calls for practical, if unconventional, alternatives. But in addition, it permits us to learn directly something about rural practices and establish better links with city and countryside.

The Dutch have made some interesting calculations of maintenance costs based on their woodland approach to urban design in comparision to more highly maintained traditional parks. Taking the maintenance of woodland landscape as the index against which other forms of maintenance are evaluated, the Parks Department at Rotterdam has made the calculations shown in Table 4.1 for different types of plantings. From the table it is evident that woodland landscape is the cheapest form of planting against which all other materials are judged. It is interesting to note that turf maintenance is over twice as expensive, while annuals are 68 times as costly as woodland. These figures relate to the Dutch experience and highly developed traditions in park management. Also, many landscape developments incorporate a mixture of all or many of these categories. But they provide an interesting guide for comparison with other approaches, bearing in mind the unique problems that every city must face. They also have lessons for us in the development of low maintenance landscapes. Existing urban woodlands, transformed into parks, need not be demeaned through an over-zealous concern for tidiness. Forest planting in unused spaces like highway interchanges can replace turf and transform the city environment. Grasslands themselves can be treated and managed as meadows in many places. It becomes evident that the principles under discussion in this chapter are not only socially and ecologically desirable, but have a practical and economic basis for action. Established tradition, at least in the short term, often speaks louder than economics or environmentally sound approaches to urban design. The opportunities for better ways of using urban plants or managing woodlands and grasslands for overall social benefits are none the less within easy grasp. There are indications that economics, if not a better appreciation of environmental problems will, over time, affect tradition.

Table 4.1: Comparative costs of maintenance

Type of Open Space	No of Hours/100 m^2	Index
Woodland	1.7	100
Shrubs	1.8	118
Groundcovers	8.0	475
Roses	15.2	1,075
Rose gardens	18.8	1,291
Annuals	61.9	6,855
Perennials	29.9	1,842
Hedges	22.0	1,303
Lawns (overall maintenance)	3.3	210

Source: *Aannemerij Plantsoerien van de Gemeete, Rotterdam* (Department of Parks, Rotterdam, 1980).

In this chapter we have examined the natural systems of the city from the perspective of its natural, fortuitous and cultivated plant associations. It becomes clear that the conventions that create the cultivated landscape have been based on technological imperatives that are in confrontation with the realities of urban nature. They relentlessly overpower even the simplest observation of natural process at work under our very noses, from which much can be learned. We have the anomaly of a design process dedicated to urban quality but instead creating impoverished environments. Naturally diverse places are replaced by a landscape of turf and cultivated plants, dependent on man, that minimises ecological diversity and social options. The alternatives available to us are rooted in an ecological view of plants and an integrated management framework for plants drawn from rural practice. The concepts of urban forests, planting design based on natural succession and alternative grassland management strategies provide benefits in a more diverse environment, greater economic and environmental productivity and enhanced social, educational and aesthetic values. In addition, the economies over current landscape practice are undeniable. It is also apparent from our discussion up to this point that climate, water and plants are indivisible parts of the natural process of cities that must be seen as a whole in design and management. In this way they provide us with a useful and enriching urban environment and a means of closing the perceptual gap between the city and the larger non-urban landscape. A framework for aesthetics and design becomes available that is responsive to ecological, functional and social criteria.

As we have seen, plants are a fundamental component of the urban scene. Their significance as habitat for wildlife, as well as for people, varies in proportion to the complexity and variety of their associations. Thus the ideas discussed in this chapter have a direct impact on the diversity and stability of animals, birds and insects and thus on the quality of the human environment. Since the health of the city must be gauged by the sum of its life processes, we must turn now to an examination of wildlife.

Notes

1. Eugene P. Odum, *Ecology* (Holt, Rinehart and Winston, New York, 1963).
2. Eugene P. Odum, 'The Strategy of Ecosystem Development', *Science*, vol. 164 (Apr. 1969).
3. Peter Farb, *The Forest* (Time-Life Books, New York, 1963).
4. Thomas S. Elias and Howard S. Irwin, 'Urban Trees', *Scientific American* (Nov. 1976).
5. Erik Jorgensen, *Urban Forestry: Some Problems and Proposals* (Faculty of Forestry, University of Toronto, Sept. 1967).
6. Michael Laurie, 'Nature and City Planning in the Nineteenth Century' in Ian C. Laurie (ed.), *Nature in Cities* (John Wiley, New York, 1979).
7. Faculty of Environmental Studies, York University, Toronto, 'Urban Wildlife Workshop 1974-5', unpublished.
8. Nan Fairbrother, *New Lives, New Landscapes* (Architectural Press, London, 1970).
9. Herbert Sukopp, Hans-Peter Blume and Wolfram Kunick, 'The Soil, Flora and Vegetation of Berlin's Wastelands' in Laurie, *Nature in Cities*.
10. John A. Livingston, *Canada* (Jack McClelland, Toronto, 1970).
11. Sukopp *et al.*, 'Soil, Flora and Vegetation'.
12. David Bellamy, *Bellamy's Europe* (British Broadcasting Corporation, London, 1976).
13. Fairbrother, *New Lives*.
14. Hough, Stansbury and Associates, *Design Guidelines for Forest Management* (Ministry of Natural Resources, Government of Ontario, Toronto, 1971).
15. W. G. Teagle, *The Endless Village* (Nature Conservancy Council, Shrewsbury, 1978).
16. F. T. Last *et al.*, 'The City of Edinburgh — its Stock of Trees: a Continuing Amenity and Timber Resource', *Scottish Forestry*, no. 30 (1976).
17. Sukopp, *et al.*, *Soil, Flora and Vegetation*.
18. Carl E. Whitcomb, 'Factors Affecting the Establishment of Urban Trees', *Journal of Arboriculture*, vol. 5, no. 10 (1979).
19. Ibid.
20. R. S. Dorney, Paul F. J. Eagles *et al.*, 'Ecosystem Planning, Analysis and Design in Ontario as Applied to Environmentally Sensitive Areas', paper to American Association for the Advancement of Science Meeting, Toronto, Jan. 1981.
21. Jorgensen, *Urban Forestry*.
22. Ir. J. L. Guldemond, 'City Woodlands', talk to Department of Town and Country Planning, University of Manchester, Sept. 1978, unpublished.
23. H. J. Bos and J. L. Mol, 'The Dutch Example: Native Planting in Holland' in Laurie, *Nature in Cities*.
24. Ibid.
25. Hough Stansbury Michalski Ltd, 'Naturalization Project', unpublished report, National Capital Commission, Ottawa, 1982.
26. Ecological Parks Trust, *The William Curtis Ecological Park* (1st Report 1977-8, London).

27. James A. Schmid, *Urban Vegetation* (University of Chicago, Department of Geography, Research Paper no. 161, 1975).

28. Emil Fröhlich, Forest Engineer, Stadtforstamt, Zurich, personal communication.

29. W. O. Morrison *et al.*, 'Avi fauna Survey of Vacant Grasslands' (National Capital Commission, Ottawa, 1981).

30. R. A. H. Smith and A. D. Bradshaw, 'Use of Metal Tolerant Plant Populations for the Reclamation of Metalliferous Wastes', *Applied Ecology*, no. 16 (1979).

31. Lyndis Cole, *Nature Conservancy in Urban Areas*, report for the Nature Conservancy Council, Land Use Consultants (May 1978).

32. J. E. Lowday and T. C. E. Wells, *The Management of Grassland and Heathland in Country Parks*, Report to the Countryside Commission by the Institute of Terrestrial Ecology (Countryside Commission, West Midlands Region, Shrewsbury, 1977).

33. Ian C. Laurie, 'Urban Commons' in Laurie, *Nature in Cities*.

34. Weaver Liquifuels, Downsview, Ontario, personal communication.

35. Charles Thomsen, Department of Landscape Architecture, University of Manitoba, personal communication.

Chapter FIVE

WILDLIFE

The Dodo used to walk around,
and take the sun and air.
The sun yet warms his native ground —
the Dodo is not there!
The voice which used to squawk and squeak
is now for ever dumb —
Yet may you see his bones and beak
all in the Mu-se-um.[1]

Introduction

This verse from *The Bad Child's Book of Beasts*, by Hilaire Belloc is, indirectly, a relevant comment on city nature. Driven to extinction in the seventeenth century, the Dodo, together with numerous other extinct, rare or unusual creatures, is mounted and preserved for posterity in city museums. At one time museums and zoos provided the citizen with the only opportunity of seeing animals he had read about in books. They were collectors' items, curiosities to be admired for their size, ferocity, brightly coloured posteriors, or strange shape. Today museums are depressing reminders of an increasing number of species that have vanished from the scene. Zoos have become more sophisticated in the way animals are exhibited and more enjoyable as entertainment; some are concerned with the preservation of endangered species. Television has raised the educational level of the public with a host of informative programmes on the nature of the living world. But one may question whether the urban experience of nature is still not largely focused on the exotic bird in a space frame cage and the elephant secure behind the well designed moat. Most of our knowledge comes to us second hand through television programmes and the media. Direct contact with nature and the animal world, apart from resident starlings and pigeons, is confined to non-urban experience. It is to be had from the weekend at the cottage, or on occasional school visits to the rural interpretation centre. Most of us know more about nature in the countryside than in the places where we mostly live. Can the city itself provide us with a direct experience of nature and wildlife? Why is this important? To what extent does the city provide habitat for wildlife? How are these questions relevant to urban design? These are some of the concerns that will be explored in this chapter. To do so we must review some aspects of natural process with respect to food and habitats; how these are altered by the city and how the urban environment has shaped attitudes and perceptions towards wildlife.

Natural Processes

Woodland and forest, grassland and meadow, marshes and water, are the habitat for wildlife. The diversity, structure and continuing evolution of plant communities, their interaction with landform, soils and climate, dictate the diversity and stability of wildlife populations.

The layering or structure of forest vegetation provides distinct environments that support different groups of species. Some feed and breed on the forest floor, some inhabit the understorey and others live in the canopy. Warblers have been found to populate well defined nesting niches according to species, thus reducing competition and enabling a large variety of species to occupy the same forest.[2] Different plant associations provide places for different groups of species. Plant succession produces, over time, a range of habitats from open field to mature forests. Each successive stage is home for different associations of insects, birds and animals. Studies in Maine showed how different species of birds are attracted to these different habitats.[3] Open land was populated by savannah sparrows, song sparrows and bobolinks. In low brush these were replaced by field sparrows, Nashville and chestnut-sided warblers. Pioneer forest attracted ovenbirds, warblers in the succeeding evergreens. Woodpeckers and kinglets appeared with the climax forest.

Similarly, in aquatic environments, the increased productivity of a lake as it proceeds from an oligotrophic (nutrient-poor) condition to a eutrophic (nutrient-rich) one attracts an increasing number and variety of wildlife species. Thus wetlands, being highly productive ecosystems, provide habitat for vast numbers of birds and other wildlife. Places that have many different plant associations tend to be richer in species than those that have only a few. The composition and numbers of wildlife species are also affected by other factors. The edge, or interface between one habitat and another is often more diverse than the interior of the habitats themselves. Continuity of habitat provides essential migratory routes and helps maintain wildlife populations.

The disturbance of the natural landscape through human activity sets

162

Blackburnian warblers; hemlock tops

Redstarts; sugar maple

Magnolia warblers; lower hemlock branches

Chestnut-sided warblers; low shrubs

Ovenbirds; the cover of the forest floor

Habitat The layering or structure of forest vegetation provides distinct environments for different groups of species. Different birds live at different levels of the forest depending on their nesting and feeding habitats. Generally the greater the layering of foliage on a vertical profile the greater the diversity of species

Bobolinks
Song sparrows
Savanna sparrows

Nashville and
chestnut-sided
warblers
Field sparrows

Towhees
Ruffed grouse
Red-eyed vireos
Redstarts
Ovenbirds

thrush
Olive-backed
warblers
blackthroated
Blackburnian and
Magnolia, myrtle

Cape May warbler
Kinglets
Woodpeckers

Rojer Tory Peterson's study of bird fauna in Maine showed how different species inhabit different successional stages of a forest from open land, low brush, pioneer forest, mature spruce forest (from Farb, 1963)

163

up imbalances in plant and animal communities. Equilibrium is maintained by an elaborate system of checks and balances. The loss of habitat on which a species depends for food and shelter and to breed may mean that it has to adjust to the new conditions or abandon its chances of survival. Some species more adaptable than others may survive and flourish. Those less adaptable may disappear. Some modified landscapes where woodland, field, scrub, wetland and open water are associated may enhance species diversity. The old complex agricultural landscapes and fields have traditionally been rich in wildlife. The increasingly industrialised agriculture of today is widening imbalances and simplifying habitat, favouring explosions of a few species at the expense of diversity.

Urban Processes

Urbanisation and Wildlife

The city has radically altered both natural habitat and wildlife communities. Studies in the United States of the effects of the urbanisation of agricultural land on wildlife have documented the changes that take place.[4] Farmland, field and woodland species declined drastically as urbanisation advanced and as suitable habitat was reduced. A few species, however, increased dramatically. House sparrows and starlings, virtually absent prior to urbanisation, become the most abundant species. The total number of bird species declined, but the total bird population increased. It has been found that there are many more birds in cities, in a numerical sense, than in rural areas outside. Taken as a whole, however, the urban environment is a patchwork of many habitats. The relative numbers, distribution and diversity of animals and birds in various parts of the city are directly related to the diversity and structure of vegetation, which determine habitat quality. The plant groups discussed in the previous chapter, therefore, provide a useful guide for an understanding of this question.

The Cultivated Urban Landscape

The habitat of heavily built-up areas is an environment of buildings, paved surfaces and cultivated landscape. The ornamental and biologically sterile tree and lawn landscapes of downtown parks offer little in the way of food, shelter or breeding places. The herb and shrub layer of natural woodland becomes the paved or grassed floor of the city, trampled by people and permanently hunted by cats and dogs. The intermediate layers have been eliminated. The canopy also disappears where trees have been planted as separated individuals. Ornamentals often lack insect life or fruit on which birds can feed. It is reported that the number of recent and threatened extinctions of higher animals in Sweden is directly attributable

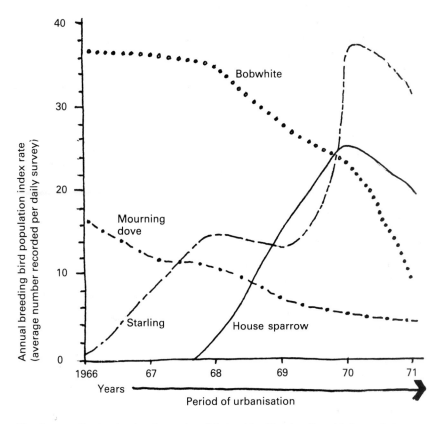

The impact of urbanisation (new city of Columbia, Maryland) on bird populations. The typical farmland species such as bobwhite and mourning dove showed rapid decline. Starlings and house sparrows, virtually absent from the area before development, showed the most striking population increases (information for graph derived from Geis 1974).

to urbanisation and the tendency to manicured parks.[5] The disappearance of native animals and birds favours a few aggressive species that are readily adaptable to this habitat. Thus pigeons, sparrows and starlings all thrive in large numbers, feeding off the city's wastes and living and breeding in its buildings. All have been introduced. In North America, the house sparrow was introduced in the mid-nineteenth century. The starling was imported and liberated into New York's Central Park in the 1890s. Old world rats and mice arrived in ships accidentally. It is estimated that there may be as many rats in a large city as there are people.[6] The ancestral form of the domestic pigeon is the rock dove. Urban structures, being a man-made substitute to its original windswept Scottish cliffs, provide it with ideal places to roost and nest.[7]

Changes of habitat structure
Substitution of turf for
natural ground layers,
elimination of intermediate
layers, disappearance of
the canopy and substitu-
tion of native plant species
for non-food-producing
ones create a hostile
environment for native
wildlife. Diverse native
populations are replaced
by a few aggressive exotic
species

166

As the density of building reduces beyond the city core, however, more vegetation survives, or is planted along the streets and gardens of residential areas. Robin, redwing blackbird and grackle are common birds of urban gardens and local parks. Even though these are heavily populated by people and domestic pets, the more adaptable native species have gained a foothold. The squirrel, racoon and skunk have flourished. Raccoons dine on the contents of garbage cans and take up residence in attic and chimney. Ducks and geese in many waterfront parks have become resident and proliferated, feeding in summer on handouts from park visitors and wintering in patches of open water, created by an industrial plant or generating station. Other species, not normally tolerant of urban conditions, have taken to the city, where the warmer climate and altered habitat provide the right environment for survival. Rooks have formed colonies and bred in urban areas in England; the main shopping mall in downtown Cheltenham is a splendid example. Hawks prey in most cities on the small animals that inhabit waste places. The black redstart has adapted to urban industrial areas where it now chiefly lives.[8]

Remnants of Natural Habitat

As we saw in the last chapter, many cities still retain elements of native vegetation diversity which can be found in the ravines, cemeteries, golf courses and campuses. Mature and dead trees, open grassland, scrub and young growth, water and wetland are often present, supporting a variety of native birds and animals. A small natural area in central Toronto that had been neglected for many years was found to include 63 bird and 23 animal species.[9] A major problem, however, is that these remnant environments often become islands, disconnected from the rural landscape and from each other by the expanding city. And so, where they remain isolated, the chances of maintaining high wildlife diversity are relatively small.

Linkages

Cities are not closed environments, but are connected to rural areas through natural and man-made corridors. Natural corridors include streams and rivers bordered by vegetation or steep banks. Man-made ones include railway connections, canals, highways and transmission lines. These corridors have greatly influenced the migration and perpetuation of wildlife in cities. They maintain the links between natural habitats, parks and the open countryside, and have increased uncommon or non-tolerant species. The ravine system in central Toronto still supports foxes, a relatively non-tolerant animal. London's corridor routes permit movement of animals in and out of the built-up area. Within a 20-mile radius of St Paul's cathedral 314 vertebrate species were recorded by the

167

London Natural History Society between 1960 and 1970.[10]

Problems and Conflicts

The imbalances and stresses created by urban activities have many repercussions. Diseases transmitted from wildlife to man and from man to wildlife occur more easily when people and animals share limited space in the absence of natural controls. Some diseases are carried by wildlife and transmitted to people. For instance, rabies is widely distributed in rural areas in North America, skunks and foxes being the principal maintenance hosts. The free movement of animals into cities makes the disease a continuing threat to urban and rural people and is expensive to control. Salmonella occurs in English sparrows during cold weather and can be transmitted to pets and people.[11] Some diseases may be carried by pets and transmitted as well. Toxoplasmosis is particularly infectious to children and is picked up from the faeces of domestic cats in sandboxes and play areas.[12] Urban pets create problems of health and security in crowded city conditions. Feral or stray dogs attack people, defecation is injurious to plants and is a major source of stormwater pollution. New York, London and other major cities now regard this as a health hazard, since stormwater is discharged into receiving rivers and lakes untreated. Consequently, over-population and uncontrolled breeding, particularly among strays, have become a major management problem. The conflicts between people and wildlife range from questions of safety to aesthetics. Birds are hazardous around airports; squirrels damage telephone lines; pigeons make a mess of building cornices and statues in squares; moles tear up the lawn; racoons and rabbits enjoy garden produce. This raises questions about what is valuable or a nuisance and thus of one's perceptions and values of wildlife.

Perceptions and Values

Our discussion in the last chapter focused on the inherent conflicts of values and priorities that are reflected in the design and management of the urban landscape. These concerns are equally relevant to our discussion of wildlife since we are dealing with inseparable issues. What makes a pet poodle loved and a house mouse persecuted has the same relationship as the garden rose to the dandelion in the lawn. The acceptance of nature is a function of how it conforms to a predetermined set of values and to what extent it is under control. It is tolerated on our own terms, within the limits of convenience and aesthetic conventions. The conflicts are heightened, however, with wildlife. Animals, birds and insects are more difficult to control. Their presence is more obvious. They are also potentially more damaging to human health and welfare. Getting rid of aggressive weeds is less frustrating or demanding than trying to stop the raccoons from spreading the contents of a trash can over the street on pick-up day. Those same raccoons make charming pets as babies, but fully grown they are a menace in the attic or with the pet goldfish. Pigeons being fed in the park are desirable and very much a part of the urban scene. But in and around public buildings they are messy and a nuisance. Wildlife is worthy of study in the nature centre out of town but is largely ignored in the city. Urban man is perceptually disassociated from the cycles of nature, and city dwellers have come to believe that nature can be found only in unspoiled forests and rural areas. Even the natural science disciplines, until recently, avoided the urban environment, preferring 'unspoiled' sites beyond the city limits where nature could be studied without the interference of man.

Two examples of this are interesting. The raccoons population in the city of Toronto has flourished and there are undoubtedly substantially more animals than there would be in any non-urban environment. No one, however, knows how many there are in the city. Neither the Ministry of Natural Resources nor the Canadian Wildlife Service has ever attempted to carry out a population count. 'We're only interested in doing a census if there seems to be a problem,' a Ministry biologist is reported to have said. 'People often have a problem with individual raccoons. But the raccoons aren't having any problems. Why should we count them when they seem to be doing very well?'[13]

The *Globe and Mail*, a Toronto newspaper, carried an article in 1981 on 'Scavengers in the City'. It read in part:

As descendants of the nature-bashing pioneers, Canadians are especially susceptible to the fear that someday, soon, the beasts of the field and the fowl of the air, will have their revenge. Without determined vigilance, the cities, skyscrapers, subways and cathedrals may slip back into the bosom of nature, to be overrun by creeping vines and crawling creatures, and the eerie cry of the loon will echo through the empty hallways of abandoned public works projects.

Even at the core of the urban control centre and the heart of civil intelligence, our own Nathan Phillips Square, the panic has begun to eat at the nerves of our leaders. In a novel civic ceremony . . . they'll be hanging fish line . . . between the arches, across from the ramp to the snack bar and over the top of the pool. To strollers in the square, it will appear invisible but, the theory goes, it will frighten any passing pigeon and gull who is looking to do what birds do in public squares.[14]

The black redstart, mentioned earlier, is one of Britain's rarest breeding birds, and had taken readily to urban and industrial settings. Yet it is the least thoroughly studied, despite the fact that it lives mainly in cities full of bird watchers.[15]

169

What gives rise to these conflicts and human attitudes towards nature is subject to much philosophical debate in the literature. Hall has shown the basic territoriality of man in the resentment he shows at intrusions, which may extend to unwanted encounters with wildlife.[16] More suggests that the literary encounters with wildlife by urban children greatly influence anthropomorphic values and popular misconceptions about non-human beings.[17] Worster has shown that responses to nature over the last two centuries have shifted from the Arcadian view of peaceful coexistence to one that expresses the utilitarian view of nature as resources.[18] Livingston suggests that we must consciously re-establish an ethic of co-operation and humility towards nature. Since man is governed by culture and culture evolves more rapidly than non-human life, this must be achieved by a conscious act of will.[19] But while studies of urban attitudes to nature are few and inconclusive, there is a general consensus that contact with natural environments and wildlife has undisputed value.

Of immediate importance to the thesis of this book is the search for ways in which the city and nature can be brought more closely together to promote alternative values. First, we can act on the notion that greater environmental literacy at home about living things and the way they interact with human life in cities is essential to promoting greater understanding about wildlife as a whole. Second, there is the question of diversity and choice. If choice is the key to a healthy social environment, then a rich and varied wildlife environment is one way of achieving it. Varied habitats that benefit wildlife will also have spiritual benefits for urban man. Third, there is the more utilitarian view of wildlife and plants as indicators of urban health. Monitoring the reproduction of shore birds may give us a clue to the condition of the city's aquatic environment. The presence or absence of lichens is an indicator of habitat condition and diversity and therefore a reflection of its suitability for people. How these concerns become part of urban design must be examined in the light of the strategy outlined for plants and in the inherent opportunities the city provides.

Alternative Values: Some Opportunities

The last chapter suggested that the integration of objectives in forestry and other rural occupations adapted to the city environment provides an alternative framework for urban design. These same principles hold true for wildlife as they do for plants. While the preservation of rare or endangered species has become a major preoccupation of biologists and landscape planners, the emphasis on this approach has tended to ignore the fact that the maintenance and enhancement of *representative* associations are also educationally vital to the urban scene and may be achieved more realistically in culturally shaped landscapes that have become a patchwork of remnant habitats. It is only through an understanding of the interactions of living beings with their habitat in our own backyard that we can understand the significance of nature as a whole. In addition we are concerned here not only with the preservation of habitats but with opportunities for their creation. These considerations form the basis for the following sections of this chapter.

Natural Remnants and Fortuitous Habitat

The habitats with the most obvious wildlife potential are the rivers, streams, canals and pre-urban landscapes that still exist within the city's boundaries (see Chapter Four). Those that retain sufficient species and structural diversity of vegetation and are linked to larger natural areas are likely to have the greatest faunal diversity. They are, therefore, among the city's richest and most precious places. But the very process of urban growth may itself inadvertently create complex environments which will become places for wildlife. It is these that provide the *unexploited* opportunities for urban design. They are to be found in the less obvious places that lie behind the city's façades and public travel routes and often go unnoticed.

Some are everywhere around us in the waste places and vacant lots that have been colonised by the plants of the city. Associations of plants and animals are everywhere in evidence. Weedy places abound with voles and mice together with the hawks that feed on them. Dock leaves are food for the painted lady butterfly; stinging nettles are food for the larvae of red admiral butterflies;[20] monarch butterflies associate with milkweed. Old rooftops may combine standing water and soil and patches of vegetation that become fortuitous wetland habitats for visiting and resident birds. The natural or contrived impoundments that result from stormwater run-off in many urban areas create new wetlands from open water habitats. Explore the old industrial sites in many a downtown area and you will find unexpected and surprising landscapes behind the junk yards and chain link fences, where a combination of a poorly drained site and the natural colonisation of aquatic plants have made an ideal marshy breeding place for ducks and geese.

We must look to those places where energy is concentrated to find other rich wildlife resources; to environments that have been created by the processes and functions of the city. The waste heat from electricity generating stations that is pumped into lakes every day amounts to millions of gallons of hot water. In cold climates the raised temperature is sufficient to maintain open water all winter. This fortuitous aquatic habitat is the wintering ground for thousands of ducks off the Toronto waterfront and a potential urban wildlife reserve. Rubbish disposal sites attract rodents and other small animals which in turn attract the hawks

171

Plan of Outer Harbour Headland, Toronto Waterfront

City of Toronto

Ontario Place

Toronto Islands

Lake Ontario

Outer Harbour Headland (Leslie St. Spit)

Outer Harbour Headland vegetation communities (from McNab, 1978)

Field community – moist soil
Field community – dry soil
Field community – very dry soil
Ridge community
moist sand meadow
Wet sand meadow
Beach strand
Wet barren ground

Foraging areas for birds, Outer Harbour Headland, 1978 (from McNab, 1978)

Foraging area for terns and swallows

Foraging area for redwing, blackbirds and sparrows

Foraging area for warblers and other migrant songbirds

Disused industrial areas often become flooded and provide breeding places for ducks
and geese

and owls that feed on them. The availability of food, shelter or heat may create a niche for a species of bird to breed or benefit migratory flocks and winter visitors. Among the most spectacular man-made habitats inadvertently created by city processes are its sewage treatment centres. These are among the city's most concentrated energy resources (see Chapter Two) and a favoured habitat for birds.

Wildlife and Waste-water Treatment

Many urban communities with space available have adopted a lagoon system for sewage treatment. Lagoons work on the principle that water and soil bacteria cause oxidation of organic solids, producing carbon dioxide. It is used by green algae in photosynthesis which in turn releases oxygen. This is then available for further aerobic fermentation. The function of the sewage lagoon is to provide large surfaces for the growth of organisms responsible for the oxidation process. In effect, it is a eutrophic aquatic system that closely parallels natural wetland eco-systems. Large amounts of organic material increase the supply of nutrients that become available to aquatic plants and micro-organisms. They are, therefore, highly productive environments for enormous numbers of worms and insect larvae that live in the sludge and feed on micro-organisms. These in turn attract diverse species of shore birds and waders.

A scientific study carried out in 1976 in the regional municipality of Ottawa Carlton, Ontario, compared the birds inhabiting six of the city's sewage plants with an adjacent stretch of natural shoreline along the Ottawa river.[21] Its purpose was to describe the various sites with particular emphasis on the type of sewage treatment used and how this might affect the diversity and numbers of shore birds attracted to the site. Systematic censusing of each area provided important information on the variety and abundance of shore birds passing through the region during spring and autumn migrations.

It became evident that the sewage treatment centres attracted far larger numbers and a greater variety of birds than the much larger natural stretch of shoreline, which for over a hundred years has been the most popular habitat for breeding ducks. They were particularly important as a stop-over point for the spring and autumn migrations. Fourteen shore-bird species were recorded in the autumn. They included, among others, plovers, yellowlegs, sandpipers, phalaropes, snipe and woodcock. Some evidence from the major shore-bird stop-over centres along Lakes Erie and Ontario for 1979 indicated that Ottawa's sewage lagoons system is attracting as many or more birds than the established wildlife areas. The summary of autumn migration visitors drawn from this study in Table 5.1 shows clearly that birds preferred the lagoons to the natural shoreline. This was so even though available space is more limited in the lagoons system. One reason for this is the greater abundance of available food in the lagoons; another relates to habitat diversity.

Table 5.1: Comparison of visits by birds to sewage lagoons and Ottawa Bay (no. of species)

| 22 July | | 29 July | | 5 Aug. | | 12 Aug. | | 19 Aug. | |
SL	OB	SL	OB	SL	OB	SL	OB	SL	OB
15	6	10	6	18	8	12	11	19	12

| 26 Aug. | | 2 Sept. | | 9 Sept. | | 16 Sept. | |
SL	OB	SL	OB	SL	OB	SL	OB
19	11	18	11	19	12	15	9

Note: SL: Sewage Lagoons.
     OB: Ottawa Bay — natural shoreline.
Source: Hamel, 1976.

Many species of wildlife depend on wetlands. The destruction of natural wetlands has been particularly severe in and around most densely populated urban regions. Land drainage, industrial development and human disturbance have all taken their toll. In the face of such widespread disappearance of wetland habitat it is significant that man-made resources are, in some situations, creating new habitats to replace the natural ones urban processes have destroyed. In fact, in Ontario, there has been a significant improvement in recent years as many new artificial wetlands in the form of waste-water treatment lagoons have been created. These lagoons are more productive and beneficial to wildlife in many cases than natural water bodies. For many communities the system is the cheapest form of sewage treatment available, provided that there is sufficient land available in the immediate area. In Ontario, between 1956 and 1968 the Ontario Water Resources Commission spent over $1 billion in water-supply and sewage treatment facilities, and over two hundred municipalities have undertaken sewage disposal projects, many of them for the first time.[22]

The concentration of energy and resources in and around cities generates by-products that are often accidentally beneficial in other ways. The sewage lagoons serving Ottawa have created a landscape richer in species diversity than the agricultural lands that preceded them and richer than an adjacent area of natural shoreline. As an urban habitat the lagoons have provided a place *not* for the exotic species found in cities such as house sparrows or pigeons, but for native species that inhabit

A polishing lagoon; part of the sewage disposal system for Ottawa. Until 1961 it was a large marsh on the Ottawa river. It has been cut off from the river by a gravel berm to form a tertiary sewage lagoon. It has a number of temporary and semi-permanent shallow marshes interspersed with deep marshes and open water. Located within two miles of the historically most productive stretch of shoreline along the Ottawa river, the area attracts more bird species than the natural shoreline. It is considered to be the best area for birds in the region

A forest of cottonwood colonising the harbour headland. A few groves have reached a height of 6 metres in six years and provide good cover for small birds

natural marsh and pond habitats. It will be evident, therefore, that far from being wastelands in the city, places that are considered necessary but unmentionable, the sewage treatment lagoon is a highly productive area, lending great diversity to the urban environment and thus of immense potential value to the study of birds and animals within the city. It is one of the city's greatest interpretive and educational resources for naturalists, school groups and the community at large.

Its educational potential is not limited to ecology, but also includes the biology of sewage treatment and the interdependence of natural and human processes. Hamel notes that problems that have received little attention from biologists could also be studied at sewage lagoon sites, for instance: the possible harmful effects to feeding birds from toxic chemicals; the problem of parasites such as tapeworm and roundworm found in some feeding species; the vulnerability of birds to botulism that results from eating decaying vegetation in which the anaerobic bacterium *Clostridium botulinum* has grown.[23] As scientific laboratories sewage lagoons have much to teach about the specific and general interrelationships of natural processes.

The presence of sewage lagoons has other connections with agriculture. At a sewage farm near Melbourne, Australia, the treatment process has been exploited to raise beef cattle and sheep on the adjoining land fertilised by the waste water. A wildlife sanctuary has also been developed at the centre which is visited regularly by large numbers of shore birds, waders and ducks.[24] In Vancouver, British Columbia, the Greater Vancouver Regional District sewage treatment plants in Richmond keep two gaggles of geese on the properties. The first geese were placed at the Lulu Island plant in about 1977 and in 1981 numbered 50 birds. A second gaggle of about 45 birds was later installed at the Iona Island plant. Their function, as farmyard livestock, is to mow the grass and act as guards. By eating the grass at the two treatment plants they were reported in 1981 to be saving some $15,000 a year in grass-cutting costs.[25] As guard animals, farmyard geese are extremely effective, making a racket when intruders enter the property that can be heard for a considerable distance, as well as unnerving the intruder.

There are some intriguing implications in these examples that provide an entirely new perspective on the value of treatment plants to the city. The concentration of energy resources provides the natural connection to farming operations, while being at the same time a valuable wildlife habitat and environmental education centre, protected from unwanted intrusion by farm animals. Such a scenario provides an elegant example of symbiotic relationships.

Wildlife and Regenerating Waterfronts

The Outer Harbour Headland referred to in previous chapters is a spit of land nearly 5 km long enclosing the new Toronto harbour on Lake Ontario. Begun in 1959, it was intended to accommodate the increased shipping expected from the St Lawrence Seaway. The shipping boom, however, never materialised. The port, in fact, now handles 1.5 million tons less than when the Seaway opened,[26] and the future of the Headland has continued to be debated for many years.

From the beginning the Headland started to evolve into a complex natural environment and is a fascinating example of the regenerative processes of nature. This is an evolving landscape. Its soils consist of an unconsolidated mixture of fill and rubble, brought from city construction works and from sand dredged from the lake bottom. Dredged sand was dumped along the sheltered side of the lake forming four new low-lying peninsulas and protected lagoons. Over the years water, wind and wave have been grinding the rocks and debris along the shore into smooth shapes and sands. During its short history an astonishing total of 152 species of vascular plants have naturally colonised the barren soils, brought by wind, birds and people. Of these, 88 represent introductions into southern Ontario and the remainder are native.[27] Some are rare within the metropolitan Toronto region and two species have been identified by botanists as the first record for the region — golden dock (*Rumex maritumus*) and sticky groundsel (*Senecio viscosus*).[28] A new forest of cottonwood has appeared which in six years reached a height of 6 metres. Plant communities are evolving in response to site conditions, including various field associations; ridge community, moist and wet sand meadow, beach strand.[29]

This evolving landscape soon began to attract migrating and wintering birds — owls, shore birds, ducks and songbirds. By 1976 185 species had been sighted at the Headland.[30] Of the mammals, raccoon, skunk, muskrat, rabbit, Norway rat and groundhog have been recorded.[31] With spectacular rapidity the Outer Headland has become the host to great numbers of nesting gulls and terns. In 1973 10 pairs of ring-billed gulls attempted to breed. By 1977 some 20,000 pairs were nesting on the peninsula. Other breeding birds include the herring gull, common tern and rare Caspian tern.[32]

This remarkable place has become one of the most significant bird colonies in the Great Lakes region. How and why did this happen? Studies of nesting success here have shown that it is high in all four species. A much larger proportion of eggs was hatched at the Headland than in other colonies in Eastern Lake Ontario where reduced success has been linked to high toxic chemical levels. Biologists also strongly suspect that it is the loss of nesting habitat elsewhere on the Great Lakes that has contributed to the colonisation of the Headland.[33]

Urban growth and development have destroyed many of the places that birds require and have rendered others toxic. Before large-scale harbour developments began in 1912, Toronto's waterfront was one of the richest marshlands on Lake Ontario. These were filled in to create the harbour, industrial lands, railways and expressways that are the legacy of the city today. But the creation of the Headland has, by accident, recreated some of the very habitats that were destroyed earlier in the century. Its existence has permitted many birds to recolonise. Without the construction of this peninsula biologists believe that the common tern would no longer be nesting in the Toronto area.[34]

The opportunities that occur fortuitously as a result of urban processes have great relevance in our search for an alternative urban design philosophy. I have already suggested that the principle of diversity offers variety of place and social opportunity. It is apparent if one begins to observe the city with an ecological perspective that this is occurring unwittingly in many places and in many ways. It needs only to be recognised and exploited. I have also suggested that the principle of least effort is a relevant and important objective. It is perhaps best summed up in a leaflet distributed by a group of Toronto citizens, in an effort to preserve the Headland as a nature reserve.[35]

What do we want . . . and how much will it cost?
— Keep the place as it is without any major development.
— Let it develop naturally into an increasingly secure wilderness.
— Jettison the [Metropolitan Toronto and Region Conservation Authority] master plan approach.
— The nice thing is that to do these things will cost very little. And millions of taxpayer dollars can be spent instead on more pressing social and economic needs.

The implications of these principles and opportunities for urban design are equivalent to those for plants, viz.:

— capitalising on the habitat created by city processes provides unparalleled opportunity for enriching city wildlife;
— design for wildlife forms part of the multi-functional objectives for urban open space;
— design and management that integrate wildlife objectives with recreation, vegetation and environmental education, together with urban functions, provide greater benefits at less cost in environmental and social terms.

Amphibian and Reptile Habitats

Another aspect of the wildlife scene in urban areas, and one that has been almost completely ignored, is the habitat that the city does and could provide for frogs, snakes, lizards, turtles and other amphibian and reptile species. These animals, like the more obvious ones that we have been examining, not only rely on remnant areas of undisturbed habitat, but also on altered sites. Riverine marshes, for instance, may support many species of turtle; the gabion baskets forming urban stream banks may be habitat for garter snakes; old gravel pits and fortuitous water impoundments are often places where frogs, toads, turtles and snakes are found. While amphibians and reptiles have conventionally been among the least recognised of the urban fauna, it will be evident that their continued existence in viable populations is critical to the maintenance of species diversity and stability. The presence of herons is dependent on wetland habitats that support the frogs and fish they feed on. A survey of amphibian and reptile species and habitats was conducted in metropolitan Toronto in 1982 as a first step to identifying sites for preservation and creating habitats for introducing extirpated species.[36] The survey identified 24 species which included five turtles, seven snakes, five tailed amphibians and seven frogs or toads. A comparison between the 1982 survey and one conducted in 1913 shows consistent decline in populations and an increase in uncommon and rare species (see Table 5.2). Five (17 per cent) of the species recorded in 1913 were extinct in the area in 1982. Four species (turtles) not recorded in 1913 were excluded due to uncertainties in observation and distribution.[37]

Table 5.2: Comparison of 1913 and 1982 surveys on amphibians and reptiles

Status	1913 Survey	1982 Survey
Common	18 (72%)	7 (29%)
Uncommon	5 (20%)	7 (29%)
Rare	2 (8%)	10 (42%)
Total spp	25	24

Source: After Johnson, 1982.

The survey indicates the need not only for preservation of undisturbed and altered sites from total destruction where these species are to be found, but also for reintroducing species into the urban environment through a programme of captive breeding and release and habitat creation. This latter issue is discussed in the next section of this chapter.

Design and Management

A Strategy for Design

The naturally occurring urban wildlife resources that we have been examining are the basis for purposeful design strategy. At the heart of the matter is the fact that the city has innate capability for complex wildlife habitats. As the city evolves and as agriculture industrialises, there is a tendency for rural areas to become simpler ecologically and the city more complex. This provides us with a basis of a strategy for urban design. Its fundamental objective should be the enrichment of the city's natural wealth; to make the maximum use of what is inherently there. This is, in fact, one of the significant attributes of cities of the western Netherlands. The great diversity and richness of its park system, canals and streets, the mixture between old and new, is in marked contrast to its agricultural hinterland. This is a modern, working, food-producing landscape that has little ecological or visual diversity, or natural recreational interest. The Dutch have embarked on a programme of enrichment of the urban landscape which counterbalances this contrast between urban and rural environments. While limited space is the crux of the problem for the Dutch, elements of such a strategy are highly relevant to other cities.

At a broad level of open space planning the urban resources that have special value for wildlife must be integrated into the open space planning network for the city. This must include not only the parks and recreational areas, but essential natural and man-made connections and the exterior environment as a whole. This is particularly significant in view of the fact that many of the most ecologically important urban resources are not currently included in park planning. The identification of habitat types provides a start to identifying highly valued places requiring restricted or carefully controlled access. Others may be identified in descending order of significance or sensitivity to disturbance. Special areas include:

(1) Remnant rural landscapes enclosed within the city's boundaries that maintain an existing community of wildlife species or harbour locally rare or unusual species. Examples include woodland associations, old field and meadow, water courses, marshes, natural corridors.
(2) Man-made resources that have high potential. Examples are the city's sewage treatment lagoons, abandoned lands, naturally regenerated or unimproved construction projects, industrial lands, aquatic wintering sites.
(3) Areas of potentially high wildlife significance and sensitivity where the management of stormwater impoundments and wildlife habitat can be integrated. These might occur in association with residential open spaces, major city parks, wetland reserves, flood plains and water courses.

WILDLIFE HABITAT TYPES
Remnant rural landscapes

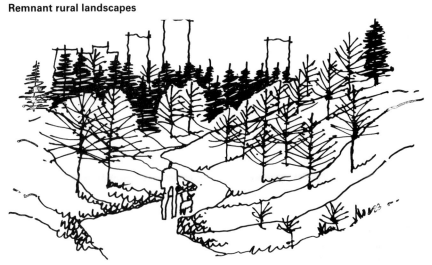

Remnant woodlands and corridors within the city's boundaries

Remnant marshes

Man-made resources

Abandoned industrial sites

Aquatic wintering grounds

Wildlife habitat integrated with storm water impoundments and water courses

Major city parks that have wildlife potential

Water courses

Places where wildlife habitat and human activity may be integrated

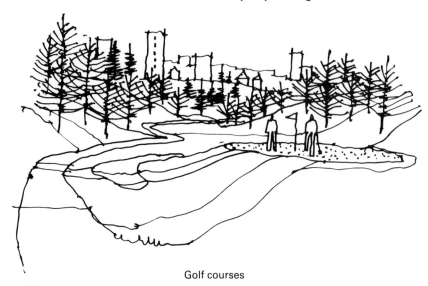

Golf courses

City parks and institutional lands

Places not barred to the public, but having little or no direct use

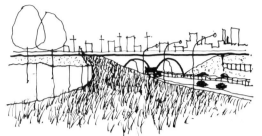

Road edges

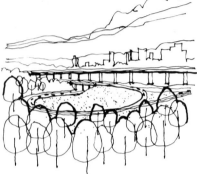

Expressway interchanges

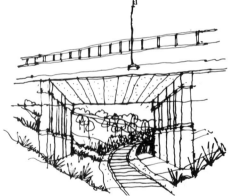

Abandoned railway lines

Disused canals

Places barred from the public, or having restricted access

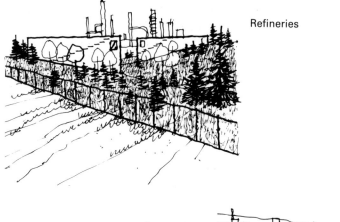

Refineries

Reservoirs

(4) Other areas less sensitive to a human presence. These may include open spaces with a wildlife potential that could, with management, accommodate a combination of human activities and wildlife. They might include public parks, cemeteries, golf courses, institutional lands, industry, public works property and other areas.

The ability of wildlife to survive urban pressures depends on the complexity, productivity and quality of habitat. It also depends on the intensity and kind of public use and the varying degrees of restriction imposed on the site. The best habitats in cities are often those with the greatest impediments to human use. For instance:

— places that are open to the public but have little or no direct use. These include travel corridors, such as main roads and urban expressways, abandoned railway lines and canals.
— places that are restricted to the public for social or security reasons. These include private properties and gardens, golf courses, public works property such as sewage treatment plants, water reservoirs and

some high-security industries such as refineries and airports, electricity generating plants and many rooftops.

Incorporating these into a city-wide wildlife network is critical to the overall enrichment of the city. At the detailed level of design and management, the task is twofold; first, to enhance wildlife habitat through adaptation and design improvement of high-value sites; second, to create new habitat where urban land offers potential opportunities for this to occur.

Adaptation and Improvement This may involve a number of measures:

— providing maximum variety of habitat, plant associations and edge conditions through vegetation management.
— planting to provide a diverse vegetation structure for breeding, cover and food sources. There are a variety of excellent publications on these topics.[38]
— maintaining vegetation diversity where it exists. For instance existing old and dead trees, ground litter, brush piles and thickets in woodland parks and open spaces provide appropriate conditions for a variety of species. The frequent practice of clearing and tidying up, where safety is not involved, minimises natural diversity and needlessly increases maintenance costs.
— providing nesting boxes, bird feeders, water sources.
— providing places and paths for people to minimise conflicts and disturbance.

Private property. The long-term stability of private property is a question that has considerable bearing on wildlife and one that makes urban situations different from rural ones. Some types of property tend to imply a vested interest in the protection of natural areas within the context of human use. Golf courses that are located in valley lands provide one example, where a complex pattern of vegetation — woodlands on valley slopes, copses, water, brush and golf greens — have mutual benefits in the maintenance of a variety of wildlife habitats and added enjoyment and variety of the course. Golf courses also tend to incorporate fairly large areas with a low intensity of use. Similarly, some older cemeteries have the same types of qualities. Private residential property that incorporates natural and valuable wildlife habitat such as ravine lands may, on the other hand, be subject to improvement by diligent and tidy-minded gardeners, which has been known to include cutting of trees, clearing of underbrush and forest litter, regrading of land, installation of lawns and flowerbeds. Such activities, apart from being inappropriate and destructive of habitat, may also pose threats to bank stability from water erosion and human intrusion, alteration of drainage and soil characteristics by irrigation and application of fertilisers. These garden-oriented activities not only destroy the immediate environs but have extended impact on the ecology, drainage patterns and soils of the large valley areas. In such situations, legislated controls to protect natural areas on private property are often necessary. A case in point is the city of Toronto by-law that imposes restrictions on property owners whose land encroaches on ravine slopes. The by-law forbids owners from altering or interfering with bank slopes by grading, filling or dumping, cutting of trees and similar alterations to their natural state.[39]

Planting to provide a diverse vegetation structure and an adequate food and cover supply on private property could greatly enhance the diversity of wildlife in the city and is a creative alternative to prevalent horticultural methods of gardening. Tall trees provide an upper-storey canopy for birds preferring this habitat, including such birds as vireos, tanagers and orioles. Smaller trees attract other species of the intermediate canopy. Ground cover and shrubs provide places for species preferring habitats closer to the ground such as song sparrows. Food sources may be provided by planting fruit and berry-bearing shrubs and trees, patches of wild or cultivated flowers that are a source of food for seed eaters in the fall and winter. Cover and a water supply should also be provided to create a varied and useful habitat that will attract a large number of animal and bird species at different times of year.

Sewage treatment plants. The potential of sewage treatment lagoons would be enhanced by simple management practices. Nesting boxes would encourage birds to breed. Planting low shrubs below lagoon dykes would provide cover for land birds. Well sited look-out points, blinds and trails would permit observation of birds without disturbance and control access and movement. Interpretive signs and pictures of birds that may be seen would enhance visitor experience. This is normal practice for wildlife reserves in urban parks in Britain and Europe. Other simple interpretive techniques might include walking trails illustrated by pamphlets or tape recorders. This latter method is both effective and inexpensive and has been used for a number of years at the outdoor trail system in the Petawawa National Forestry Institute near Ottawa.[40] The necessary controls for distribution and return of materials might be incorporated into existing security facilities of the treatment plants.

City park wildlife. Setting aside areas as wildlife reserves would enhance many city parks and would reduce maintenance costs as well. The lake in Stanley Park in Vancouver is a favourite place for visiting and breeding birds. Disturbance to breeding swans from people and domestic pets has been minimised by incorporating simple fences between the footpaths and nesting sites along the lake edge. In this way the enjoyment and educational value of seeing nesting birds is maintained easily and effectively. One of the most famous parks in London, Regent's Park, has incorporated a protected wildlife area within its boundaries. A densely wooded island in the lake provides undisturbed sanctuary for many species of ducks and other birds. The island is home for a permanent colony of herons that live and nest in its mature trees. These normally shy birds have become accustomed to living in a park environment, surrounded by the noise and traffic of the city and the everyday coming and going of park users. The whole of the area surrounding this part of the lake is separated from the footpaths by water and a fence. But the sanctuary is close enough to allow people to observe the activities of its inhabitants. To see these great birds flying low over the water, or feeding their young at treetop level in April, with the sounds of the city in the background, is an extraordinary and quite unforgettable experience.

In the urban parks of the Dutch cities, the well known image of tulip beds and beautifully tended lawns is only one part of a great diversity of habitats that are considered essential to a good park environment. These habitats serve many purposes, including a climate function, active and passive recreation, education in natural sciences, horticulture, animal husbandry and allotment gardening. Every major park in the large cities contains wildlife sanctuaries and interpretive centres where animals and birds may be observed and studied in their particular habitats. In The Hague about 300 different bird species live in or visit the city, with some 95 species breeding there. There are five or six local nature reserves of different kinds, including woodland and dune landscapes. One, accessible only to members of the Association for Bird Protection, is an area of old dune landscape where green woodpeckers, owls, finches and jays may be found together with wild plants that have ceased to exist anywhere else.[41] It must also be remembered that there has been painstaking reconstruction of natural areas in some cities in the western Netherlands, whereas many other cities have existing natural and man-made resources that can be incorporated into the fabric of an open space system at considerably less effort and cost.

The habitat of abandoned industry. The rehabilitation of industrial areas in, or on the fringes of, urban areas is a problem facing most cities and is particularly relevant to British cities where nineteenth-century exploitation has left a legacy of abandoned and unused land. Some of these have regenerated naturally and have become immensely rich, diverse landscapes (see Chapter Four). Many of these are being considered not only for rehabilitation as open space but also for industrial and residential development and new mining operations. Such is the case in the Blackbrook Valley in the industrial Midlands of England known as the 'Black Country'. This area, some 3 square kilometres in extent, was chosen by several environmental groups in 1981 to become a conservation project as part of the European Campaign for Urban Renaissance.[42] The

191

purpose of the project was to collaborate with the various public and private agencies involved to achieve a comprehensive plan, so that the land uses proposed — residential, industrial and mining operations — could be integrated with the conservation of the rich natural habitats that have regenerated on this once exploited landscape. The principles proposed for the area are significant because they provide lessons for the rehabilitation of similar urban fringe areas in other cities.[43] They include:

— biological surveys of the area's natural resources and incorporation of ecological planning into future decision making in its redevelopment (this included the involvement of amateur enthusiasts and school groups in field work);

— consideration of the valley as a whole which would include the identification, exploitation and enhancement of ecological corridors of landscape significance, so that the conservation of wildlife and provision for a rich human experience can be integrated;

— the preparation of a comprehensive landscape plan for the valley;

— involvement of the local community living on the edge of the valley. Experience has shown that involvement in landscape improvement can provide a catalyst for a more general social revival (see Chapter Six);

— the development of the valley as an educational resource. With the sense of history that exists in the Black Country, the project could provide a stimulus to local schoolchildren and make a valuable contribution to the valley's renaissance;

— the opportunity for creating employment in the area through landscape rehabilitation. There is a realisation that 'the landscape could hold the key to a new age. When the dreaded long awaited three day week is recognised to be the long awaited four day week-end, then areas like the Blackbrook Valley will begin to function as real community landscapes. There is great pressure to create low maintenance landscapes with quick-spend intensive capital. So much of the management of a landscape like this is far better done by hand.'[44]

— proposed new industrial development will generate a dramatic increase in stormwater run-off which could have severe impact on water courses. The concept of retention lakes represents very considerable economies and valuable habitat.

It is principles such as these that provide a framework for a realistic alternative to the consistent problems of urban rehabilitation; which is the problem of creating new ecologically derelict landscapes from naturally rich ones in the name of rehabilitation planning.

Creating New Wildlife Habitats The methods used by the Dutch and other European countries that were discussed in the last chapter are relevant here. Planting design that provides the maximum diversity of species, structure, edge condition, continuity and food is also a continuing management process. The key to wildlife habitat design is creating the conditions where conflicts between people and wildlife are minimised. The survival of creatures and their enjoyment by people are not incompatible objectives. As we have seen, some of the best potential places for wildlife are those areas that have visual access but are otherwise physically restricted. I have also suggested that the most valid basis for open space planning is a multi-functional approach where many compatible uses can be integrated. Two examples will illustrate the principle.

Rooftops. The flat rooftops of many commercial and industrial buildings are an example of often highly visible, but publicly inaccessible, places. They could, with some adjustment to roof design, provide the ideal sites for upper-level urban wetlands. A few inches of water allowed to pond in some areas and places for marshland vegetation to become established, when designed with the same care as decorative rooftops, could provide stop-over places for migratory birds and nesting sites for resident species. The rooftop wetland would, in effect, be replacing some of the natural habitat lost to urbanisation. Referring back to previous chapters, there are other benefits that make the urban rooftop a valid expression of an alternative design form. Retention and controlled release of rainwater to drainage systems reduce the impact of sudden storms on water courses, a problem that is of increasing concern to many urban municipalities. The presence of water and vegetation at rooftop level assists in the control of heat build-up during the summer months, through direct evaporation into the air, and evapotranspiration by plants. Wetland habitat, by providing physical and biological solutions to many problems, becomes the basis for a vernacular urban landscape and an aesthetic derived from the integration of technology and design.

Industry. The principle of visual access but physical separation for wildlife areas is highly relevant to high-security industries. An example of this is the case of the Gulf Canada oil refinery in Clarkson, Ontario.[45] This 550-acre industrial complex is abutted by urban development on three sides and Lake Ontario on the fourth. In 1975 the refinery, faced with the realities of having to live in harmony with the communities that surround it, initiated a landscape plan around its edge as a part of a continuing plant modernisation programme. The plan, conducted in co-operation with neighbouring communities, included extensive screening with earth berming and planting and the creation of a wildlife area of approximately 30 acres within the refinery's fenced boundaries. This came about at the request of the community, many members of which were keenly interested in wildlife. People had over the years witnessed the continuing deterioration of the environment where they lived. Analysis of

Community   Public park   Wildlife area   Lakeshore   Refinery

MARSH

Connecting reforestation

Gulf Canada Clarkson Refinery, location plan

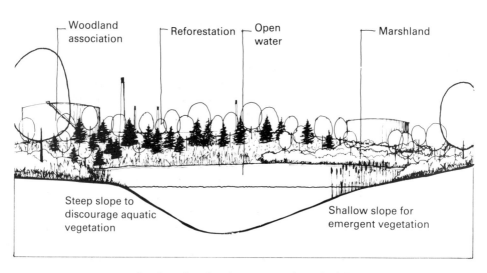

Woodland association   Reforestation   Open water   Marshland

Steep slope to discourage aquatic vegetation

Shallow slope for emergent vegetation

Pond section showing construction principles

Modified mowing regime maximises habitat and minimises maintenance costs.
Mowing is confined to areas adjacent to housing

natural conditions revealed some interesting features. The site was close to a remaining lakeshore wetland and woodland that extended to its easterly boundary. Thus a reforestation of this boundary strip would create a natural corridor linking the marsh to the proposed wildlife site. The site itself had been disturbed by landfill and other refinery operations. It was, therefore, in poor physical shape. But a natural drainage channel running through the site had created a small area where aquatic vegetation could flourish. There also remained the vestiges of old field communities of wild grasses and flowers from the old agricultural landscape that had previously existed.

The plan that grew from these resources included the creation of a number of distinct wildlife environments. A pond was dug adjoining the existing wetland, combining open water and aquatic vegetation. The old field community was retained and expanded. A small woodland of mixed deciduous and coniferous species was planted, which over the years will provide contrasting habitat. A linear wooded strip along the refinery boundary was planted to link the wildlife area in a continuous corridor to the adjacent lakeshore wetland.

A key element was management. Wildlife habitat is dependent on a minimal maintenance regime in the normal sense of horticultural maintenance. An initial periodic cutting of grass during the summer was initially undertaken to reduce competition to shrubs and small trees. As they developed a natural balance evolved as natural succession took over, making it possible to reduce maintenance. Over the years careful adjustments to the environment may be undertaken to ensure that habitats remain distinct. But normal upkeep on an everyday basis is now discontinued.

Outside the boundary fence within the existing park separating the community and refinery, a large hill was built to permit wildlife viewing at a distance. Other views of the pond were designed to permit closer observation by local residents.

Time will tell how this experiment will develop. In less than a year, though, there was evidence of new life in this regenerated piece of refinery land. Pheasants began to return. Shore birds and ducks were seen at the pond edge. There were signs of raccoons and muskrats. This is a place where a practical attempt to re-create a natural habitat in urban surroundings has been made. The association of wildlife and industry is a symbiotic one. Industry benefits from a landscape buffer between it and the community that needs little or no upkeep. The community benefits from the educational and enjoyable resource that is available on its doorstep. And wildlife flourishes, protected from direct intrusion on its territory by security fences.

Some Other Aspects of Management

The imbalanced ecological conditions caused by urbanisation create problems as well as opportunities. An example is the vast increase in exotic species of birds and rodents. Bringing technology to bear on environmental problems is often difficult and expensive. In some cases it may be a question of minimising hazards, or being aware of the problem and living with it. 'We don't destroy wild birds because they carry encephalitis viruses. Instead we try to control the mosquito vectors — by means that will not injure the birds.'[46]

There are many situations where a greater balance could be brought to the city environment by a greater respect for natural processes in design and management. Several examples will illustrate.

The overwhelming reliance on a few, mostly exotic, species of trees for urban parks and gardens is based largely, as we saw in the last chapter, on horticultural, engineering and decorative criteria. Their relationship to such factors as insect and animal diversity is rarely considered. So, while they won't clog the drains, or cause a problem with the telephone wires, the habitat created is generally sterile. A study of the common trees in Britain, together with their history and the insects associated with them, is revealing.[47] A few are summarised in Table 5.3, and show that the native trees have the largest numbers of associated insects (oak with 284) and those introduced by far the least (plane with 0). From the perspective of wildlife diversity alone the incidence of insect communities related to plants has some significance for selection and the creation of viable habitat.

Table 5.3: Common trees in Britain

Tree Species	History in Britain	Total No. of Associated Insect Spp.
Oak (*Quercus robur* L. and *Q. petraea* (Matt.) Liebl.)	Native	284
Birch (*Betula* spp.)	"	229
Willow (*Salix* spp.)	"	266
Hawthorn *(Crataegus* spp.)	"	149
Lime (*Tilia* spp.)	Native and introduced	31
Horse-chestnut (*Aesculus hippocastanum*)	Introduced c. 1600	4
Acacia (*Robinia pseudo acacia* L.)	Introduced c. 1501	1
Plane tree (*Platanus orientalis* L.)	Introduced c. 1520	0

Source: Southwood, 1961.

In central urban areas buildings are bird habitat, but the communal roosting and nesting habits of pigeons and starlings create problems. The large quantities of droppings they produce deface buildings and floor surfaces and are expensive to clean up. For many historic cities, like Venice, this is a serious matter. The sculptural surfaces of historic buildings and statues make fouling more obvious. At the same time one of the great attractions of Venice is its famous pigeons in the Piazza San Marco. It is ironic, however, that recent studies have shown that guano protects limestone from sulphur dioxide, the industrial pollutant to which Venice and other ancient cities are highly prone.[48] In modern industrial cities the solution is to design buildings to inhibit nesting and perching. Crevices, cornices, ventilation shafts and similar holes and projections could be simply protected and bird numbers reduced by reducing available habitat.

The use of predators may control or reduce the number of common birds that have either become a nuisance or are a hazard in certain situations. For instance, snowy owls are regularly used at some airports where the danger from birds to aircraft taking off and landing is potentially an extreme safety hazard. Peregrine falcons have been introduced into some cities to prey on pigeons, starlings and sea-gulls.

Many city parks, particularly those on waterfronts or associated with fresh water, have been invaded by large flocks of geese and ducks. These birds, finding the urban climate and secure food supply to their liking, have adopted new habits. Traditionally migratory birds, many now reside in the cities all year round. The Toronto Island park, across the bay from the city, has a burgeoning population of Canada geese. From one gander and goose planted in 1959, one flock rose to 1,000 by 1974.[49] They have continued to increase and have spread to other waterfront parks. Canada geese have now become a management problem, competing with people for space on the beaches and grass lawns, making clean-up a constant chore. Management to cull them has included spraying eggs with kerosene or removing them, but the numbers continue to grow with the assured food supply from a devoted public. An obvious solution would be to harvest the geese on a yearly basis and sell them as dressed birds, in much the same way as deer are harvested and sold as venison in Europe. In this way the beginnings of a farming industry could be started.

But it is curious how urban people accept without question their right to hunt wild and half-starved geese struggling to exist hundreds of miles from the city, but look on the harvesting of well fed home grown birds, themselves a product of the city's energy, with disapproval. This anomaly raises some of the basic questions that I have referred to throughout this book. There is the problem of environmental attitudes and literacy. The tendency to make urban pets of wildlife that has successfully adapted to new environments is deep rooted. The true value of wildlife in the city is the lessons it can teach us about the balance of nature and how human life is a part of that balance. Study of human and natural urban systems is perhaps the best way of coming to grips with the wider issues of vanishing species and pollution. Hillaire Belloc's poem about the dodo is, therefore, an apt reflection on our problem and the need for city nature. There is the perceptual dissociation between urban and rural environments that has radically influenced the way urban people view wildlife and nature in general. Cottaging, camping, hunting and most other leisure-oriented activities that are pursued in the countryside are basically exploitive occupations when there is no long-term investment in nature or the land. Yet our examination of wildlife and its dependence on the other elements of nature's processes shows that many of the city's most biologically productive environments are to be found where energy and nutrients are concentrated — which brings us to the question of how this phenomenon may become a way of *regaining* an investment in the land. The productivity of land, growing food and our ultimate dependence on the soil for survival strike at the heart of the problem. What implications does food growing have for cities in the light of ecological and conserver values? What are the connections between soil productivity, energy and nurtrients, and the alternative framework for urban design that we have been exploring? These are questions that now deserve our attention and will be addressed in the next chapter.

Notes

1. Hilaire Belloc, *The Bad Child's Book of Beasts, together with More Beasts for Worse Children* (Duckworth, 1974).
2. Peter Farb, *The Forest* (Time-Life Books, New York, 1963).
3. Ibid.
4. Aelred K. Geis, 'Effects of Urbanization and Types of Urban Developoment on Bird Populations' in *Wildlife in an Urbanizing Environment Symposium* (Co-operative Extension Service, University of Massachusetts, Amherst, June 1944).
5. Urban Wildlife Research Centre, *Urban Wildlife News* (Mar. 1979).
6. John A. Livingston, *Canada* (Natural Science of Canada, Toronto, 1970).
7. Ibid.
8. Gina Douglas (ed.), *The William Curtis Ecological Park*, Second Report (Ecological Parks Trust, London, 1979).
9. The Ravine Developers, Citizens Committee, *Foxes and Watercress* (published by means of a grant from the Civic Improvement Foundation, Toronto, 1972).
10. Penelope A. Bonnett, 'London: an Examination of the City as a Wildlife Area' in Gerald McKeating (ed.), *Nature and Urban Man* (Canadian Nature Federation Conference, University of Western Ontario, 1974).
11. Lars Karstad, 'Disease Problems of Urban Wildlife' in David Euler *et al.* (eds.), *Wildlife in Urban Canada, Symposium* (University of Guelph, Guelph, Ontario, 1975).
12. Ibid.
13. *Globe and Mail* (Toronto) 18 July 1981.
14. Ibid.
15. Douglas, *William Curtis Ecological Park*.
16. Edward T. Hall, *The Hidden Dimension* (Doubleday, Garden City, New York, 1966).
17. Thomas A. More, 'An Analysis of Wildlife in Children's Stories' in *Children, Nature and the Urban Environment*, Symposium proceedings (USDA Forest Service, General Technical Report NE 30, US Dept. of Agriculture, Washington, DC, 1977).
18. Donald Worster, *Nature's Economy* (Anchor Press/Doubleday, Garden City, New York, 1979).
19. John A. Livingston, *One Cosmic Instant* (McClelland and Stewart, Toronto, 1973).
20. Livingston, *Canada*.
21. Peter J. Hamel, 'Wastewater Treatment and Shorebird Ecology in the Regional Municipality of Ottawa-Carlton', unpublished student paper, Faculty of Environmental Studies, York University, Toronto, 1976.
22. Ibid.
23. Ibid.
24. Ibid.
25. *Greater Vancouver Regional District Newsletter* (Nov. 1981).
26. Bruce Kidd and H. Roy Merrins, 'Keep it Primitive if you Want a Really Modern Park', *Globe and Mail* (Toronto), 12 Aug. 1978.
27. Paul M. Catling, Karen L. McIntosh and Sheila M. McKay, 'The Vascular Plants of the Leslie Street Headland', *Ontario Field Biology*, vol. 31, no. 1 (1977).
28. Ibid.
29. Ian D. McNab, *An Environmental Survey of Aquatic Park* (Metropolitan Toronto and Region Conservation Authority, Toronto, 1978).
30. Hans Blokpoel and Gerard T. Haymes, 'How the Birds Took Over the Leslie Street Spit', *Canadian Geographic Journal* (Apr./May 1978).

31. Ibid.
32. Ibid.
33. Ibid.
34. Ibid.
35. The Friends of the Spit, 'The Eastern Headland and Aquatic Park', produced by the Friends of the Spit, Toronto, unpublished.
36. R. Johnson, 'Inventory of Amphibians and Reptiles in Metro Toronto', unpublished paper, Faculty of Environmental Studies, York University, Toronto, 1982.
37. Ibid.
38. A few publications on planting for wildlife include: US Department of Agriculture, Forest Service, *Wildlife Habitat Improvement Handbook 1968* (US Dept. of Agriculture, Washington, DC); Daniel L. Leedy *et al.*, *Planning for Wildlife in Cities and Suburbs* (American Society of Planning Officials, Report no. 331, Chicago, 1978); NE Forest Experiment Station, *Shrubs and Vines for NE Wildlife* (USDA Forest Service, General Technical Report NE 9, US Dept. of Agriculture, Washington, DC, 1974); James R. Vilkitis, 'Wildlife Habitat as an Integral Component of a Planned Unit Development', *Urban Ecology*, vol. 3 (1978); Gerald B. McKeating and William A. Creighton, *Backyard Habitat* (Ministry of Natural Resources, Toronto, n.d.).
39. Ravine Control Bylaw No. 332-81, City of Toronto.
40. Hough, Stansbury and Associates, *Public Awareness Program, Petawawa Forest Experiment Station* (Canadian Forestry Service, Ottawa, 1972).
41. *Groot Haags Groenboek* (Hague Municipal Public Relations Bureau Publication, The Hague, 1971).
42. Chris Baines and George Barker, 'The Blackbrook Valley Project', *Landscape Design*, no. 134 (1981).
43. Ibid.
44. Ibid.
45. Hough Stansbury Associates, 'Gulf Canada, Clarkson Refinery', unpublished Long Range Master Plan for Landscape and Site Development, 1976.
46. Karstad, 'Disease Problems'.
47. T. R. E. Southwood, 'The Number of Species of Insects Associated with Various Trees', *Journal of Animal Ecology*, vol. 30 (1961).
48. David Bellamy, *Bellamy's Europe* (British Broadcasting Corporation, London, 1976).
49. K. C. Faulkner, 'The Egg Snatchers', *Ontario Fish and Wildlife Review*, vol. 13, nos. 1-2 (1974).

Chapter SIX

CITY FARMING

Introduction

A 1980 issue of the British *Farmers Weekly* journal offered some
alternative guidelines to the Countryside Commission's Country Code on
how urban visitors could cement friendships with country folk.[1] Here are
a few of them:

> Gates: a modern technique called zero grazing has made all gates
> redundant, so there is no need to bother with them. Never open a gate
> if you can climb over it first. If it is locked, take it off its hinges.
>
> Join in the fun: eartagging is a common practice in almost all
> livestock enterprises. Try catching some animals to see whether they
> have any tags. A farmer will roar with friendly laughter if he finds they
> have been removed.
>
> Share a good laugh: no one likes a practical joke better than a
> farmer. When passing a farm, call in and tell him his sheep have got
> out. Remember, if they have, never direct him to the right field.
>
> Bulls: contrary to popular belief only one breed of bull is dangerous
> — the savage Hereford. The majority are warm-hearted amiable
> creatures loving nothing better than to munch grass and attend shows.
> When out walking, why not try scratching a Friesian bull behind the
> ears with a blunt stick? The results can be interesting and rewarding.

While tongue in cheek, these comments reflect the basic conflicts
between urban and rural values and social perceptions towards land. To
most urban people, the countryside exists primarily for their benefit — as
a recreational resource — a place to escape to from the city. The
connection between food and the land on which it is produced has
become increasingly remote as an issue that directly concerns urban
welfare. The food that appears in the shops has little direct connection
any more with the fields adjacent to the city. Rather, it is dependent on
world-wide marketing and distribution networks operating on fossil fuels.

But increasing fuel and food costs and shrinking farmlands will, over time, influence current patterns of consumption and priorities. Indeed, there are signs of a return to home-grown versus 'factory-made' food as more and more people convert back yards into vegetable plots. In this chapter we are concerned with how the links between people and food-growing and the values that these represent can be creatively re-established. The relevance of food-growing as one of the functions of urban open space and its environmental and social values will also be examined.

Agriculture — Process and Practice

Productivity

Agricultural systems are man-made communities of plants and animals, interacting with soils and climate. Unlike self-perpetuating natural systems, they are inherently unstable. Cultivation and harvesting and the biological simplicity of a few species inhibits recycling of nutrients and makes them susceptible to attack from pests. The degree to which they can be stabilised depends on factors such as soil fertility, the extent to which animal nutrients are recycled and the diversity of the plant and animal species under cultivation. Traditional mixed farming practice, while varying widely in the type of cultivation, has maintained a certain degree of ecological balance. The enclosed field systems of European agriculture relied on nutrient input from farm animals, crop rotation and crop variety and the natural communities of hedges and woodlands to offset nutrient output from the harvest and the depredations of pests. Energy inputs to the system before the age of fossil fuels were limited to horses and men to pull the ploughs, sow the seed and thresh the grain. Fossil fuels provided the fundamental breakthrough. The rubber-tyred tractor replaced human and animal labour. Chemical fertilisers and pest control agents have substituted for earlier biological methods of maintaining stability. Fossil fuels enable agriculture to increase its efficiency and size and decrease its labour inputs. The increasing trends in this direction have had immense environmental, social and economic impact, both in the countryside and in the city.

The evolution of new technologies based on a plentiful supply of energy has made possible an ever increasing agricultural productivity. Between 1910 and 1970 farm output in the US doubled, producing in 1970 twice the amount of food on less land.[2] In a ten-year period up to 1975 output per worker in Britain increased, on average, by 6 per cent a year, more than twice the rate of the average industrial worker.[3] The technology of machinery, fertilisers, herbicides and pesticides that makes this growth possible depends on larger land areas for an efficient operation. So the trend towards larger, more efficient commercial farms and fewer small ones has been growing in all industrialised countries. Nitrogen and other fertilisers replace organic manures and extend the productive capacity of soils over a larger area. Relatively few, but highly productive, plant hybrids replace the more diverse but less productive plants of earlier farming. World-wide, man now relies on eleven plant species for about 80 per cent of his food supply.[4] Herbicides and pesticides provide the protection against pests for large areas of a single crop originally provided by crop and livestock diversity and natural communities.

Larger farms increasingly specialise in either crops or livestock. Animal feed-lots and battery poultry have intensified farm output, converting feed into meat and eggs. New breeds of mechanical harvesters have been developed for harvesting grains, fruit and vegetables with minimum labour. An entirely new agricultural industry has evolved, of which farming is only a part. What is commonly known as 'agribusiness' is based on three major components:

— an input processing industry that produces seed, machines, fertilisers, fuel and related products required for large-scale farming;
— the farm itself;
— the food processsing industry which transports farm products, processes food, markets and distributes products to wholesale and retail outlets.

Thus modern farming is dependent on fuel energy not only for growing food, but for processing and distribution. In 1966 agriculture and food processing used 28 per cent of all petroleum products marketed in Canada. Agricultural use of petroleum products doubled between 1961 and 1971.[5] A large portion of energy is used in intensive fruit and vegetable growing and in the production of animal and dairy products. In general the intensive nature of agriculture near large cities consumes more energy than in more distant rural areas.[6]

Over the last century agriculture has evolved from a labour-intensive, low-energy, small-scale and mixed farming operation to a vast industry that is capital- and energy-intensive and requires fewer and fewer people. But the benefits of high production — being able to feed more people cheaply, and less grinding labour for the farmer, also bring considerable costs, in environmental and social terms, that affect both rural areas and the city.

Environmental Costs

The first and most basic issue that is receiving increasing attention is non-renewable energy. Continued expansion of production, subsidised by an increasingly costly and diminishing resource, is a short term policy. As Odum has observed, man eats potatoes partly made of oil.[7] Commoner has pointed to the law of diminishing returns, where, as cultivation becomes more intensive, greater amounts of energy subsidy must be used to obtain diminishing increments in yield.[8] The cyclical flow of energy resources through natural systems is simplified in industrial agriculture, which is sustained by non-renewable energy at high environmental cost. High concentrations of fertilisers and chemicals used to maximise homogeneous crops threaten soil life and deplete the humus needed for the maintenance of biological health. Streams, rivers and groundwater receive nutrients and chemicals that lead to pollution and threaten human health in the cities. Heavy machinery and tilling contribute to soil compaction and erosion and consequently the reduction of soil fertility.

The complementary benefits to the soil of an animal/crop relationship disappear when crops and livestock become separate industries. Concentrating animals into feedlots involves high energy inputs, disposal of wastes and chemical agents to prevent disease in constricted spaces. This type of industrialised agriculture has been shown to have inbuilt inefficiencies.[9] Feed must be transported to the site. Enormous quantities of manure produced by the animals (estimated at 40 to 70 pounds per day per animal) are often uneconomical to transport back to the fields and must, therefore, be disposed of. Once fattened, the animals have to be transported long distances to urban markets.

The replacement of manpower by industrialised food production decreases the energy value of various food crops. In 1972 figures for the energy efficiency of different crops grown in California showed the ratios of crop energy over input energy illustrated in Table 6.1.[10] It will be apparent that despite high yields, generated by industrialised agricultural systems, there does not appear to be a viable net energy return to society. That is, the amount of energy that goes into growing, shipping, packaging and marketing the food we eat is greater than the energy we get out of it. Research conducted on farmland in upland areas of Britain suggests that as farms get larger they tend to produce *less* food per acre on average than more.[11] This suggests that policies aimed at amalgamating smaller farms into bigger ones in the interests of efficiency and increased production may, in fact, be counter-productive.

Social Costs

Biological stability and the sustainability of agriculture are directly related to social issues. The development of modern agriculture over the last seventy-five years has been accompanied by a progressive replacement of human labour for a capital-intensive agricultural industry. The labour-intensive farming of an earlier time maintained viable rural populations. But relatively low-cost technologies, fertilisers, chemicals and machinery

Table 6.1: Energy efficiency of Californian crops

Crops	Crop Energy/Input Energy
Field crops	3.9
(barley, corn, rice, sorghum, wheat)	
Raw vegetables	0.77
Raw fruits	0.54
Average of all raw foods	1.36
Canned vegetables	0.25
Canned fruits	0.25
Frozen vegetables	0.22
Dried fruit and nuts	0.63
Average of all processed foods	0.47

Source: The New Alchemist Institute, 1974.

of modern farming have become an effective substitute for labour. For instance, a New York farmer in the early part of this century spent 150 minutes producing a bushel of corn. In 1955 it took him only 16 minutes. In the 1970s it took him less than 3 minutes per bushel.[12]

An increasing number of people have moved from the rural areas to the cities in search of urban jobs. The statistics are disturbing. Between 1950 and 1955 more than 1 million workers in the US left the farms. No other important food-producing country in the world has reduced its farm labour to the same extent.[13] In 1976 US farms were reported to employ only 5 per cent of the work force.[14] In Canada the farm population decreased 50 per cent in 30 years and by 1971 only 6.9 per cent remained on farms.[15] In 1958 19 million people in nine countries of the European Economic Community made a living from agriculture. By 1977 this had dropped to 8½ per cent of the total working population.[16]

The reasons for declining numbers have been credited to increased competition, more capital to run economic operations, amalgamation of farms into larger units, the centralisation of agriculture and increased mechanisation needing fewer people to manage more land. But these factors work against the maintenance of healthy rural communities. Many once flourishing rural areas have been brought to economic ruin and have been unable to support or house their remaining population.

The steady disappearance of farmland in the face of urban growth has decreased the capacity of the rural areas to supply their local urban regions. There is a growing preference for foods of tropical origin, and city dwellers now rely almost exclusively on the major food-producing regions of the world for their food. Only 9.5 per cent of all food consumed in Massachusetts is produced in the State. Many of these regions, however, are undergoing similar development pressures and consequent loss of farmland. Recent estimates suggest that by the year 2000 California and Vermont may lose 15 and 43 per cent of their prime farmland respectively. By 1971 Massachusetts' farmland amounted to only 8.6 per cent of the state's total land area compared to almost 60 per cent at the beginning of the century.[17] In the face of such land losses and rising costs of petroleum and food costs the security of supply becomes a potential problem as reduced surpluses force the key food-producing regions to place priority on their own needs rather than on export. While rising food costs may be little more than a nuisance for the affluent, they represent real hardship for low-income urban families. It is estimated that the number of families making less than $5,000 in Boston is 22 per cent city-wide, and in many neighbourhoods the percentage is well over that.[18]

The dehumanisation of the processes of food growing affects patterns of consumption. It is a well known fact that the food problems of the wealthy industrialised countries stem from over-consumption and mal-nutrition, which have led to enormous waste and poor health. North Americans consume nearly 1 ton of grain per person per year, of which only 150 pounds are eaten directly. The rest is consumed indirectly in the form of animal protein.[19] Agriculture Canada research in 1973 compared nutritional diet to actual Canadian consumption patterns. It was found that 50 per cent more meat, fruit, tomatoes and sugar were eaten than is required for a healthy diet. Eggs, flour, cheese and poatoes remained roughly the same, but vegetables, legumes, nuts and butter were eaten less than required for a healthy diet. In particular, milk and vegetables would have to increased by 60 per cent to meet dietary needs.[20] In addition, the proportion of the diet of tropical origin, imported at high energy cost, has continued to grow at the expense of such cool-climate crops as potatoes and cereals.[21]

Urban Processes

Problems and Perceptions

The problems that confront rural areas are urban based. Rural occupations, such as fruit growing and dairy farming, which once were common in cities, are largely a thing of the past. As the cities grow larger, the vast majority of people have ceased to have any knowledge of rural values and skills. For urban people the country is seen as an urban playground, a recreational resource of fresh air and peaceful scenery, not as a working environment for producing food. Many have returned to live or retire; others to find a weekend cottage; many more to camp, hike, water-ski or sightsee. So urban activities in the countryside are essentially exploitative in terms of their environmental and social effects. For the farmer the holidaymaker with his dog, camper and urban values is a potential menace, interfering with crops, setting fires, chasing cattle and leaving hazardous garbage that can damage property and livestock. Separated as we are from the sources and processes of our food supply, we carry around a burden of expectations and ignorance that may be often as destructive as it is well meaning. Cats and dogs are permitted to proliferate in the cities and are cherished, but animals kept for food are regarded with suspicion or outright hostility. Two official recommendations to government pertaining to livestock-keeping in cities make an interesting comparison of attitudes; the first, during the early years of the Second World War in England, reads as follows:

[It is recommended] that provision should be made . . . for town dwellers to keep pigs and poultry and in general to continue those rural occupations which have proved to have social, economic and educational advantage in time of war.[22]

The second, in the city of Toronto, in 1981, reads in part:

a farm animal may be described as any animal commonly or historically used in the production of food . . . Almost by nature of their purpose these live animals and poultry require extensive space, constant supervision and present obvious problems with regard to defecation and perhaps noise . . . The typical city home and lot does not provide anything approaching an appropriate setting for such animals. It is proposed, therefore, that ownership of live animals and poultry within the city be banned.[23]

In 1978 Vancouver city officials were reported to have forced a citizen to get rid of the chickens she claimed were necessary to provide her children with an adequate diet. This occurred in the very city that twenty-seven years before had urged its citizens to 'plant a wartime garden'.[24] The meat bought at the supermarket was once livestock, but few know of the preparation processes that precede the packaged product. We have little idea of how to handle or manage the animals that are the source of our food and impose sentimental value on 'fluffy baby animals', which prohibits a straightforward acceptance of their use as farm livestock. It is clear that there is a need for education in where our food comes from for urban children and adults alike. The city itself presents biological problems that cannot be ignored without at the same time sterilising the minds and habits of its inhabitants. The slaughter of farm animals for food is an unknown and unwanted experience. We don't know how to manage unwanted insects or plants without employing lethal poisons, a

The working environment of the countryside is invaded by urban people who see it as a place for fresh air and leisure. The recreationist, too often ignorant of rural functions and values, becomes a menace to livestock and a hazard to the environment

practice that is about as sophisticated as swatting a fly with a sledgehammer. Most of us rely on high-energy technologies beyond the control or influence of the people they are supposed to serve. Our perceptions of the urban environment and the things we do there have, as I showed in Chapter One, been moulded by the increasing isolation of modern urban life from rural values. The preoccupation with leisure and aesthetics as the exclusive function of urban parks and open spaces and the inherent assumption of their non-productivity have remained since the nineteenth century, the unquestioned dicta of parks departments, designers and the public.

Redressing the Balance

With rising costs of food and energy, heightened environmental concern and an increasing consciousness that fossil fuels cannot go on for ever, there are signs that agricultural processes are changing. There is renewed interest in soil conservation and modern versions of traditional farming practice of using the 'experience of generations of farmers working as closely to the soil as possible, but now supported and explained by advances in soil biology and taking advantage of modern machinery'.[25] In most European countries with long traditions in farming and scarce oil resources soil fertility has always been a primary concern. The spiralling costs of artificial fertilisers make the fullest use of cheaper organic manures necessary. In the Netherlands much of the organic manure produced in the eastern half of the country from intensive livestock farming areas is transported to the west and used on crop lands. In Britain farm slurry is commonly used on the land to offset commercial fertilisers' costs.

In the cities, waste disposal from sewage treatment has become a problem of major proportions. In the US there is interest in the application of composted sewage to the land. There are a number of examples of this recycling process in operation. One of the best known is the Muskegan County project in Michigan referred to in Chapter Three. Started in 1973, the Muskegan system recycles 43 million gallons per day on to formerly unproductive lands, totalling 10,300 acres. The waste water irrigates 4,500 acres of corn which in 1975 yielded 65 bushels per acre.[26] The sewage treatment plants around London that are controlled by the Thames Water Authority have solved the problem of sludge disposal for many years in a similar fashion. Approximately 5,000 hectares of farmland surrounding the city are regularly treated with the waste water from treatment plants, transported by tankers to the farms. The land is monitored on a regular basis in accordance with government regulations to ensure that heavy metal content does not rise above prescribed levels.[27]

There is growing public awareness of environmental and health problems inherent in chemical food production, a concern for a greater control over personal destinies in the face of an inhuman and violent technology. It is being expressed in the groundswell of organisations that have been created in search of gentler, more humane approaches, alternative life-styles, solutions to social problems and rural employment. Many thousands of people are once again taking to the land to grow food uncontaminated by chemical additives or preserved in tin cans. The Friends of the Earth report that the rising price of vegetables in the 1970s has been a contributing factor in the upsurge in home vegetable growing in Britain. The waiting lists for allotments have grown by over 100,000 in under a decade.[28] There is a search for greater self-reliance, a more direct connection with land, the satisfaction of having more control over personal diet and health. So the question must be asked: how is urban design relevant to the problems of food and farming? The answer may lie in the fact that, fundamentally, rural problems are urban based.

If we look back in history, it becomes obvious that the dichotomy of urban man and the land is a malaise of the last half century. In earlier cities, urban and rural values were integrated by necessity. Mumford notes that a good part of the population of medieval cities had private gardens and practised rural occupations within the city. In addition, burghers had orchards and vineyards in the suburbs and kept cows and sheep on the common fields under the care of a municipal herdsman.[29] Pigs and chickens were kept which in early days acted as town scavengers. Until provisions for street cleaning were effected the pig was 'an active member of the local Board of Health'.[30]

The New England towns maintained a similar balance between rural and urban occupations up to the end of the nineteenth century. Prior to the First World War a thriving dairy industry existed in Liverpool. Many families from the Yorkshire Dales went into the business of supplying milk to a fast-growing urban population, keeping cows in the city and selling the milk to homes on the city streets. The story of these enterprising families is told through one family who stayed in Liverpool for twenty years before retiring to a farm in the Dales that they bought with the profits of their Liverpool milk business. The business started with 2 cows and ended with 46 cows and 3 horses. The Liverpool house where they lived was at the end of a row, and the front room formed a dairy where people arrived at all hours to buy milk. A short distance away were the buildings housing the cattle. The daughter took a horse-drawn lorry to the local cemetery in the summers to collect loads of grass cuttings which had been put into piles by the cemetery maintenance men. Hay for the animals was obtained from a local farmer who would dump a load on his way to the city market and load up with manure on his way home.[31]

The necessity of pursuing rural occupations in the city has been no more clearly demonstrated than during times of war and emergency. During the German occupation of Denmark in the Second World War, it was the food grown in gardens that saved the citizens from starvation.[32] In Britain efforts to make the most of limited resources led to the setting up of the Pig Keeping Council in 1939 by the Ministry of Agriculture. Its original purpose was to move pigs from the farms, which were threatened by shortages of imported feedstuffs, to the villages to encourage the use of household wastes for feed. These efforts, however, were soon reflected in an *urban* livestock movement. Since the bulk of edible waste came from the cities, pig and poultry keeping naturally evolved as a major urban activity. Pig keeping spread on to bombed sites, in back streets and allotments and included policemen, firemen and factory workers among the devotees. There was a pig club in London's Hyde Park and another within two hundred yards of Oxford Circus. In 1940, in response to the increasing demand for eggs, the Domestic Food Producers Council set up a Poultry Committee which recommended households be encouraged to keep poultry for egg production. The backyard food production movement became officially accepted with an Order in Council which suspended restrictions in keeping pigs, chickens and rabbits, subject to certain public health requirements. By 1943 there were 4,000 pig clubs comprising some 110,000 members keeping 105,000 pigs. While the promoters of the pig-keeping movement originally intended it to be a rural activity, it became urban because the food wastes of modern society were mainly in urban areas. Prior to this, the disposal of waste food levied a heavy charge on public rates. Many of the clubs were organised into co-operatives, livestock being fattened collectively, rather than by individuals, lending greater efficiency and organisation to the activity.[33]

By 1942 there were 916,000 registered poultry keepers keeping 1 to 12 chickens and nearly 264,000 with 13 to 50 chickens with a total poultry production of some 16 million. Domestic rabbit clubs were formed which by 1943 amounted to 2,700 keeping 252,000 breeding does. Other livestock activities included bee keeping and goats. In England and Wales at that time there were about 30,000 beekeepers controlling some 429,000 colonies of bees. While bee keeping is not an urban pursuit by nature, there were many that were distinctly urban or semi-urban in character. One of the most progressive associations of beekeepers was in the city of Birmingham, where facilities for an instructional apiary were provided in

In Order to continue the work of the late John Morgan during the summer and autumn of 1940 in focussing the varied activities of small producers on a national objective; and to preserve the spirit of co-operation with which people of diverse interests united at the microphone to inspire their own followers with the true significance of their various fancies; and to maintain the position of all those people who truly desire to foster home livestock interests and to preserve the usefulness and fertility of our land and towns, the undersigned have formed a Club to be named after the series of broadcast talks in which they appeared together.

Its objects shall be to include like-minded persons and to exercise a common influence in fostering and safeguarding the activities mentioned above.

The Charter of the 'Back to the Land' Club, formed early in the Second World War by John Green, who was in charge of farming and gardening broadcasts at the BBC in London. The Club provided a focus for the various organisations concerned with food production, including the Pig Clubs, Domestic Poultry Keepers, the National Allotment Society and others. The Club also served as a technical forum and defensive organisation to solve problems such as urban by-laws, treatment of wastes, administration of rationing, livestock in schools and so on. The Club lasted 26 years, until rationing was discontinued in Britain

one of the public parks. It is interesting to note that the planning of parks and gardens was of particular concern to the beekeepers, since the selection of plants in the city's parks would have considerable impact on nectar supply. The maintenance of plant diversity that was discussed in Chapter Four can be seen to be a crucial factor in a functional and productive urban landscape. In addition, the value of bees as pollinators for allotment and backyard gardens is, in the opinion of modern beekeepers, much more important than their value as producers of honey. Goat keeping was practised intensively partly due to the shortage of fresh milk and partly because the wastes on which goats thrive were not in competition with the diets of other animals. Milk yields averaged over a gallon a day throughout the year from goats that were entirely stall fed and with a yard of some 20 square yards for exercise.

The 'Dig for Victory' campaign during the last war in Britain and other countries showed that the production of fruit and vegetables in or near cities could have a significant influence on food production when people are in need. Production from allotment and garden plots in Britain reached a peak when the number of allotments almost doubled from a pre-war figure of 740,000 to 1.4 million. In a parliamentary debate reported in Hansard in 1944 it was estimated that 10 per cent of the food grown in Britain came from this source.[34] During the years when urban food production was at its height agricultural shows took place in a variety of places, including the basement of John Lewis's shop in Oxford Street, in industrial areas and on football fields. John Green, founder of the 'Back to the Land' Club and in charge of BBC broadcasts on farming and gardening at the time, has recorded visiting Bethnal Green after one of the worst air raids of the war and seeing the people feeding their ducks on the canals and visiting a poultry show at the Working Men's Institute. The inner city had acquired a new unity with the countryside.[35] In Canada, Vancouver citizens urged by the government to 'plant a wartime garden', and aided by a city decision to rent vacant land at a nominal fee, produced some 31,000 tons of fresh vegetables and fruit in 1943. This was equivalent to $20 million worth of supermarket produce at 1979 prices.[36]

It is clear then that in terms of crisis and shortage urban land can be put to functional and productive use. The brief period of plenty that has been made possible by cheap energy has been the root cause of our current urban condition. An affluent society, less concerned with basic living needs, has turned to alternative pursuits that are the product of leisure rather than necessity. Food is readily available, imported, canned or frozen. The migration from farm to city, the return to the countryside to find recreation and second homes, the dissociation of urban and rural occupations, industrialised food systems and current attitudes to land: these are the legacy of the cities. The price and future use of agricultural land are based on political decisions made by people who live in urban areas and who follow urban life-styles. We face a future of increasing energy shortage that will eventually bring about a greater concern for conservation in urban life and the way land is used.

So we must begin where most people live. The city is the place to re-establish constructive links with the land and the natural processes that are tied to the food we eat. It is the place where alternatives to destructive technologies can be explored and demonstrated through direct experience with food growing and through education. We can learn about energy and food production, farming practices, market gardening techniques, rural affairs as well as urban ones. To do so requires that food growing and farm management at an appropriate scale become an integral part of the city's open space functions. The resources and opportunities for doing so should, therefore, be explored.

Resources and Opportunities

Contrary to what might be supposed, the city has significant potential for productive farming. The disillusionment with the urban environment as a place to live has the effect of blinding one's view of the resources on one's own doorstep. Many have forsaken the city in search of a plot of land in the country, where communion with nature and the trend to self-reliance seem more assured of success. But for the majority of urban dwellers concerned with these ideals, such a radical shift in life-styles is unrealistic. The place to start building a richer life and re-establishing contact with the land must remain, as I have suggested, in the familiar environment of the city.

This fact is borne out by many cities in the less industrialised nations that must produce food for large populations with limited energy and space. China offers perhaps the best example of urban food production. With an urban population of 150 million people and limited transportation facilities, government policy has aimed to create producer rather than consumer cities.[37] At least 85 per cent of the vegetables consumed by urban residents are produced within urban municipalities. Shanghai and Peking are self-sufficient in vegetables, producing over 1 million tons per annum. Many Chinese cities also produce large quantities of poultry and pigs and other essential foods. In Hong Kong 16 per cent of the total consumption of fresh-water fish was produced from local fish ponds in 1978.[38] But one does not have to go far to see land used productively where there is need. For those less affluent and ethnic minority groups living in many Western cities, home farming has always been a way of life. They do it, not because of any environmental conscience — this is a middle-class ethic — but because it is necessary.

In Chapter One I showed how two landscapes exist side by side in

a

Food production by necessity and tradition in a North American city. Every available space is cultivated and used to the maximum in many ethnic areas. Front and backyards supply vegetables for the family – some families being almost self sufficient. Flowers, religious icons and decoration fill ground plots and rooftops; small cafés and backyards are sheltered from sun by grape vines that are also grown for wine making. This rich urban tradition is a far cry from the standard park provided by the municipality. Installed and maintained at public expense, it has little diversity and provides no productive uses

(a) rooftop landscape; (b) the municipal park; (c) backyard neighbourhood sheltered by grape vines, which provide wine and shade; (d) food growing on the street

214

b

c

d

cities; the one (the pedigree landscape) a product of conscious design, the other (the vernacular landscape) a product of spontaneous natural forces. We find similar patterns if we look at the urban landscape from a cultural perspective. The pedigree of public parks, gardens, civic spaces and well-to-do residential neighbourhoods is the symbol of civic pride and care, reflecting the city's public face. It is none the less wholly dependent on energy and horticultural technology for its survival and produces no energy return for energy invested. The vernacular is hidden away in alleys, rooftops and backyards, in ethnic neighbourhoods all over the city. Here one finds an extraordinarily rich variety of flourishing gardens and brightly painted houses. The front yard turf of the well-to-do neighbourhood gives way to a rich array of sunflowers, daylilies and Michaelmas daisies, bric-à-brac, religious icons and fences that express ideas of personal territory and a rich urban tradition. Over the backyard fence one will find productive vegetable gardens, grapevine-covered trellises, providing both summer shade and grapes for the fall wine making, chickens, ducks, goats and a variety of other livestock, kept for food rather than as pets. These vernacular landscapes of the city reflect still surviving rural skills and cultural connections with the land. They are the consequence of individual effort and group co-operation; they are self-maintaining and provide economic returns. By contrast, the conventional open space provided by the municipality through public taxes is at high design and maintenance cost, has little diversity and provides no economic returns. This strongly suggests that it is time to rethink the basic nature and function of open space in cities.

Physical and Energy Resources

It is plain that modern urban tradition has been moulded by a combination of economics, technological and aesthetic influences and values. This is reflected in the fact that vast amounts of nutrient energy and land are currently conceived of as waste. The idea that the city itself should be required to contribute to the production of such basic essentials as food involves a shift in values to an ecological/conserver frame of reference. From this perspective, the urban environment may be seen as a generator of vast *resources* in nutrient energy and land. The sewage treatment plant, food industry, and the leaf litter collected by the parks department provide potential resources for enriching soils for gardens, parks and rehabilitation sites. Wasted land created by urban expansion, planning regulations, inefficient use that precludes other functions, and the economics of unfinished urban renewal may in fact be regarded as invaluable resources for the future when necessity will dictate its more productive and intelligent use. Open space may be seen as having value beyond the recreational and aesthetic purposes generally ascribed to it.

a

b

The land resources in the city These may be seen as an opportunity for the future, rather than a problem of urban growth. Two examples are: (a) industry, electricity rights of way, rooftop space; (b) cemeteries

217

Land. Urban land resources are potentially enormous in almost all major cities. Railway, public works and public utility property, vacant lots, cemeteries and industrial lands form a major proportion of unbuilt-on land that remains sterilised or ineffectively used, often through a lack of co-ordination between the various private and public agencies that control it. In 1971, 2,500 acres of electrical utility rights of way existed in the city of Toronto.[39] A land utilisation survey in 1974 of the London Borough of Tower Hamlets revealed that the amount of waste land had quadrupled in a decade. Another estimate has put the total area of vacant land in London as 31 square kilometres.[40] Such figures may be considered typical for many cities and are depressing reminders of the vast areas of land that most cities have. As they expand on to agricultural land, more and more land lies vacant within it — a resource that could be brought into productive use.

Backyards. At the smallest, personal scale, the backyard provides some of the best opportunities for food growing in terms of energy, efficiency and direct benefit. As I showed earlier in this chapter, commercially grown and processed vegetables and fruit are the most energy-intensive of all crops. It requires more energy to produce them than the energy benefit they return; i.e. there is no net energy return. A comparison between the yearly energy budget of a residential lawn, 20 square metres in area, and the use of the same space for productive crops has revealed some interesting results. Each unit of energy invested to maintain the lawn, in human work, fuel for the mower, fertiliser and pesticides, returned 6 units of energy as lawn clippings. If the clippings were discarded, the net production efficiency of the lawn could be described as zero. With the same area planted with alfalfa, each unit of energy invested returned 22 units in crop production. In addition, the alfalfa produced enough digestible nutrient per square metre to support the production of one pound of rabbit meat.[41]

With respect to diet, most North Americans eat insufficient vegetables. An increase of about 60 per cent of fresh vegetables would have to be eaten to meet nutritional standards.[42] Backyard food is a small-scale operation that is appropriate to the size of most residential areas. For some less affluent levels of society, growing food has definite economic advantages, as the price of food continues to rise. For others it affords opportunities for productive spare-time work, which is a form of recreation increasingly sought by urban people. The educational advantages of direct contact with plants and soil are interwoven with a need for greater self-reliance and less dependence on the centralised food systems of agriculture. The residential garden provides readily available opportunities for urban farming at a small scale and personal level. They range from simply growing a few vegetables to more intensive and integrated

218

Yearly energy budget of a lawn compared to an alfalfa patch

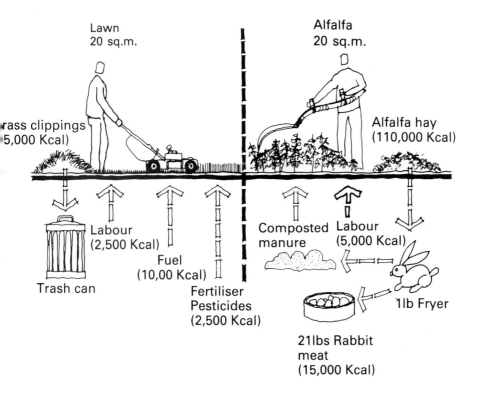

	Energy input Kcal	Energy yield plant	Kcal: Human food
Lawn	15,000	95,000	–
Alfalfa	5,000	110,000	15,000

Note: All notation represents annual totals.

A comparison of two equivalent-sized residential yards of 20 square metres, the one producing lawn grass, the other alfalfa. For every unit of energy invested (exclusively human labour) in the production of alfalfa, 22 units of energy were returned in crop production. In the case of the lawn, the net production efficiency (assuming the grass clippings are discarded) is zero. It has been calculated that the rate of energy use for the maintenance of some 16 million acres of lawns in America exceeds the rate for the commercial production of corn on an equivalent amount of soil (from Fallarones Institute, 1979)

systems, where small energy-intensive livestock such as rabbits and chickens are combined with plants in a balanced natural system. While home food production is a question of personal choice, it is clear from an increasing number of publications and organisations concerned with food in cities that there is growing interest in the concept of self-reliance and an improved quality of life. Originally begun as a rural movement to escape from the city, interest is now focusing on the city itself. Among the organisations concerned with urban problems is the Farallones Institute in Berkeley, California, which is attempting to demonstrate by practical means how life-support systems can be integrated in an urban house in such a manner as to conserve energy and resources and provide a healthy environment in the city. Another, the Institute for Local Self-Reliance, Washington, DC, provides guidance to local communities in recycling of wastes, energy efficiency, urban agriculture and related issues. A similar organisation in Wales is the Centre for Alternative Technologies. In Canada, McGill University has experimented with urban rooftops as an open space resource for growing food (see 'Wastelands and Allotments' below).[43]

Thus, residential resources for urban farming are considerable and include private properties, apartment balconies, rooftops, in fact almost any space where the individual can grow a few tomatoes or lettuce. The increasing interest in private food growing does not affect public space directly, but the city is richer and more productive because of it.

Wastelands and Allotments. The demand for allotment gardens in or near the cities has been rapidly growing for the last ten to fifteen years, particularly among those who live in apartments or in locations where open space is at a premium. In Britain, the lists for allotments rose by 100,000 in a decade[44] and demand is equally high in other European and North American countries. Increased leisure time, early retirement and unemployment are credited with the increasing demand for a plot of land. In addition, rising food costs and a rejection of frozen or canned foods have contributed to the growing interest in organically grown produce. Allotments can be fitted to any shape of property. The small-scale and labour-intensive agriculture of the allotment is ideally suited to the small or awkwardly shaped space that has little potential for many other uses. Allotment food production is also more concerned with high-value crops such as tomatoes, onions and lettuce that give better financial returns for labour than crops such as potatoes and legumes, which may be cheaper and plentiful in the shops. The productivity of such a method is potentially high. It has been estimated that the standard allotment garden of 300 square yards may yield, under experienced management, 20 tonnes per acre or approximately 3.5 tonnes per plot per year.[45] The Friends of the Earth calculate that this level of performance, repeated on the

250,000 acres of land estimated by the Civic Trust in Britain to be lying idle, would yield some 5 million tonnes of food.[46]

Another study of the economic development potential of community-scale gardening in Boston reported estimates that a gardener producing 500 lb of vegetables on a 600-square-foot plot could save a minimum of $235 at average 1979/80 market prices.[47] In addition, the study found gardeners producing the same quantity of crops on a third of the area. It compared the value of these crops to the average 1979 tax revenue per square foot in the city of Boston. The 600-square-foot garden plot producing $235 worth of food would yield 47.5 cents per square foot. The 200-square-foot plot would yield $1.43 per square foot. The former figure of 47.5 cents was found to be more than the 27c, 30c or 44c return for residential one- to three-family units and over half the amount produced by the industrial square footage of 92c. The latter figure of $1.43 was higher than all land uses except for mixed residential/commercial at $1.54 and commercial at $1.60. The amount of crop production in both cases is far greater than the amount the city was getting in 1979 from its vacant lands (12 cents per square foot). This suggests, as the study points out, an entirely new valuation of land use for food production in the city.[48]

Table 6.2: Tax revenue per square foot in Boston, 1979

Type of property	Tax revenue per sq-ft ($)
Single family residential	0.27
Two-family residential	0.30
Three-family residential	0.44
Four or more unit residential	0.97
Mixed residential — commercial	1.54
Commercial	1.60
Industrial	0.92
Agricultural/horticultural	0.01
Vacant land	0.12
All types, all wards	0.63

Source: Wagner, 1980.

Other urban wastelands are, of course, the hundreds of acres of rooftops that for the most part lie desolate and forgotten in every city. Yet they present opportunities as open space resources that could be turned to productive use as community gardens. This idea has been the basis for practical experiments at McGill University, Montreal, where a community garden project was begun in 1975 on a community centre roof in downtown Montreal. The 1,000-square-metre area was intended to serve as 'both a demonstration of rooftop potential as well as a living classroom

Rooftop gardens Experimental community vegetable gardens in Montreal by McGill University. These highly successful gardens were built to test the limitations and opportunities of rooftop space for productive purposes. An example of a response to the lack of space at ground level and consequent contribution to the quality of city life (photo: Centre for Minimum Cost Housing, McGill University, Montreal, Canada)

for the organic gardening courses that formed an important part of the [community centre's] activities.[49] It included gardening containers, cold frames, several small greenhouses, a compost bin and shaded sitting areas. The value of gardening to the social life of a community was demonstrated by the enthusiasm for working with the soil by participants. New skills were acquired, practical problems solved and friendships formed. The conclusions of the study after two years showed clearly that the use of rooftops for productive purposes is realistic and practical in situations where little space at ground level is available.

Heat. In Chapter Two we discussed how the prodigious amount of heat energy pumped into the city atmosphere from heating and cooling systems and industry has a major impact on its climate. This same energy must, however, be regarded as a resource rather than a problem in the context of urban farming. The wasted heat energy from buildings and generating stations may be considered in several ways. One is the question of conservation, about which there is increasing discussion and application on saving energy through better design and insulation. Another is to capture waste heat and make use of it for other purposes. Sweden harnesses approximately one-third of the waste heat from its power plants for commercial purposes.[50] The Pimlico housing development in London for years derived hot water from the adjoining Battersea Power Station. The same principle of tapping waste heat has great potential for food growing, particularly in cold countries where the growing season may be limited to four or five months of the year. In agriculture, the greenhouse has been used for many years to increase crop production, particularly in highly intensive market gardening. Greenhouse agriculture has been based, however, on abundant energy for heating and is now facing an increasing cost burden that in cold regions threatens the economic survival of the industry. Conventional greenhouse design is, in addition, inefficient and dissipates heat freely in all directions. With increasing scarcity and rising costs of energy the resources of the city can be put together to create an integrated urban agricultural system, using waste land, heat and energy-efficient greenhouse design. Year-round food growing can thus be greatly enhanced. The need for greater self-reliance in the future may well become more significant as food, imported during the non-growing season and based on high-energy inputs, becomes more costly. This potential has application at various levels, both at the domestic and commercial scale. The explosive growth of domestic food growing all over the Western world has also been accompanied by a growth of self-reliant organisations. The New Alchemists, for example, are experimenting with the practical application of integrated living systems in the US and Canada, where greenhouse agriculture becomes part of a total biological cycle of life systems. In the urban context the heat pumped out from industrial processes may be connected directly to food-growing industries. The use of flat rooftops of many industrial buildings, using lightweight hydroponic (soilless agriculture) techniques, could begin to make more efficient use of both space and energy resources that are currently discarded as useless. The industrial parks of many North American cities would become agricultural as well as industrial producers, combining functions that have traditionally been separated. A project initiated in the 1970s by the Ontario government aims to revitalise the greenhouse industry by making use of waste heat from a nuclear power station to heat greenhouses and develop a fish-farming operation. Whisky distilleries in Scotland cultivate eels (a highly prized delicacy in Europe) in large tanks using the heated waste water from the production process. This is proving to be commercially successful.[51] The same principle could have even greater relevance to the city since the costs of transportation can be minimised and agricultural produce can be grown in direct association with local markets.

Nutrients. A key factor in urban farming is the question of soil enrichment and management. Many urban soils have been sterilised through constant disturbance and pollution. Consequently they have little fertility. But the move to a thriving agricultural industry during the war years in many countries was made possible by the immense inherent wealth of nutrient resources that is available in the city. The wastage of such resources, as the North American experience shows, is usually a consequence of overabundance. About 14 million tons of human sewage (dry matter) are produced in the US annually.[52] Resources that are limited tend to be used more wisely. Modern China has demonstrated the importance of human waste to agricultural development and provides practical approaches to treating them with minimum health hazards. In spite of the introduction of artificial fertilisers, organic fertilisers brought from the cities remain today by far the most important source of nutrients.[53] The intensive use of manure in fish farming is standard practice in China. The technique, which requires growing fish of different feeding habits for its effective utilisation, has been so perfected that from a third of the world's area of fish ponds, the Chinese production is close to two-thirds of the world's yield of farmed fish.[54] In the US there is interest in composting of wastes and their application to land, as an alternative to the current practice of dumping. Some of Britain's major sewage treatment plants compost sewage for sale to horticulturalists, gardeners and allotment owners. The properties and composition of compost are advertised at the Mogden sewage treatment works, London, as follows:[55]

Moisture	10%	Nitrogen	3%
Organic	50%	Phosphorus	2-3%
Inorganic	34%	Potash	less than 0.2%

While somewhat deficient in potash, it is an excellent soil conditioner and fertiliser. Its organic content provides a source of humus, opening pore spaces in clay soils and improving soil aggregation in sandy soils. It has also been used in Britain and the US as a basic treatment for rehabilitation of mining land and the creation of new parks.

Other nutrient resources of the city are the organic wastes generated by the food industries, the enormous quantities of leaf litter collected every autumn by urban municipalities and other organic resources that are currently disposed of by dumping or burning. They are and will continue to be a mounting financial burden on urban municipalities. Yet the need for soil is a major problem facing all urban gardening operations. The composting of such material would provide a valuable soil amendment for increasing the organic matter of poor soils, or a water-conserving mulch for vegetable plants. In Boston work to develop a large-scale year-round composting facility began in 1978. It has been established that there is enough suitable organic waste generated in the city to supply a composting facility which can handle 40 cubic yards per day, five days a week.[56] The city of Berkeley, California, operates a municipal composting site capable of recycling a large mix of materials from municipal and private agencies. An average of 100 to 150 cubic yards of material is delivered daily to the site, producing a finished compost with a collective nutrient content of 2.3 per cent and a bulk density of 600 lb per cubic yard.[57]

Implications for Design

The Basis for Form

Historically speaking, the form of early towns and villages was dictated by their relationship to the agricultural fields where food was produced. The symbiotic relationship between the fields that produced food for the town and the town that returned its refuse to enrich the fields was necessary to ensure survival. The role of open space *within* the town, as Mumford has shown, was primarily a functional one; it was important to citizens for growing useful produce or for livestock. The agricultural co-operative settlements (kibbutzim) in Israel show a similar pattern; a direct relationship between habitat and food-producing land. It was initially for survival in a harsh environment that the kibbutz system arose.[58] But new towns are few and far between and have little impact on the problems of existing cities. It is with the reshaping of the existing city landscape —

with the productivity of its soils — that we must be concerned. The breakdown between people and direct connection with the land began as a consequence of industrialisation, growth and mass migration into the cities for non-rural work. The creation of urban parks in the eighteenth and nineteenth centuries were based on spiritual and leisure needs rather than the functional necessities of food growing. This perception of open space, to provide recreational and aesthetic amenity at public expense, that satisfies the soul rather than the stomach, has persisted as the main objective of the parks. While recreation is obviously an important and necessary facet of urban life, it is, as I have tried to show, only one of the many functions that urban space must serve as we move towards a conserver society. Urban agriculture will increasingly become a necessary function of open space to which urban design should be addressed. We have the beginnings of an environmental concern expressed in the explosive growth of interest in food growing; in a better diet and health; in current recreation trends that have a connection with the land; in greater self-reliance and the therapy of working with the soil. Ethics, however, are dictated by need. Where necessity or the spirit of enterprise prevails, the producer city becomes a reality.

In many European cities the allotment garden, located on the edge of the city, on railway land and any other piece of ground that can be leased, is a precious resource. High demand and limited land have made it so. The garden plot in Europe is the citizen's summer cottage, often within cycling distance from home. Each plot is laid out with loving care. A two-room shed not only stores the tools but includes a living area where people can spend a weekend at work or lounging in a garden that is usually beautifully laid out and cared for. On a larger scale other examples offer fascinating insights into the potential of urban agriculture making productive use of derelict land while providing fortuitous alternatives to the treatment of industrial land.

Farming in Cities — a Commercial Venture

An examination of the city's open spaces has shown that industrial lands take up very large areas, particularly on its fringes. These neglected places contribute to its visual blight, particularly when they become encircled by development. One such area lies in the borough of North York in metropolitan Toronto. Once on the fringes of the city, it has seen tremendous growth over the last ten years. The York University campus, first located here, was followed by major industrial, residential and commercial development. The industrial area adjacent to the university, which was owned by four oil companies, totals 224 acres, 108 acres of which have been developed as tank farms and related plant. The remaining 116 acres have not been built on, and await possible future expansion. The visitor to this part of the city will be greeted by two landscapes as he drives north. On one side is the university laid out with immense open spaces of mown turf and shade trees, the product of conventional design vocabulary. On the other are the oil company lands which have been transformed into fields of corn, tomatoes, zucchini, squash and green pepper. These lands, surrounded on all sides by industrial and residential development, have been leased to several Italian farmers who over the last four or five years have developed a thriving market garden operation. The produce is sold primarily to the surrounding community that now provides the farmers with their main market. And so a direct relationship exists here between producer and consumer in the middle of a highly developed urban area.

The stimulus to turn formerly vacant land to productive use of this kind lies in provincial land tax laws. Under the Ontario Assessment Act, land that is in use for agriculture is exempted from full land taxes levied by the local municipality. This act was introduced some years ago by the province to protect farmland from the skyrocketing taxation that always follows urban development. On this basis the oil companies pay $80 per acre for the unbuilt land used for farming rather than the industrial rate of $400 an acre.[59] The municipality, furious over lost tax assessment, has taken the companies to court, but has been unsuccessful in its efforts to force them to pay full industrial rates.

The anomalies in this case raise some interesting issues. A tax loophole has provided an opportunity for turning waste industrial land into a productive, visually pleasing, self-sustaining landscape. It upgrades the general quality of the urban environment and has direct benefits to the surrounding community in fresh produce. Connections between agriculture and the city establish new potential patterns of landscape development in urban areas. At the same time this inadvertent phenomenon may be seen as an unrealistic mechanism for achieving these ends in the existing political framework, where a municipality is denied the taxes it needs to provide public services. There is a further anomaly in the fact that if the oil companies were required to pay full taxes, the primary stimulus for farming their vacant lands would disappear. In this case the land might either revert to the status of urban blight or be subjected to 'landscaping' to improve its aesthetics. The task of being a good corporate citizen seems to imply adherence to accepted aesthetic standards over a productive use of land. While this may be an unusual example, it is a problem for which solutions must be found within the unique legal and political framework for each region. It points to the fact that intelligent and creative policies are needed to create the useful and productive landscape that will help provide cheap sources of food and point the way to an alternative approach to urban land planning and design. An example of this planning approach may be found in the integrated urban forest parks system of Zurich, Switzerland, described in Chapter Four.

a
Productive market gardening on industrial land in a densely urbanised area, city of North York, metropolitan Toronto. (a) the York University campus grounds; landscaped in accordance with prevailing aesthetic conventions. A perpetual investment of energy for no energy return;
(b) on the other side of the road, the market gardens. A productive well-tended landscape that returns food energy for energy invested. Landscape with edible plants; an example by default of a new interdependence between city and land that has been absent since the pre-industrial city

b

Here we find commercial agriculture being practised within the city's parks system. Farmers rent space on the common lands surrounding the city and use the land for crops, pig farming and related agricultural pursuits that can be carried out on a small scale. The recreational trail system of the park provides access through these areas as well as through the managed forests. In both Dutch and Swiss parks the concept of farming on a residential and commercial scale has been integrated as a basic function of the parks system. On both these scales farming is privately undertaken with the city providing and leasing out the land. The city's parks, therefore, function as food producers and for leisure and are administered on this basis. The aesthetic appeal of carefully managed and well kept gardens and farmland is one that is derived from this function in the same way that well managed rural landscapes are appreciated. The aesthetic is derived from the product of the work.

These examples show what long tradition and intelligent planning at the municipal level can achieve — a multi-functional self-sustaining landscape that provides social, environmental and economic benefits. A key concept here is the idea that parks systems can be, at least in part, *economically* self-sustaining, contributing in ways other than recreation to the public good. Other possibilities spring to mind. Greenhouse market gardening has a viable potential on industrial rooftops and other unproductive space, drawing its energy from industrial waste heat. Fish ponds become another productive and recreational use of city parks, making use of heated water generated by industrial or building cooling systems. In the parks of Shanghai, for example, it is reported that fish ponds generate enough income to allow the parks system to be self-financing.[60] Waste places could be used for allotment gardens, which occur in some cities under transmission lines. Roadsides and other communications links could be mown to provide hay, as occurs in some western Canadian provinces. Livestock such as sheep, feeding on the city's grasslands while maintaining and fertilising them, can provide the basis for a low labour-intensive and balanced urban farming operation that is geared to the peculiar conditions of the urban environment. This, as we have seen, existed in the past and can still be found where necessity dictates.

The urban farmer who is producing food as a part of his livelihood or to support himelf is enriching and maintaining soil fertility, providing a self-sustaining land use with considerable public benefit in produce and amenity value. It is the kind of landscape that we have come to accept in the countryside as a matter of course. But the concept of productive urban land also brings to bear the notion that plants that can be eaten can also have a role in landscape design. The observer of city gardens cannot fail to notice that not one of the plants that are grown in most urban residential areas, or that appear on planting plans, have the slightest nutritional value. Conventional landscape design has no place for cabbages, runner beans, squash or any other edible plant. But these have aesthetic qualities too in texture, form and colour if we stop to look at them with a designer's eye. The consciously designed landscape of the city, as we have seen earlier, is one that has been created by a leisured class that has no need or desire to grow its own food. Food plants, in fact, are usually relegated to the allotment garden. The ornamental flowering crab, cherry, almond and mulberry replace the plant that used to produce real fruit, ensuring that their purpose in the accepted design idiom remains an aesthetic one.

However, the opportunities for using edible plants are just as great as using those that are purely ornamental. Tree planting along city streets could include fruit-bearing species. Orchards could be grown on unproductive land and provide a return in city-grown fruit. The city of Adelaide, Australia, grows olive trees which are harvested by people who use the olive oil and preserve the fruit.[61] In the Netherlands old orchards that have been encroached on by urban development have been used as recreational open space, integrated with picnic areas and children's playgrounds. Vines grown on trellises for shade in public places, on buildings, terraces and in gardens can be selected to produce useful crops such as grapes, beans and scarlet runners that have colourful flowers and strong texture. The opportunities for the residential gardener to landscape his property using hundreds of trees, shrubs and groundcovers that produce edible produce are limitless and have been well documented in Rosalind Creasy's book, *Edible Landscaping*.[62] The potential and implications for design, however, go beyond the private garden and into the larger public landscape of the city.

Community Action and Urban Form

The commonly held belief that parks should be provided at public expense by authorities and at little or no direct public involvement is a legacy of the past that requires re-examination. This belief dates from the growth of the industrial city in the nineteenth century and the creation of the public park by men of social conscience who saw parks as an essential component of urban reform. In England J. C. Louden's writings advocating public parks contributed to the support by the middle classes of the concept of gardens for the less fortunate. Andrew Jackson Downing and Frederick Law Olmsted in the United States both saw contact with nature as a source of pleasure and benefit to society and a necessary way to improve the cities.[63] Olmsted himself was convinced

'that the larger share of the immunity from the visits of the plague and other forms of pestilence, and from sweeping fires, and the larger part of the improved general health and increasing length of life which civilized towns have lately enjoyed is due . . . to the gradual adoption of a custom of laying them out with much larger spaces open to the sunlight and fresh air'.[64]

Today we recognise that the nineteenth-century Romantic view of the park as a piece of natural scenery for contemplation and spiritual renewal has lost the validity it may have once had. The whole physical, technological and social structure of urban life has changed. Changing economic conditions, new demands and attitudes towards recreation, and reduced priorities with respect to urban parks have made it increasingly difficult to maintain the existing parks systems acquired over more than a century, or to expand them. There has, in addition, been a radical shift in the way people view authority and government. A growth of public interest and concern in public affairs as they affect the everyday life and environment of the common man has begun to shift the balance of power in favour of greater public participation in the affairs of the city. Paternalistic authority that imposes solutions on the community in the community interest but without its input is giving way to a much greater public involvement in decision-making. The days are fast disappearing when expressways could, without public protest, cut through the city, divide neighbourhoods and create havoc with its fabric and environment. The halting of urban expressways in San Francisco and Toronto by concerted citizen action in the 1960s is testament to the increasing political power of urban community groups. The demand for greater control over one's life and surroundings on the part of urban people is reflected in a changing view of parks and open spaces. Local communities are becoming involved in the design, building and maintenance of their parks and recreation areas. As a case in point, Central Park has long been regarded as sacred ground to New Yorkers who feel personally possessive and protective about this 840-acre oasis in the middle of the city. Olmsted himself referred to it as a people's park, his original purpose being to create a public place rather than an aristocratic reserve. This attitude has given rise to highly vocal public debate with respect to its proposed restoration, to which the planners must listen and respond.[65]

The growing grass-roots determination among people to be participants in decision-making where it affects them and the increasing incapacity on the part of public authorities to provide for social needs with public amenities that have traditionally been their responsibility are creating new conditions in cities today. Experience in Britain has shown that the current physical decay and social need prevalent in cities are best tackled by those who have their roots, their families and their futures in the neighbourhood. The development of a new kind of park has been initiated — one that combines small farm holdings and other multiple community activities, such as crafts, theatre, auto repair workshops and so on. The combination of rural and urban activities, planned, built and managed by the community, is seen as a means of enriching the environmental and social places of the city. They also obviate problems that frequently accompany well meaning but often inappropriate efforts by public authorities to provide amenities that are often at high capital and operating cost. These often do not satisfy needs and are subject to vandalism. In practice, inflation and poor economic times lead to the deterioration of many urban parks due to the inability of authorities to maintain them. The importance of direct involvement with plants through gardening in neighbourhood pride and morale has been demonstrated in Britain and the United States. Cultivating gardens in low-income areas of Chicago, Philadelphia and New York is reported to have encouraged residents also to improve the surroundings of their neighbourhoods.[66] In planting, growing and protecting a garden, people find opportunities for social contact with neighbours. A sense of community is created. The existence of vegetable gardens in many communities may be seen as an indicator of social health and neighbourhood cohesion. A crop of tomatoes growing in the front yard facing the public street is only there because people are protecting it. The following case study from Britain provides an appropriate illustration, among many, of how community action and urban farming can shape a new landscape that is relevant to people's needs.

The City Farms

On a one and a half acre piece of railway land in north-west London there exists a small urban farm run by local residents. Established in 1972 by the community, this fascinating experiment in community agriculture has demonstrated how a derelict site with no commercial value can be put to creative use and bring life back into a neighbourhood. In a farmyard and stables, converted from derelict buildings, there are to be found horses, sheep, a cow, goats, chickens and rabbits. The number of animals varies. Adjoining is a piece of land containing community allotments. Created from reclaimed land, these produce vegetables and are run by a gardening club. The animals are looked after by the children under the supervision of permanent staff, also members of the community and trained in animal husbandry. The riding school is a central feature of the project and children ride the horses on the adjoining heath. Management of the farm animals is done in association with local farmers outside the city, who bring in the larger animals for the summer, dip the sheep and undertake the farm tasks that cannot be done in the city. The animals are taken back to the countryside in winter, but the rabbits, chickens and horses are kept all the year round. Sanitation and health requirements are monitored by health inspectors from the city who make regular visits to the farm. Manure is stockpiled and distributed regularly to the vegetable

The City Farm, Kentish Town, London A new kind of park created through community action, where local children can learn about horses through direct experience in the local park. In addition, many barnyard animals, including chickens, goats and sheep are looked after by the children and adults (photo: Inter-Action Advisory Service)

Part of the Kentish town city farm is devoted to allotment gardens looked after by the elderly members of the community. Leased from British Rail, the site was originally a derelict piece of railway land which has now become a productive multi-functional park through the efforts of the community. It is, in addition, economically self-sustaining, making no demands on the public purse (photo: Inter-Action Advisory Service)

233

allotments in the neighbourhood. The project is self-financed through earnings from the farm (riding school fees, eggs, etc.), from donations and gifts in kind. In addition to farm operations, the project also includes other community activities such as an auto repair workshop, tea room, meeting room, pottery and leather workshop.

In 1979 there were well over twenty of these community urban farms in Britain, started by local groups and assisted by the Inter-Action Advisory Service. Its task is to facilitate planning approvals, help obtain funding, establish links with farmers and provide expert help and advice. The 'city farms' concept, therefore, has provided a basis for community revival in depressed urban areas and an educational link with rural occupations in practical farming demonstrations within urban neighbourhoods. As an alternative framework for urban parks, the concept is significant. It returns derelict land to creative use; and through community effort it is self-supporting, offering facilities otherwise unavailable in inner-city areas. It therefore adds nothing to the burden of public expenditure for city parks, which in many housing developments are simply not being provided. In contrast to the normal city park, running costs are considerably less. Vandalism is reduced to a minimum as a consequence of community action and the unattractive target of rough-hewn sheds and paddocks. An interesting comparison between the capital and running costs of a community urban farm and an adjacent London local authority park is given in Table 6.3.

Table 6.3: Comparative costs of local authority park and urban farm

	Statutory Authority	Voluntary Agency
Name	Lisson Green Estate Playground	City Farm 1
Date of completion	31 July 1972	1 July 1974 but continuing development
Capital cost	£75,000 plus demolition costs	£5,690
Vandalism cost	Approx. £24,000 building entirely vandalised	Approx. £20, 4 break-ins
Closure period for refitting	8 months	None
Running costs 1st year	£10,176 (direct fees for equivalent of 4 workers exclusive of on-costs, back-up staff, security and maintenance)	£4,200 (inclusive of on-costs, back-up staff and maintenance)

234

	Statutory Authority	Voluntary Agency
Source of finance	Ratepayers	Earnings from users plus donations
Construction agency	Westminster City Council, Eng. Dept.	NUBS
Location position	Border of council housing estate	Border of council housing estate
Size	Approx. 3 acres	Approx. 3 acres
Child pop. in area	2,500	2,500
Facilities	Play hut, football pitch kick about area, 3 mounds with swings, slides and nursery area	Stables (11 horses), tack room, indoor riding school, pony club, community gardening for elderly, greenhouse, 20 kitchen gardens, caretaker's house, storage block, household repair workshop, auto-repair workshop, farmyard (58 animals), tea room, meeting place/rehearsal room
Adult visits p.a.	Nil	19,000 estimate
Child visits p.a.	35,000	49,640 organised plus 25,000 random
Mode of construction	Comprehensive redevelopment; tax-payers' investment	Renovation with voluntary labour, donations in kind from local industry
Mode of organisation	Council Eng. Dept. (until May 1974, after the vandalism, handed over to voluntary organisation with council funding)	Voluntary organisation with users' management committee for each activity

Source: *City Farms*, Inter-Action Advisory Service pamphlet (London, n.d.).

The lessons are self-evident. The comparison shows that the community farm concept is far less costly to build and maintain than the public park under the city authority. It is socially more viable, educationally more pertinent and physically more diverse. This example of the city farm in operation also demonstrates that urban wasteland is a resource out of place and that its creative and productive use does not necessarily depend on high capital investment. The implications for urban design are clear.

A new approach to our concept of the urban landscape is needed, requiring radical conservation measures to ensure our future survival in cities. What we are concerned with is an urban design philosophy that integrates the ideal of urbanism with nature and rural skills and values. It brings us closer to the land and the biological systems from which urban people have been alienated, and gives us the practical tools with which to sustain ourselves in the future. The principles of productivity and diversity, the integration of environment and culture in the planning, design and management of urban landscapes flow from this philosophy. What logically follows is a view of urban land as functionally necessary to the biological health and quality of life in the city. Outmoded standards and design criteria for parks must be revised to permit a wider view of their purpose and function. We need a policy for urban land as a whole that encourages the creation of both commercial and community gardens; that makes productive use of currently wasted energy and land resources; that encourages the perpetuation of self-sustaining urban spaces; that provides real economic benefits to the needy in times of economic depression and high unemployment and accounts for the changing recreational needs of the more affluent; that contributes to the maintenance of cohesive and stable neighbourhoods. As working environments parks must also be seen, to a greater or lesser extent, as economically self-sustaining, providing returns for investment in food and contributing to the evolving needs of people.

For many, urban farming is an alternative way of renewing contact with the land and nature through therapeutic and healthy work. For others it is an increasingly necessary method of obtaining food at reasonable cost. Everyone should be familiar with the broad scientific principles of production, handling and use of the food that appears on the table. So for everyone it teaches through direct experience something of rural occupations and the basic elements of human survival. It provides us with the basis for alternative conserver-oriented values. The concept of productivity in urban design terms, therefore, has wide implications. Drawing its inspiration from ecologically sound management practice and understanding of human aspirations, it deals with the maintenance of diverse natural and cultural environments. It is from this that its aesthetic inspiration is derived. This inherent variety and richness of purpose are the imperatives that will shape a new urban vernacular and provide the foundation for the alternative design language we seek.

Notes

1. Frank N. Hopkinson, 'Country Code, Unauthorized Version', *Farmers Weekly* (UK) (Feb. 1980).

2. Earl O. Heady, 'The Agriculture of the US', *Scientific American*, issue of Food and Agriculture (Sept. 1976).

3. National Union of Agricultural and Allied Workers, *Outlook for Agriculture and its Environment* (NUAAW Policy Document, London, Oct. 1976).

4. Heady, 'The Agriculture of the US'.

5. Barbara J. Geno and Larry M. Geno, *Food Production in the Canadian Environment* (Perceptions 3, Science Council of Canada, Ottawa, 1976).

6. Ibid.

7. Howard T. Odum, *Environment, Power and Society* (Wiley-Interscience, New York, 1971).

8. Barry Commoner, *The Closing Circle* (Knopf, New York, 1971).

9. Geno and Geno, *Food Production*.

10. The New Alchemist Institute, 'Modern Agriculture: a Wasteland Technology', *The Journal of the New Alchemists* (1974).

11. Geoffrey Sinclair, 'Upland Landscape Study', unpublished address to the Employment in the Countryside Symposium, New Mills Study Centre, May 1980.

12. Denis Hayes, *Energy: the Case for Conservation*, Worldwatch Paper no. 4 (Worldwatch Institute, Washington, DC, Jan. 1976).

13. Heady, 'The Agriculture of the US'.

14. Ibid.

15. Geno and Geno, *Food Production*.

16. Commission of the European Communities, *The Common Agricultural Policy* (Commission of the European Communities Directorate General for Press and Information, Brussels, rev. edn, Dec. 1977).

17. Judith Joan Wagner, 'The Economic Development Potential of Urban Agriculture at the Community Scale', unpublished Master of City Planning thesis, Massachusetts Institute of Technology, June 1980.

18. Ibid.

19. Geno and Geno, *Food Production*.

20. Ibid.

21. Rodjer D. Schwass, 'Food Production in the Autonomous Community', unpublished paper, May 1977.

22. John Green, 'Memorandum on Domestic Livestock Keeping in Urban Areas', unpublished report, 1943.

23. Animal Control Sub-committee, *Proposals for Animal Control* (City of Toronto, 1981).

24. *Globe and Mail* (Toronto), 29 Nov. 1979.

25. Sam Mayall (ed.), *Farming Organically* (Soil Association (UK), Haughley, Stowmarket, Suffolk, 1976).

26. Jerome Goldstein, *Sensible Sludge* (Rodale Press, Emmaus, Pa., 1977).

27. Thames Water Authority, London, personal communication.

28. Peter Riley, *Economic Growth, the Allotments Campaign Guide* (Friends of the Earth, London, 1979).

29. Lewis Mumford, *The City in History* (Harcourt, Brace and World, New York, 1961).

30. Ibid.

31. W. R. Mitchell, 'The Cow Keepers', *The Dalesman*, vol. 43, no. 11 (1980).

32. Lawrence D. Hills, *Fertility without Fertilizers* (Henry Doubleday Research Association, Braintree, Essex, 1975).

33. John Green, 'Memorandum on Domestic Livestock Keeping in Urban Areas', unpublished paper, June 1946.

34. Riley, *Economic Growth*.

35. John Green, personal communication.

36. Harrowsmith Report, 'The City Farmers', *Harrowsmith*, vol. 3, no. 20, p. 8 (July 1979).

37. Isabel Wade, *Urban Self-reliance in the Third World: Developing Strategies for Food and Fuel Production* (World Futures Conference, Toronto, 1980).

38. Ibid.

39. Michael Hough, *The Urban Landscape* (Conservation Council of Ontario, Toronto, 1971).

40. Riley, *Economic Growth*.

41. The Farallones Institute, *The Integral Urban House. Relf-reliant Living in the City* (Sierra Club Books, San Francisco, 1978).

42. Geno and Geno, *Food Production*.

43. Susan Alward *et al.*, *Rooftop Wastelands* (McGill University, Montreal, 1976).

44. Riley, *Economic Growth*.

45. Ibid.

46. Ibid.

47. Wagner, 'Economic Development'.

48. Ibid.

49. Alward *et al.*, *Rooftop Wastelands*.

50. Hayes, *Energy*.

51. BBC Television, 'Tomorrow's World', 21 Feb. 1980.

52. Hayes, *Energy*.

53. Michael G. McGarry, 'The Taboo Resource', *Ecologist*, vol. 6, no. 4 (1976).

54. G. W. Wohlfarth and G. L. Schroeder, 'Use of Manure in Fish Farming — a Review', *Agricultural Wastes* (1979).

55. Mogden Sewage Treatment Works Pamphlet, *Morganic Pulverized Heat Treated Digested Sludge* (Thames Water Authority, London).

56. Wagner, 'Economic Development'.

57. Farallones Institute, *The Integral Urban House*.

58. Ruth Lumley-Smith, 'The Road to Utopia', *New Ecologist*, no. 1 (Jan.-Feb. 1978).

59. *Toronto Star*, 20 Nov. 1979.

60. Wade, *Urban Self-reliance*.

61. Bill Mollison and David Holmgren, *Permoculture 1* (Corgi, Condell Park, New South Wales, 1978).

62. Rosalind Creasy, *The Complete Book of Edible Landscaping* (Sierra Club Books, San Francisco, 1982).

63. Michael Laurie, 'Nature and City Planning in the Nineteenth Century' in Ian C. Laurie (ed.), *Nature in Cities* (John Wiley, New York, 1979).

64. Albert Fein, *Landscape into Cityscape* (Cornell University Press, Ithaca, NY, 1968).

65. *New York Times Magazine*, 5 Sept. 1982.

66. Charles A. Lewis, 'Human Perspectives in Horticulture', in *Children, Nature and the Urban Environment*, symposium proceedings, USDA Forest Service, General Technical Report NE 30, US Dept. of Agriculture, Washington, DC, 1977).

_____

Chapter SEVEN

MAKING CONNECTIONS

_____

Introduction

Thus far, we have examined the city in the context of its natural resources as connected elements of a puzzle. The processes of climate, water, plants and soils, wildlife and food growing have been examined first, as balanced natural systems, or in association with man; then the ways in which these have been modified, warped or transformed by the processes of the modern city have been discussed. It has become evident that each of these components offers, individually and collectively, opportunities for an urban design form reflecting the needs of a conserver society. We need now to see the puzzle as a whole. So the purpose of this chapter is, first, to review the themes that have surfaced in this inquiry, and, second, to suggest how an integrated design philosophy for the urban landscape may be derived from them.

Some Central Issues and Concepts

The Conserver View

The fundamental objective for this book has been to search for a design form for the modern city that derives its inspiration from urban natural processes (urban ecology) and the ultimate necessity of a conserver ethic. This philosophy was originally espoused by the Science Council of Canada in its 1977 publication *Canada as a Conserver Society*.[1] Its roots, however, may be traced to the awakening of environmental consciousness in the Western world in the 1960s. The conserver society view is based on a recognition of the need to come to terms with resource scarcity, environmental pollution and the associated social issues. In many fields the continuing expansion of current practice will not be possible in the future. New perceptions are evolving of human beings as biological creatures, immersed in vital ecological relationships within the earth's biosphere; of the earth's finite capacity as an ecological system; of the need to understand the limits of the system. These perceptions lead us to the view that there must be a transition from a society preoccupied with consumerism and exploitation to one that gives priority to a more sustainable future. Recycling of resources, greater self-reliance, smallness of scale, economy of means, and a harmonious coexistence between man and nature are its goals. The principles on which urban design must rest reflect these goals and are inspired by insights offered by natural process. Process and change, economy of means, diversity and the enhancement of the environment altered by man are the principles that have pervaded all the essential concepts that have arisen from this inquiry.

The Investment in Nature

Pre-industrial settlement depended on the land in a direct way for its livelihood and survival. Soil fertility, the conservation of energy and nutrients that would perpetuate the productivity of the land, therefore, assumed priority. A symbiotic relationship between land and settlement dominated urban and rural life, which gave physical form to the town and its surrounding countryside. The destruction of rivers and lakes, forests and soils that so often accompanies the growth of the modern industrial city and the increasingly uninhabitable quality of its open spaces are signals that this investment no longer has high priority. Recreation, while an essential component of urban living, is an activity that has contributed little to the land on which it occurs. The key to the concept of investment in nature is the notion that the urban landscape is a place of work as well as play; that is, as a useful environment for achieving a number of conservation and productive objectives. Its primary thrust must be based on functional, social and environmental motives. The design alternatives for managing urban natural resources discussed in the preceding chapters may, when seen in the light of biological imperatives, become valuable, to be conserved because of their functional and spiritual benefits; not discarded as costly liabilities.

Rainwater, stored in impoundments of various kinds, is environmentally and economically superior as a solution to urban drainage over conventional storm drainage systems. Modelled on natural processes, run-off is released slowly, dangers of flooding are reduced, water quality is improved and groundwater is maintained. Man-made water cycles that closely follow natural processes, therefore, perform a valuable hydrological function and are also less costly, invoking the principle of economy of means. The principle of diversity is invoked when permanent impoundments, appropriately designed, provide habitat for wildlife and fish, and create recreational environments that enrich the social and aesthetic nature of the city. The principle of enhancement of the environment is invoked when the development process contributes to the environment it changes, enriching it ecologically and socially. Similarly,

240

Pre-industrial Settlement

Industrial Settlement

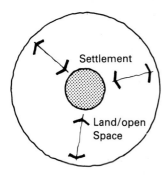

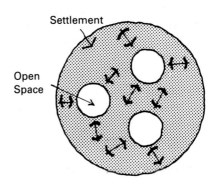

The investment in nature The symbiotic relationship between land and settlement in pre-industrial times.................must be re-introduced in new ways in the modern city's open spaces

urban farming, which combines animals and garden produce, taps wasted heat, nutrients and organic resources for productive purposes, enriches unproductive land, contributes significant social and economic benefits to the city, and helps re-establish links with the land. The integration of an urban natural process with social values brings people into direct everyday contact with the continuum of natural events and provides the most relevant basis for environmental education. Thus the integrative process of design best symbolises the investment in nature.

Multi-functional Landscapes

The original purpose of the urban park was to bring back the countryside to the city whose growth had broken the bond between town and countryside. It has been seen primarily as a place for leisure. The functions and values of rural areas as working environments in close proximity to the town have, however, been excluded from the concept of the urban park. The physical and psychological isolation of urban people from the countryside and processes of nature has contributed to the attitudes towards resource use, design values, energy, nature and technology that have made the city environment what it is. Urban plants are conceived more as decorative elements than their potentially useful function to enhance urban climate, create wildlife habitat, provide wood or produce

241

food. Nutrients, heat, rainwater, food and other energy resources are disposed of in the sewer system or released unprofitably to, and to the detriment of, the larger environment. The physical and social value that a resource represents to the urban environment becomes apparent when it is seen in an ecological context, which involves connections with other resources. This implies a management strategy that will integrate and link the various resources of the city, and exploit their environmental and social benefits.

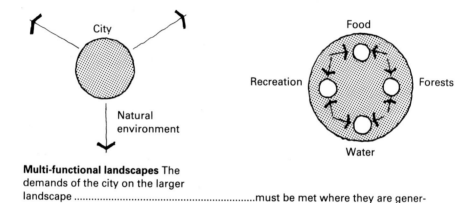

Multi-functional landscapes The demands of the city on the larger landscape ....must be met where they are generated by making use of urban resources to create multi-functional landscapes

An appropriate model is the integrated resource management objectives of rural occupations that are based on a long-term investment in nature. The integration of objectives of forestry and farming, applied to urban conditions provides the basis for the management of the city's open spaces and provides the underlying framework for design and aesthetic values. Thus it becomes possible to manage the city's resources functionally to produce a variety of benefits. Plants will function to improve urban climate and air quality; produce wood; encourage wildlife diversity; provide diversity of place and amenity values. The enrichment of the soil from sewage treatment plants and other unused city resources will form the basis for an urban agriculture and a productive landscape. Rainwater will assume social benefits while solving environmental problems. In addition to processing urban wastes, the sewage treatment plant is connected with soil fertility, agriculture, forestry production and wildlife habitat. The underlying framework for the planning and design of urban open space should be based on an integrated management philosophy. This brings ecological, functional and economic objectives to bear on the management of open space, in addition to the recreational and aesthetic objectives on which urban parks systems are currently based. We, therefore, stand to gain in overall benefits. Opportunities are made available for richer, more diverse and more useful urban places. They assume multi-functional roles, embodying the principle of a working landscape that encompasses conservation and protection and enhancement, economic benefits from resource productivity, recreation and a new aesthetic perspective. It gives new dimensions to the form, purpose and design of open space. The inter-connections between land, energy and biology within an integrated resource management framework provide the essential strategy for the design of the urban landscape and give it renewed relevance and purpose.

The implications for urban open space are threefold. First, the environmental health of the city does not depend solely on the park system, but extends to the entire unbuilt environment which comprises by far the largest proportion of the total area. The conventional view of the modern sprawling city is that of uncontrolled growth and wasted land. In the context of this thesis, that land must now be seen as a precious resource. Therefore, all forms of open space within the city have a role in shaping its environment. Second, the city's open space resources must be seen to provide multiple values and benefits. Third, the social relevance of parks and open spaces is directly connected to the level of public involvement. A community that has an investment in sweat equity and active concern in its urban places is more likely to value them than one that has none. The urban park of the future will be seen, therefore, less and less as a free good, provided by the public authority, and more and more as an economically self-sustaining environment supported by community action and participation. This is its guarantee for diversity and future relevance.

A Vernacular Urban Landscape

Attitudes to aesthetics and design, the traditional values and perceptions that have shaped civic space, are the result of many influences. Consumer attitudes contribute to an acceptance of waste and unquestioned faith in the power of technology to provide answers for the future. Urban expansion leads to the perception that the city and the rural areas outside it are separate problems; the isolation of the city dweller from the bio-physical processes that govern his existence, his ignorance and frequent disdain for the aims and objectives of rural occupations, and the notion of nature under control are indicators of this urban/nature dichotomy.

Current design and aesthetic conventions are based on man-made values. They have created forms that have little relevance to the constraints of environmental and often social necessity. The preoccupation of architectural history with formal 'pedigree' building that was predominantly a reflection of power and wealth is paralleled in landscape history with its exclusive focus on gardens and parks for leisure. The literature ignores the vernacular forms of agricultural landscapes or urban spaces that were created from environmental, social or economic necessities. Today, the acceptance by landscape architecture of ecological determinism as the foundation of land planning is not reflected in the shaping of urban landscapes, which are still dominated by technological and gardenesque traditions of design. Design, therefore, only offers Bandaid solutions to urban problems and contributes little to the quality of life in the environment of the modern city.

Victor Papenek illustrates how design is hidebound by convention in the problem of the nine dots.[2] The task is to join them with four lines that only pass through each dot once. The problem can only be solved by extending the lines beyond the square that the dots create. Those who are unfettered by the constrictions of the square itself normally solve the problem rapidly. Conventional design thinking, restricted to solutions within the square, often takes much longer. Non-critical adherence to established rules of drainage, for instance, ignores other dimensions to design form that are added when connections to the natural processes of the hydrological cycle are made. Ignoring the enormous vigour of naturalised plants that flourish unaided by man, in favour of cultivated species that need high cost and technology to succeed, represents a doctrinaire perception imposed by brute force. Design values are still largely dictated by artistic conventions that lack the underlying basis of nature and function inherent in the vernacular landscape. The purpose of this book has been not to dismiss established and useful design criteria, but to emphasise the functional and ecological base on which they must rest. An urban design based on the precepts of necessity and environmental awareness, whether this is demonstrated in the conservation of water, urban farming or the recycling of energy, is required to re-establish biological diversity. Through diversity there comes the opportunity for greater social health and thus the creation of a landscape vernacular for cities.

Design and Urban Ecology: the Basis for Environmental Education

The isolation of urban life from the processes of nature that support the cities and day-to-day contact with the land creates destructive attitudes to the environment as a whole. Efforts to create environmental awareness through education programmes may have limited effectiveness where connections to the urban environment are missing, for several reasons.

The nine dot problem (after Papanek, 1971)

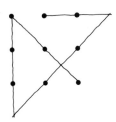

Problem: how to join the dots with four
lines that only pass through each dot once

Solution:

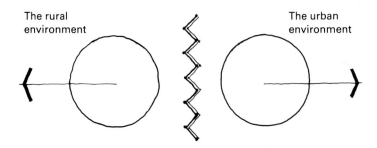

Vernacular urban landscapes The dichotomy between rural and urban values
involves the need for integration

The rural
environment

The urban
environment

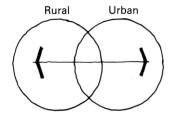

Rural   Urban

First, when the basis for education is one of altruism rather than functional necessity, it is difficult to imbue a sense of urgency to the problems of the environment; to confront people with the idea that natural process, conservation and resource management affect them directly. Second, the isolation of educational experiences from the everyday places in which people live generates an atmosphere of remoteness from the realities of issues that, while intellectually assimilated, may soon be forgotten back in the city. People learn best about life and their environment by constant and direct experience with their everyday surroundings. It is the building block on which environmental literacy and a knowledgeable concern for wider issues can most effectively be developed and where the essential connections can be made.

The urban allotment garden, through the daily process of food growing, provides a realistic basis for understanding the cycle of the seasons, soil fertility, nutrition and health, the problem of pests and appropriate methods of control. Questions of soil fertility are connected with composting, the source of nutrients in the treatment plant and the recycling of organic resources. The close proximity of food production to home is connected to the energy costs of food production on the farm. The human energy and time invested in urban farming practice provide economic rewards and social benefits as recreational time is channelled into productive endeavours. Rainwater, temporarily impounded after a storm in the park or playground, provides the basis for understanding principles of urban hydrological cycles and environmental management of stormwater. The study of urban birds in the marshland habitats created by sewage treatment lagoons provides scope for making connections between natural and created wildlife habitats required for different species. The key to environmental awareness lies in a true understanding of the totality of natural systems and the interrelationships between physical and biological and human phenomena. Experienced in the familiar surroundings of the city, these provide the basis for a rational view of nature in the larger landscape and the essential links between urban man, wilderness and the management of natural resources.

A Strategy for Design

From the central ideas that have been discussed in this book, it will be apparent that there are profound implications for urban design which represent a departure from current perspectives and practice on the function and design of open space. I have taken the view that the city, biologically speaking, displays contrasts between derelict and poverty-stricken environments on the one hand, and great richness in plant,

246

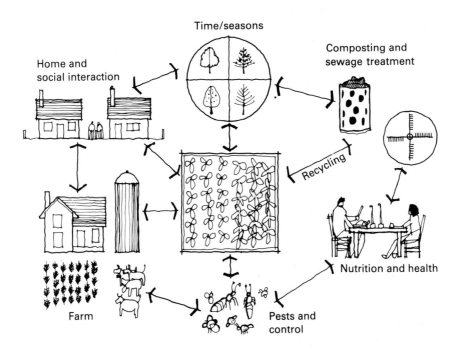

Time/seasons

Home and
social interaction

Composting and
sewage treatment

Recycling

Nutrition and health

Farm

Pests and
control

The learning experience in the allotment garden Environmental and social
connections

animal and energy resources on the other. Its derelict areas are largely
the result, not of neglect as one might suppose, but of misguided
development. There are few landscapes more sterile than the turfed parks
and open spaces, suburban housing and industrial estates that are
conceived within a fixed mould of aesthetic convention and maintenance
procedures. Those lands that have long been ignored, the abandoned
mine workings and quarries, railway embankments, vacant lots, remnant
forest land, old fields awaiting development, sewage treatment plants and
dumps, are frequently the ones with the richest flora and fauna and
nutrient resources. Our concern is with the creative rehabilitation and
conservation of the urban landscape as well as exploitation of its inherent
capabilities. Rehabilitation has two main objectives.

Objective One. To bring the landscape back to productive use. The
conservation of the city's energy and nutrients is critical to an urban
design strategy — the creative exploitation of the city's natural wealth.
The waste heat from industry becomes the basis for fish farming, market

247

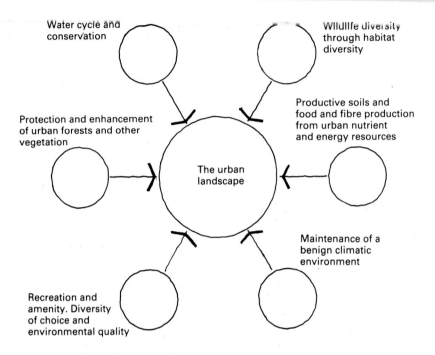

Water cycle and conservation

Wildlife diversity through habitat diversity

Protection and enhancement of urban forests and other vegetation

Productive soils and food and fibre production from urban nutrient and energy resources

The urban landscape

Maintenance of a benign climatic environment

Recreation and amenity. Diversity of choice and environmental quality

A strategy for design A self-sustaining rehabilitated urban landscape. The quality of urban life is dependent on diversity and an integrated management philosophy based on natural process

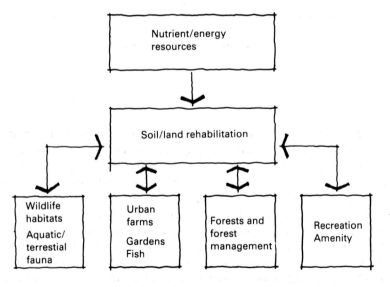

Nutrient/energy resources

Soil/land rehabilitation

Wildlife habitats
Aquatic/terrestial fauna

Urban farms
Gardens
Fish

Forests and forest management

Recreation Amenity

Design strategy: productivity

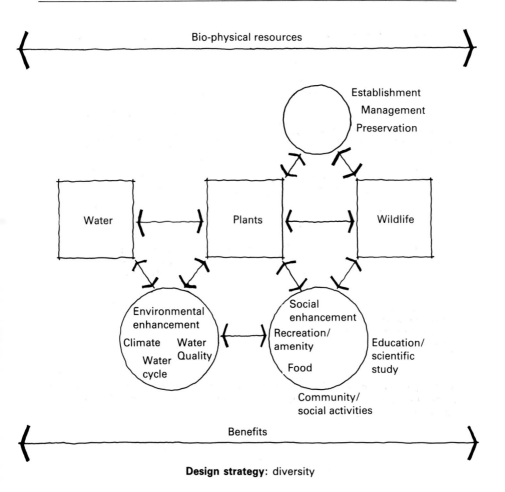

Design strategy: diversity

gardening and wildlife refuges. The recycling of urban nutrients from leaf fall, wholesale grocery distribution and other organic wastes back to the land must begin with the compost depot. The sewage treatment plant, whose current role is solely to minimise water pollution, can assume a significance appropriate to the vast resources it stores in one place. Integrated with farming and urban forestry, the management of the city's stored energy may be put to productive use on farmland, urban allotments and market gardens and to rehabilitate derelict land for recreational and amenity purposes. It produces economic benefits through enrichment of the soil and marketable products and obviates the need for disposal.

The amelioration of derelict soils through agricultural practices and related organic techniques is in itself a persuasive reason why urban farming is beneficial as an environmental function and why it is closely linked with urban biological resources and design. The development of planting design techniques, inspired by natural plant succession and speeded up through management, has helped prepare the soil through sequential plant associations. The use of clovers, alder and other nitrogen-fixing plants and grazing animals are ways in which infertile soils may be enriched with essential nutrients. These are the biologically appropriate and altogether more economical alternatives to the wholesale transport of topsoil and fertilisers from outlying sources, a practice that is akin to robbing Peter to pay Paul. Productive soils are necessary to productive and diverse landscapes.

Objective Two. To increase biological and social diversity. The conservation and creative use of key resources — water, plants, wildlife and nutrients — re-establishes natural balance and enhances the city by diversifying its environment and providing a variety of benefits. Water, stored temporarily or as a permanent feature, contributes to the re-establishment of the hydrological cycle and solves problems of water quality, groundwater recharge and stream erosion. The conservation and enhancement of remnant native forest associations and the naturalised plant communities contribute to biological stability and social usefulness by maintaining a greater diversity of plant species and wildlife habitats. The development of urban forest cover based on principles of succession and long-term management contributes to environmental protection of the urban environment by reducing loss of soil moisture, soil erosion, maintenance of stream flows, groundwater and water quality. The design and management of both stormwater and urban forests are critical to the enhancement of the city's micro-climate. Impounded water reduces the build-up of heat from paved surfaces by evaporation; plants control radiation from man-made surfaces and through evapotranspiration.

When the conservation of water is integrated with recreational, amenity and environmental awareness, it creates expanded opportunities for the social uses of open space, providing greater diversity for play, learning and awareness of the continuum of natural events. The integration of urban forestry management with recreation and economic objectives provides opportunities for marketing timber products, which in turn may reduce the cost of recreational and other public facilities. It furthers educational values by integrating the life of the city with rural forestry and by providing opportunities for demonstrating various economic, wildlife and amenity management practices.

Wildlife has spiritual and social values by increasing recreational options, promoting alternative values, and as indicators of urban health.

We are concerned with the conservation of remnant forests, wetlands and wastelands that have wildlife capability; with sewage lagoons, roadsides and ditches and similar diverse environments for animal and insect life.

Open space planning should be concerned with productivity and an efficient use of land — making the most out of what we have, which means that it is concerned with the quality of life. This implies among other things the question of choice, the ability to choose between one place and another, each satisfying a variety of needs and interests. The tendency of parks planning to downplay essential differences of place and human need and interests denies vitality to the city's open space system. The basis of planning is an approach that is multi-functional, where compatible uses and site can work together. The open space resources of the city have different potential depending on such factors as their use, physical accessibility or lack of it, character and biological value, ownership, zoning, legal constraints, costs and practical applicability.

So, as in the intelligent application of any integrated management policy, not all uses apply everywhere, or necessarily all at one time. But the application of this philosophy means the traditional *single use of open space* must be revised: i.e. recreation, in the case of parks, sports and play areas, or motor traffic on all residential streets. While different cities may have their own unique combinations of needs and resources, the basic outlines of the thesis under discussion are generally similar.

Some Design Implications for City Landscapes

Residential Parks and Public Spaces

Parks are the designated recreational places for urban people. Almost every study of urban parks systems tends to show that cities have a shortage of recreational space. Efforts to provide recreational and play spaces in many residential areas are often frustrated by lack of space and land costs. The 1970s and 1980s have seen severe reductions in the acquisition and maintenance of urban parkland by North American municipalities while at the same time many cities have inherited an ever increasing amount of vacant land.[3] The solution to the problem of inadequate and deteriorating parks must be found in a more innovative and realistic view of residential communities that parallels the ecological insights espoused in this book.

Streets. An examination of the space designated for different uses by planning regulations was made in the late 1970s in an Ottawa residential area.[4] The neighbourhood was composed of closely spaced housing having a density of 29 houses per acre. The examination revealed that the amount of space between house frontages that was taken up by streets was roughly 42 per cent of the total cross-sectional area. Not surprisingly, the streets were the focus of intensive social interaction and play by the adults and children of this Italian/French ethnic neighbourhood. The greatest social activity occurred on space officially designated in the by-law for vehicles alone. People did not seem to recognise these demarcations of space and ignored them where they interfered with their normal patterns of living. Planning, in effect, gave way to common usage. Such scenes are typical of city residential neighbourhoods everywhere. Another study of urban space in various Eastern Canadian cities has found that a very large proportion of available open space is consumed by the communications corridors that channel people and cars, ranging in residential areas from 36.6 per cent to 14.7 per cent.[5]

The tendency to use streets in this way, as social space, is spontaneous and natural. Since time immemorial the natural function of the street has been as a focus rather than as a separator of social activity. Modern perceptions of space use, enshrined in the by-law and planning regulations, imposes fixed uses and an inflexible mould on community environments that are at variance with the realities of human behaviour. The official designations of parks for recreation, roads for vehicles, and sidewalks for walking are thus ignored. People use streets because in large measure they are the best places to do certain things that parks cannot. A study of a residential area occupied by lower-income families in the inner city of Baltimore was undertaken in 1971 to determine how people used the streets and local parks. Observations over a four-month summer period showed that over half of the people counted who could be determined as residents were pursuing recreational activities. Only 3 per cent were using the parks; the remaining 54 per cent were in the streets, alleys, sidewalks and porches. Evidence suggested that people made a deliberate choice to inhabit the street front even though a park or playground was available to them. Interviews of residents during the course of the study provide interesting insights into this behaviour:

— the street is where one meets friends and where the action is;
— routine recreational activity is an extension of domestic life that naturally takes place near the home;
— many street games played by inner-city children do not require elaborate equipment. The street itself provides the necessary requirements for play. In addition, street games are not played in playgrounds since the equipment gets in the way;
— there is much greater opportunity for parental control over children playing in the streets, where they can be observed.[6]

There are similarities in the way institutionalised planning and aesthetic perceptions view the public landscape and urban nature — as something that must be brought under control; that must conform to established conventions. Similarly, William Whyte has shown how the actual use of urban spaces by people is often completely at variance with their layout and design intent.[7]

Vacant Lands. As we saw in Chapter Six, there is a growing movement in many cities in the Western world towards resident control and management of neighbourhood open space that parallels an increasng incapacity on the part of public authorities to provide public amenities. Vacant land created by uncompleted urban renewal and the abandonment of city core areas, or lands held but not in use, permeate the urban landscape and contribute to neighbourhood deterioration. In some cities residents have begun to assume responsibility for transforming unused land into productive open space for recreation, play and community gardens. The Inter-Action Trust organisation in London, England, and the Trust for Public Land in the United States are examples of grass-roots organisations that are concerned with these emerging social and environmental objectives and with practical ways of achieving them.

The community management of open space on land not designated officially as parks has important implications. It re-establishes neighbourhood cohesion and morale through participation and involvement that the public authority park cannot do. An investment in the place, in its social and physical setting, is the crucial element that makes the neighbourhood park relevant as a concept. It is clear, therefore, that new directions for urban design at the scale of the local community are dependent on an alternative valuation of open space. The problem currently is not shortage, but effective use of, land. It has value where it responds to the social patterns and needs of the people who use it. Streets provide the best places for certain kinds of social interaction and play. Similarly, vacant patches of land between buildings where colonising grasses or trees may be found, corners around parking lots, and school yards as well as designated park spaces provide opportunities that should be recognised and planned accordingly. All may serve environmental and social functions that will enrich and diversify them and provide economic, social and nutritional benefits. Consideration of the intensity and type of usage, social requirements, size and features and environmental determinants will dictate to what extent various functions can be combined. Ecologically appropriate planting and management, wildlife habitat, water storage community gardens, are approaches to park design that can be integrated with recreation and play. Recreation, however, may remain as the prime management objective with environmental and educational values enriching and diversifying the park.

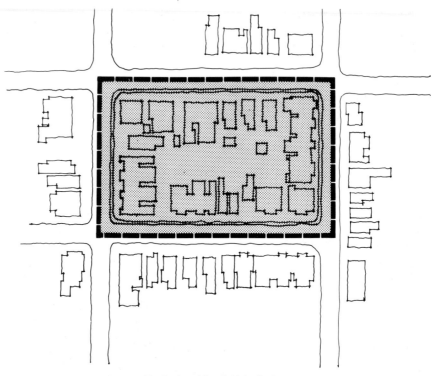

Typical residential block plan

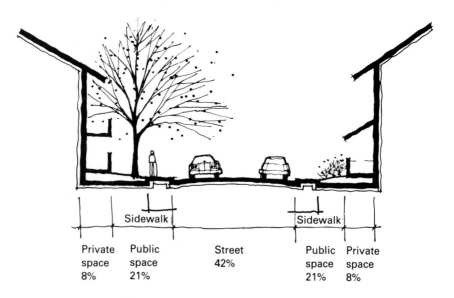

| Private space 8% | Public space 21% | Street 42% | Public space 21% | Private space 8% |

Typical section through residential street

254

Making Connections

(a) The Dutch Woonerf. Designed as a multi-functional street, it is a social place for games, meeting, growing flowers or vegetables. Cars enter on sufferance

(b)A residential street in Toronto. Here common usage often supersedes planning doctrine

Open space study of residential areas, LeBreton Flats, Ottawa, Canada
(from Hough Stansbury & Associates) The analysis of space in a typical medium-density residential area shows how much space is officially delegated to cars. People, however, don't recognise demarcations of space in such inner-city areas where planning gives way to common usage

Space allocation in residential block (Delhousie neighbourhood, Ottawa)	%	
Housing	30	
Backlots	23	No community recreational activities
Front gardens	14	
Sidewalks	6	Highly active
Streets	19	areas (total 39%)
Driveways	8	

Space allocation in residential street (Delhousie Neighbourhood, Ottawa)	%
Private space	16
Public space (including sidewalk)	42
Street	42

Communications Links

Transmission lines, railway rights of way, canals and highways are open space resources that consume enormous quantities of land and provide immense potential for urban design. These links, in particular railways, major roads and canals, have several characteristics that will determine the opportunities for alternative functions:

— they provide physical and biological links through the city to the surrounding countryside;
— for the most part they have little active use, being regarded in many cities as 'waste lands';
— public access is in many cases restricted for reasons of security or ownership.

Rights of way lands are often colonised by naturalised plant associations that have succeeded on their own where there has been little or no disturbance. Many harbour plant species which are not found elsewhere on lands subjected to horticultural management. These characteristics indicate that communications links have environmental and social value as corridors for plant and wildlife associations. Their planning and design are, therefore, associated with recreational access, education and as reserves, and management should reflect these values. Much highway land is taken up with interchanges that are often maintained as mown turf. Reforestation of these areas would reduce maintenance, provide improved wildlife corridors and create much needed visual relief from the barren 'no man's land' character that they represent. The potential contribution to recreation uses and pedestrian linkages of urban highways is often overlooked. Many could make use of underused rights of way to provide pedestrian and cycle connections through the city, a common practice in some European cities that integrates pedestrians and vehicles into planning. Left-over spaces that result from expressway interchanges could also become useful parts of the park system if connections were made to them. Links by means of underpasses or overhead connections could give such areas new recreational and environmental dimensions, as occurs in the urban expressways in Stockholm.

Railways have become, since their construction many years ago, rich in naturally regenerated habitat and are also significant natural corridors. While active lines are out of bounds to pedestrians, their location in the city often makes them the best short cut between destinations. In such conditions they should incorporate essential pedestrian linkages. The decreasing importance of railways in cities and the increasing number of abandoned lines provide opportunities for cycle and pedestrian access to link residential communities, parks, schools and commercial areas. Their advantage as natural and recreational links is the existence of overpasses and underpasses where lines meet an obstruction such as a road or an expressway. The considerable land holdings of railway companies that have lain idle for many years provide significant social and productive value. The allotment gardens on railway lands in London and other cities are a case in point.

Other linkages such as electrical transmission corridors may pose height limitations for reforestation and are frequently interrupted by roads and other obstructions which limit their value as wildlife corridors. With intelligent design, however, transmission corridors could become a major provider of open space in cities as pedestrian connections between schools, shops and parks. They could provide much needed park space, market and allotment gardens, particularly where they are associated with residential areas and such uses occur sporadically in many cities. Where they cross valleys and ravines the preservation of sensitive natural habitat is critical to maintain continuity of wildlife habitat; where they cross roads and similar obstructions to linkage, the shaping of landform may provide overpass connections for pedestrians. The land shaping, planting and management of rights of way may be designed to enrich usually sterile environments.

Communications links, therefore, have value for forestry, wildlife habitat, recreation and pedestrian connections and should be integrated into the open space planning network of the city.

Industrial Lands

Industrial lands account for a large proportion of the urban area, of which a great deal serves little productive use. A number of characteristics that are of importance to alternative uses are pertinent here.

— Many industrial plants are high-security operations and are fenced and inaccessible to the general public. Industrial structures are often surrounded by large areas of turf that have little diversity and provide no return for maintenance. Their potential for an ecologically based turf management with livestock, in particular sheep and geese, should be explored. This could, in certain situations, be associated with an adjacent livestock farming operation, providing returns for maintenance, visual amenity and public awareness of rural occupations. Examples of this practice exist in Toronto and other cities (see Chapter Four).

— The waste heat from many industrial operations has potential for greenhouse market gardening, linked directly with industrial plants, or indirectly on adjacent land. The integration of industry with agriculture has potential economies that should be explored as part of the open space system.

— Much land is unused or abandoned, often near waterfronts or in inner-city areas. Fortuitous colonisation often combined with poor drainage has, in many cases, created areas of special botanical and wildlife interest. These are also often naturally protected from intrusion by security fences. Redevelopment usually ignores the rich natural inheritance that it replaces, and reclamation often replaces natural diversity for 'green desert' recreational development and aesthetic amenity. Many of these areas have the greatest value left as they are. Alternatively some of their natural assets could be incorporated into development. Open space planning and design policies should recognise the inherent opportunities they represent to enrich urban design and provide alternative places for the study of urban natural processes — an essential part of a park system at little cost.

The 'industrial park' was conceived as a specific zone for industrial buildings to prevent conflict with other land uses and allow a more economical system of servicing. Such areas become vacant after working hours and on weekends and thus have potential as a recreational resource. In some cities these zones may provide play space in neighbourhoods where it is lacking or become a connection in a continuous open space system for walkers, cyclists or winter snow-mobilers. Closing streets after working hours and on weekends would in some situations allow uninterrupted park use. High-quality design to integrate industrial land with park usage could create an environment worthy of the name 'industrial park'. Few can be described in those terms under present circumstances, however. The concept of the industrial park as a recreational resource, like the other uses suggested here, has greater validity in urban expansion where development may be planned with multiple uses in mind. The fragmentation of open space within individual developments that usually occurs could be planned and keyed into a network of parks and linear connections serving residential areas and the city as a whole.

Waste Disposal

Sewage treatment plants, sanitary landfill sites and pollution control centres are essential city services that use large amounts of land. The sewage treatment plant is the main source of the city's nutrient resources and is, consequently, a key resource in the open space network.

— As man-made wildlife habitat, they are among the richest in the urban area. Wildlife study and education are, therefore, a logical part of the multi-functional objectives for many of these places.

— The sewage treatment plant provides potential connections to an

258

urban agricultural industry, providing nutrients to market gardening within the city and to adjacent farming areas. This is the most economical way of dealing with the products of the treatment plant that must ultimately go somewhere.

— While recognising the planning and political limitations that have resulted in the sterilisation of urban fringe lands, the potential for re-establishing a productive agricultural industry on the edges of the city has much needed economic and social advantages. The creation of urban forests that act as sewage disposal plants (the living filters discussed in Chapter Three) have immense potential where soils and land conditions are appropriate, in integrating urban forestry production, recreation and environmental management. Work in the US has shown the practical and economic benefits that accrue to the city from such practice. In addition the problems of heavy metals that might inhibit city farming in some cities are, in the case of forests, avoided. Thus farming, forestry and wildlife, when managed in association with the city's nutrient resources, can give new shape to the city's unproductive open spaces and provide amenity and educational benefits.

The works departments of large cities operate a number of sanitary landfill sites that require large land areas. The cost of preparing a site to control pollution, noise, smell and heavy truck traffic militates against the use of small areas scattered throughout the city. Landfill sites are wildlife habitats, attracting rodents and other small animals which in turn attract hawks and owls that feed on them. Landfill also produces methane gas, the product of anaerobic decomposition, over long periods of time. This has led some municipalities to tap methane as an alternative energy source. The Metropolitan Sanitary District of Greater Chicago has estimated that methane produced from sewage and sanitary landfill can be a valuable commodity from both financial and energy conservation viewpoints and should be an important factor in the design of future sewage treatment plants and sanitary landfills.[8] In addition, the long-term instability of the land surface makes it impractical to use the site for anything other than an open space type of development. Landfill therefore, offers opportunities for shaping landforms and creating new kinds of recreational landscapes. The types of recreation opportunities suited to such places include all-terrain vehicles, rifle ranges, model plane and kite flying, skiing and so on — activities that are potentially destructive of sensitive landscapes.

Miscellaneous Places

Golf courses are often restricted to golfers in both public and private courses. The limitations imposed on the public may also work to advantage where golf courses are integrated into natural ravine or valley lands and may, therefore, form a natural protection for sensitive habitat, for instance, mature woods on valley slopes. Cemeteries are often among the most valuable open space resources in cities. In many places they have traditionally been regarded as a great waste of land and a forbidden yet challenging playground for small children in search of conkers and adventure amongst the tombstones. They are now beginning to be recognised as places of quiet and repose, away from the noisy man-made parts of the city. Old established cemeteries, with their narrow roads, varied topography and vegetation, provide a secluded haven for walking, jogging, nature study and meditation. For many people old tombstones provide the best and most interesting records of local history.

The long-term cost of maintenance also poses problems that could be turned to advantage in these passive and often beautiful urban landscapes. Some cemeteries are adopting monuments that are flush with the ground which provides for dual use of the land for passive recreation as well as burial. The Toronto General Burying Grounds, which owns 1,100 acres in metropolitan Toronto, has also considered the use of sheep and geese to keep the grass mown,[9] which would, in addition, introduce a productive use to these lands. Situations such as this have occurred in the past, for instance the Liverpool urban farmers mentioned in Chapter Six, and still occur today in church cemeteries and graveyards in English towns. The role of the cemetery in conservation of wildlife habitats is also significant, since they enjoy seclusion from intense human activity and could provide a conducive environment for animals and bird populations.

Colleges, hospitals, schools and religious buildings are among the institutions that control large amounts of open space. Many acquired lands before development surrounded them and are, therefore, often located in downtown areas. The use of these open spaces by the urban community as recreation and amenity resources within the limitations imposed by the institution is of great value. The location of institutions such as universities on lands that retain natural quality may also offer some protection to rare plant and animal associations, particularly if such places have been incorporated into the academic programme of the university. Examples of this are the wooded valley slopes and cedar bogs of Scarborough College in metropolitan Toronto.

The vast amount of paved or derelict space that can be found everywhere in the city — its parking lots, streets, vacant lands and rooftops, contributes in large measure to its unfavourable climate and lack of visual cohesion. These resources also must be put to use to create new design form and visual quality.

— The re-creation of a vegetation canopy over many streets, parking lots, small paved areas and building walls radically affects the air conditioning effect on surface temperatures and hence the improvement of climate. Paved areas and deciduous planting should, in fact, be naturally associated — shading the floor in summer and permitting sunlight to penetrate in winter (see Chapter Two).

— Planting design and management must provide greater diversity at less cost than current practice. First, the inherent capacity of naturalised plants to survive urban conditions and poor soils must be recognised. Second, a management policy that ensures dynamic continuity based on natural succession must be introduced into urban planting design.

— The concept of urban woodlands should be incorporated into design where possible and where appropriate. Woodland landscape is the cheapest form of planting based on long-term upkeep and provides the greatest overall benefits. Examples are the natural valleys, parkways, railway, canal and transmission corridors that form a part of every city.

— Rooftops constitute a large proportion of the city's upper-level landscape. In addition to being highly visible from surrounding buildings, they receive high levels of solar radiation in summer and suffer heat loss in winter. Economical ways of overcoming these limitations need to be explored, for instance by the use of lightweight soils and naturalised herb plants, described in Chapter Two. The visual climatic and energy conservation benefits inherent in such an approach have important implications for design.

Regional Parks and Open Spaces

At a large scale the open spaces that include river valleys and ravine lands, private and public lands, and those that are currently dedicated in one form or another to recreational activities, lend themselves to multiple functions. In many cities, however, lack of foresight has destroyed many ravines and valley lands. A study by the City of Toronto Planning Board in 1960 revealed that 'by a process of steady infilling, 840 acres of the 1900 acres of original ravine lands in the city are now given over to houses, factories and roads'.[10] None the less, they represent a major open space resource of incomparable value that must be preserved and enhanced. As William Whyte has shown:

Per acre, linear strips are probably the most efficient form of open space . . . when they are laid out along the routes people walk or travel . . . the spaces provide the maximum visual impact and the maximum physical access. The linear concept . . . provides us a way of securing the highly usable spaces in urban areas where land is hard to come by, and in time, a way of linking these spaces together.[11]

A linked network of small parks has advantages in social terms since they can be well distributed within the city and may be more useful than a few large ones. This seems to be borne out from a climatic perspective (see Chapter Two). From a biological point of view, however, the maintenance of some uncommon species of animals and birds is dependent on large areas where these are available or can be acquired. So the large regional parks may be of greater importance as wildlife conservation and species diversity than for recreation. The significance of these and other regional park areas to the urban scene is many sided:

— Remnant natural forest communities are an irreplaceable opportunity for study of the interaction of urban and natural processes.
— The principles of integrated forest management, including reforestation, silviculture and commercial forestry, protection of rare plants and animals, recreation and amenity, should be demonstrated wherever the resources are appropriate. Economic forestry, while on a small scale and therefore not a primary objective in many cases, may nevertheless provide enough income to contribute to recreational facilities, as the experience in Zurich clearly shows (see Chapter Four).
— Where it is possible to resolve conflicts between people and grazing animals, management of grasslands by livestock reduces turf maintenance and brings an educational experience to the public landscape as some of the country parks and cities in Britain have shown.

Education

The problem of interpreting one's home environment is simply that it is so familiar. It is one thing to be taken as an organised group to the rural valley or woodland for a formal discussion on nature lore, but quite another to be made conscious of the places one lives in, or walks through, every day. The essence of environmental education in the city is understanding the bio-physical *systems* that influence it, and are influenced by it. This involves more than being aware of plants and animals or the workings of the local wetland or stream. The child in the school yard surrounded by buildings, with no tree or blade of grass in sight, survives because of natural systems that support him. The dandelion pushing its way through the cracks in the paving represents equally valid and even more persuasive lessons of nature and man as does the wooded urban ravine. So there is a need for varied environments and

A composite of open space resources in Metropolitan Toronto This map illustrates the amount and variety of unbuilt land available in cities. It includes public open space, valley and waterfront lands, golf courses, cemeteries, institutions, public works and transmission line property. Some of these places, such as the remnants of pre-urban landscapes, involve preservation. Others must involve the creation of rich and varied habitats with man and nature interacting. The key factors are diversity of choice and diversity of environment. These are in many ways synonymous. You can't have the one without the other (from Hough, 1971)

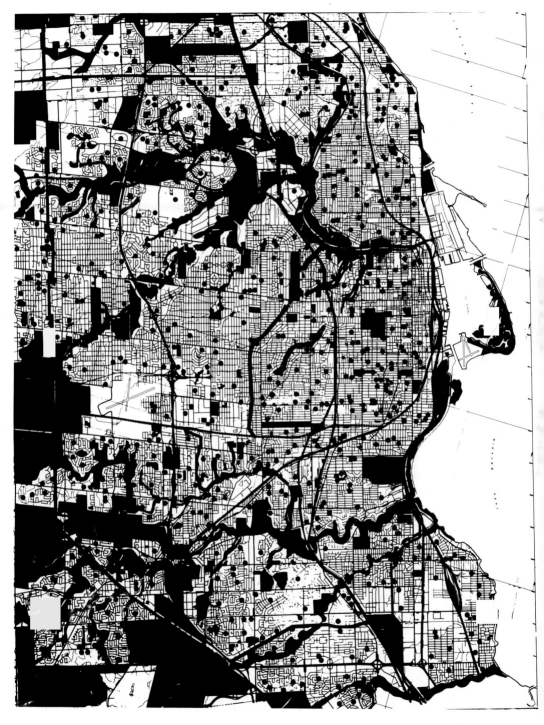

a

Educational Space The Dutch provide special places in their parks for environmental learning. Illustrated is the education park in The Hague, the Netherlands:
(a) the heath garden; (b) the deciduous woodland garden

b

education that will permit people to learn about their familiar everyday surroundings.

First, there are the places specifically designated for demonstrating the interaction between natural and urban processes. The ecological park in London (Chapter Four), whose function is to illustrate natural succession in cities, is an example. The 'Heme' parks ('home parks') of Dutch cities are built into all major parks and consist of careful and exact reconstructions of the different landscapes to be found in the Netherlands. They include such communities as sand dunes, heath bog and deciduous woodland. Geological, soil, pH and water conditions are created in accordance with each type of plant association and carefully managed to perpetuate each specific ecological environment. The parks are run by trained ecologists all the year round and every school child visits them four times a year, at each season. Here he is given insights into plant associations, seasonal changes, where in the Netherlands the particular landscape comes from, and why it is there. This kind of educational experience of an ecological heritage in microcosm in the city may be a model for other countries. But it obviously depends on different conditions and resources.

Second, there are the programmes that involve interaction and participation between members of a community to teach environmental and social messages. The Inter-Action Advisory Service in London, for example, have helped create small working demonstration farms and multiple activity parks in disadvantaged neighbourhoods through Britain (see Chapter Six). Direct learning through community action and involvement is one of the most critical needs in the development of useful social space. Communities who plant trees and flowers, dig gardens, participate in livestock keeping and learn practical and artistic skills will prove a surer way to build a groundwork of environmental consciousness than those that must accept handouts from paternalistic authorities.

A report on education dating from wartime Britain had this to say about the learning of rural occupations in urban schools:

> In our opinion [the] teaching [of science in relation to the underlying principles of life and work in the countryside] is of the greatest importance in the general scheme of cultural education for students attending schools in urban and rural areas alike. It is essential that every citizen should be familiar with the broad scientific principles relating to the production, handling and use of the various common articles of food to be seen on his table from day to day.[12]

Materialism has been said to be the product of eating fruit out of season. The learning of rural skills and food production through active urban farming in parks, schools and community places provides a way of restoring connections with the land.

265

Sewage treatment

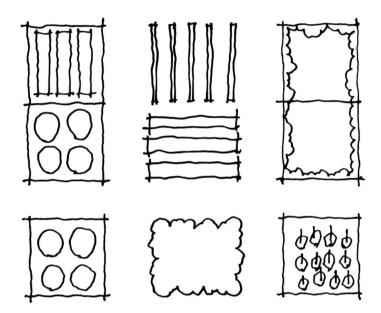

– Wildlife reserves
– Education and research
– Forest production
– Farming
– Water conservation

Third, there are educational and grass-roots organisations whose purpose is to focus on the familiar places we live in, in order to better understand the processes that make them work. An excellent example is the 'Watch' group in the United Kingdom, a countrywide organisation composed of local neighbourhood groups interested in promoting urban nature and study, enhancement and protection of local 'nature-rich' sites (usually vacant lots) in the city. Its publications for helping local groups understand urban nature focus on the small, everyday phenomena that one takes for granted in the city; for instance, small wastelands and the flowers, mushrooms, insects and animals one may find there, the history of the common pigeon introduced by the Romans for eating, and so on. All these organisations focus not only on nature *per se*, but on social interaction and the value of urban nature to communities.

266

Communications linkage

Biophysical linkage/movement

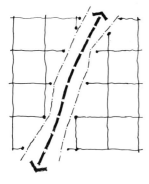

– Plant and animal corridors
– Education reserves
– Pedestrian connections

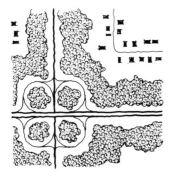

– Naturalisation/reforestation
– of road corridors/interchanges

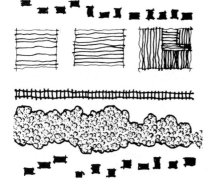

– Railway lands
– Allotments
– Wildlife corridors

Induotrial

High security

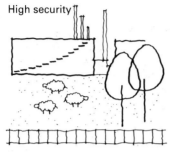

– Livestock maintenance
–Wildlife reserves

Low security

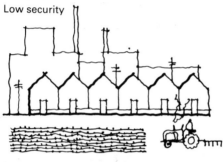

– Greenhouse farming
– Market gardens from waste heat

No public access

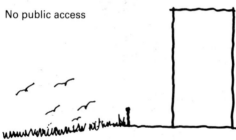

– Abandoned/unused land
– Wildlife habitat
– Protection of naturalised habitat
  in new development

Organic waste disposal

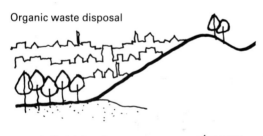

– Methane production
– Recreation
– Wildlife habitat

Industrial parks

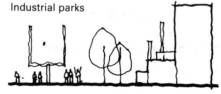

– Recreation
– Naturalisation

Miscellaneous places

Golf courses, colleges, etc.

– Valley protection, botanical and wildlife reserves

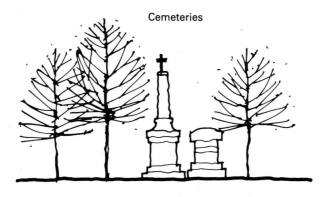

Cemeteries

– Natural areas, passive recreation, history

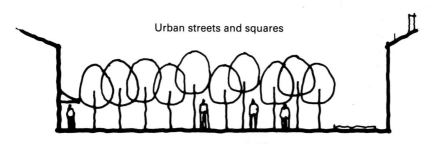

Urban streets and squares

– Woodlands, vegetation canopy, climate control

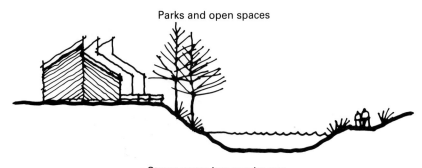

Parks and open spaces

– Storm water impoundments

Roof tops

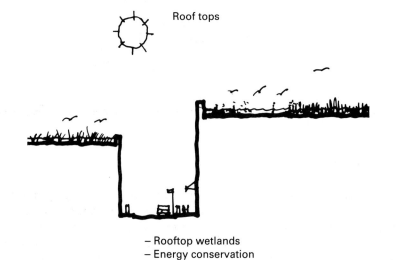

– Rooftop wetlands
– Energy conservation

Residential streets

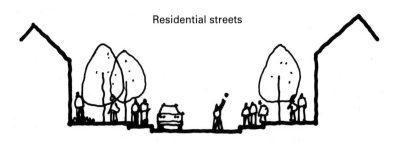

– The street as a form of park space

Regional parks and open spaces

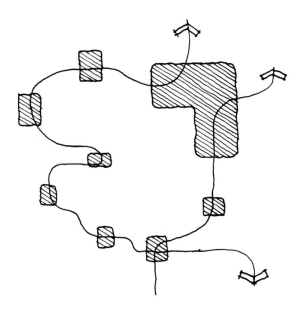

– Linked small parks for social use and maintenance of larger areas for conservation

Opportunities for Implementation

Throughout this book I have tried to show how, by bringing urbanism and nature together, a new design language emerges that has significance for the form of the city facing a conserver future. It may be thought that judging by today's values, which were formed in a climate of plenty, many of the proposals for change are unworkable, or at best unrealistic. While recognising this, my purpose has been to look to the future, with an eye to the changing times of the present.

The forces that have made the modern industrial city what it is today have been governed by unlimited energy resources and by attitudes of mind that see little need to conserve. There are also many problems that I have not dealt with that may make change difficult. Heavy metals in sewage may reduce the value of that resource for city farming; zoning, property rights and legal liability may hinder the multiple use of land. In many cities the spectre of rape and vandalism will be raised to inhibit the development of urban forests. There are problems of training new kinds of manager and the restructuring of established budget allocations and administrative procedures of the various public bodies that deal with open

271

Education

Natural Systems

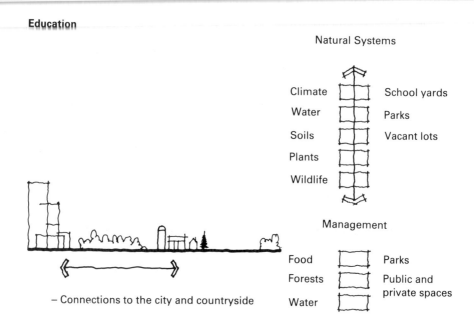

Climate   School yards

Water   Parks

Soils   Vacant lots

Plants

Wildlife

Management

Food   Parks

Forests   Public and
private spaces

Water

— Connections to the city and countryside

space. There will, undoubtedly, be practical reasons why a great many things cannot be done. But values are shifting in the face of impending necessity; and necessity is a powerful agent for change. Increasing consciousness of energy will undoubtedly modify views on long-term versus short-term investment. A long-term investment in things like soil fertility, perpetuation of forests and environmental stability may be seen to be a better bargain than quick profits gained at the expense of the future. The practical application of the principles outlined in this book will depend less on altruistic motives for the environment and more on what makes practical sense. A friend and colleague once described this situation as having 'one's head in the clouds and one's feet on the ground'. Thus most of the examples I have illustrated of alternative ways of doing things have been done for pragmatic reasons; because the alternatives provide tangible benefits, in environmental, social or health terms. Many examples are occurring fortuitously under our noses, but have simply not been recognised for what they are. The commercial use of the Zurich forests helps pay for the city's recreation; the oil company finds sheep a cheaper way of keeping its grass cut; the city that uses forests and farmland to process its sewage finds it cheaper to do it that way and can maintain essential water supply. In periods of historic necessity, such as the war years, the need to grow food and keep livestock was a matter of survival. The community urban farms in England are cheaper to run and are more socially useful than parks provided by

272

authority. Necessity combined with ideology must lead to creative design solutions. It is on this basis that the concepts outlined here become realisable and for which I make no apology. In this way we may begin to establish a language of design for the city whose base rests on the principles of natural process, economy of means, diversity and the enhancement of the environment. This underlying and indispensable structure gives support to established rules of design aesthetics and will be the guide to the future evolution of cities.

This book has been written in optimism in a climate of increasing concern about conservation and environmental issues. It is my firm belief that the key to environmental sanity and civilised life may well lie in how well we deal with our home environment. It is worth while invoking once more Patrick Geddes' remark on civics, quoted in the introduction to this book: 'Civics as an art has to do not with imagining an impossible no-place where all is well, but making the most and the best of each and every place, especially of the city in which we live.'[13] This seems pretty sound advice to follow and a good place to begin.

Notes

1.   Science Council of Canada, *Canada as a Conserver Society*, Report no. 27 (Ministry of Supply and Services, Ottawa, 1977).
2.   Victor Papanek, *Design for the Real World* (Pantheon Books, Random House, New York, 1971).
3.   Mark Francis *et al.*, *The Making of Neighbourhood Open Spaces*, Centre for Human Environments (City University of New York, New York, 1981).
4.   Hough Stansbury and Associates Ltd, 'LeBreton Flats Landscape Development, Report', unpublished report for the Central Mortgage and Housing Corp., 1979.
5.   Peter Jacobs, *Urban Space* (Ministry of State, Urban Affairs, Ottawa, 1973).
6.   Sidney Brower, 'Streetfront and Sidewalk', *Landscape Architecture* (July 1973).
7.   William H. Whyte, *The Social Life of Small Urban Spaces* (The Conservation Foundation, Washington, DC, 1980).
8.   Hugh H. McMillan, 'Digester Methane — A Fuel Not to be Wasted', paper presented at the 1980 International Public Works Congress and Equipment Show (APWA *Reporter*, 1981).
9.   M. Hough, *The Urban Landscape* (Conservation Council of Ontario, Toronto, 1971).
10.   City of Toronto Planning Board, *Natural Parklands* (City of Toronto Planning Board report, Toronto, 1960).
11.   William H. Whyte, *The Last Landscape* (Doubleday, Garden City, New York, 1968; Anchor edn, 1978).
12.   John Green, 'Memorandum on Domestic Livestock Keeping in Urban Areas', unpublished paper, June 1946.
13.   Philip Boardman, *The Worlds of Patrick Geddes* (Routledge and Kegan Paul, London, 1978).

273

INDEX